Interrogating Networks

Investigating networks of knowledge in antiquity

Edited by
Lin Foxhall

OXBOW | books
Oxford & Philadelphia

Published in the United Kingdom in 2021 by
OXBOW BOOKS
The Old Music Hall, 106–108 Cowley Road, Oxford OX4 1JE

and in the United States by
OXBOW BOOKS
1950 Lawrence Road, Havertown, PA 19083

Paperback Edition: ISBN 978-1-78925-627-7
Digital Edition: ISBN 978-1-78925-628-4 (ePub)

A CIP record for this book is available from the British Library

Library of Congress Control Number: 2021934386

Printed in the United Kingdom by Short Run Press

Typeset by Versatile PreMedia Services (P) Ltd

For a complete list of Oxbow titles, please contact:

UNITED KINGDOM
Oxbow Books
Telephone (01865) 241249
Email: oxbow@oxbowbooks.com
www.oxbowbooks.com

UNITED STATES OF AMERICA
Oxbow Books
Telephone (610) 853-9131, Fax (610) 853-9146
Email: queries@casemateacademic.com
www.casemateacademic.com/oxbow

Oxbow Books is part of the Casemate Group

Front cover: 'Cypriot daggers' from Britain. Left: Egton Moor, North Yorkshire (Whitby Museum, photo courtesy of Roger Pickles); Centre: Rubha a' Bhodaich, Bute, Argyll (Kelvingrove Art Gallery and Museum, Glasgow, photo courtesy of Dirk Brandherm); Right: Torrington, Devon (Royal Albert Memorial Museum, Exeter; photo RAMM, by permission).
Back cover: Inv. no. 59-2175, local kernos composed of three trefoil oinochoai, from the Cittadella settlement (Photo: C. Williams).

Contents

List of illustrations

Author biographies

Carla M. Antonaccio was educated at Wellesley College and Princeton University and has excavated in Greece, Cyprus and Sicily. She taught at Wesleyan University, where she served as Dean of Arts and Humanities, and Duke University, where she chaired the Department of Classical Studies for six years. Her interests are in the Greek Iron Age and in colonial archaeology in the Mediterranean, especially in questions of identity.

Lin Foxhall is Rathbone Professor of Ancient History and Classical Archaeology. Previously she was Professor of Greek Archaeology and History at the University of Leicester, and Head of the School of Archaeology and Ancient History. She has held posts at St Hilda's College, Oxford and University College London, and Visiting Professorships in Germany, Denmark and the USA. She studied at Bryn Mawr College, the University of Pennsylvania and the University of Liverpool, where she obtained her doctorate. She is an active field archaeologist and researcher currently working in Southern Calabria, Italy.

Susanne Hakenbeck is a lecturer in historical archaeology at the Department of Archaeology and Anthropology, University of Cambridge. Drawing on multiple strands of evidence – material culture, burial practice and isotope analysis – her research focuses on the social transformations that occurred along the frontier zones of the Western Roman Empire, following its demise.

Anthony Harding is Emeritus Professor of Archaeology at the University of Exeter, and was previously Professor of Archaeology at the University of Durham. In 2015–16 he was Gastprofessor für Kulturgeschichte des Altertums in the Münchner Zentrum für Antike Welten at the Ludwig-Maximilians-Universität München. A specialist on the archaeology of Bronze Age Europe, he has published several books on the European Bronze Age as well as many articles, and conducted excavations on sites in the UK, Poland, the Czech Republic and Romania.

Borja Legarra Herrero is a Lecturer (teaching) in Comparative Mediterranean Prehistory at the UCL Institute of Archaeology. His main research interests reside in early complex societies in the Bronze Age Mediterranean with special interest in the study of mortuary practices. His research interests include landscape archaeology and archaeological survey and he is currently directing projects in Crete and southeast Spain.

Julie Hruby is an archaeologist who works with prehistoric Greek material and an assistant professor at Dartmouth College. Her dissertation at the University of Cincinnati discussed the materials, including several metric tons of ceramics, from five pantries at the Palace of Nestor at Pylos. She has continued to study the same body of material since, producing articles on the relationship between class and cuisine, on ceramic variability, on the sex of prehistoric potters and on ancient typologies. She has also published on prehistoric seals, ancient fingerprints and prehistoric economies.

Katharina Rebay-Salisbury currently conducts an ERC-project on 'The value of mothers to society: responses to motherhood and child rearing practices in prehistoric Europe' at the Austrian Archaeological Institute (ÖAI) of the Austrian Academy of Sciences in Vienna. She previously was research associate at the University of Cambridge and, between 2009 and 2014, at the University of Leicester, where she managed the Leverhulme funded project 'Tracing Networks: craft traditions in the ancient Mediterranean and beyond'. Her research centres on studying the human body, identities and social relations through burial practices and representations in later European prehistory.

Roderick B. Salisbury is a researcher at the Institute of Prehistoric and Historical Archaeology, University of Vienna and the Austrian Archaeological Institute (ÖAI) of the Austrian Academy of Sciences. His research focuses on understanding the relationships between spatial organization and social organization and human-environmental interactions through a variety of archaeological and environmental datasets, in particular archaeological soil chemistry. His most recent book is *Soilscapes in Archaeology: Settlement and Social Organization in the Neolithic of the Great Hungarian Plain* (2016).

Joanna Sofaer is Professor of Archaeology at the University of Southampton. Currently she is Co-Director of the Southampton Institute of Arts and Humanities, Humanities in the European Research Area (HERA) Knowledge Exchange and Impact Fellow, Director of Archaeology for the Creative Industries, and Co-Director of the research at the Bronze Age settlement at Százhalombatta, Hungary. Previously she led the HERA-Funded Project 'Creativity and Craft Production in Middle and Late Bronze Age Europe'. Her research interests focus on the European Bronze Age; creativity, craft and innovation in material culture; and archaeologies of social identity including archaeologies of the body, age, gender and bioarchaeology.

Introduction

Lin Foxhall

Our aim in this volume is to explore critically some of the ways in which network concepts and network thinking are inspiring the study of past societies through a series of case studies drawing upon a range of different societies and time periods. The inspiration for it emerged from an interdisciplinary research programme, 'Tracing Networks: Craft traditions in the ancient Mediterranean and beyond', funded by the Leverhulme Trust. Initial versions of some chapters were presented in a conference funded by the British Academy. The contributions to this volume, however, range beyond the original research programme, which was focused on tracing networks of craft knowledge between the Late Bronze Age and the Hellenistic period across the Mediterranean and beyond into the cultures of central and northern Europe. Here we explore the strengths and limitations of network and related perspectives and methodologies for understanding interactions in a selection of societies ranging from the Neolithic through the early medieval periods across Europe.

In recent years, network approaches, including formal social network analysis, digital modelling techniques and more informal qualitative network-building, have been enthusiastically embraced by many archaeologists and historians in search of tools for understanding the links and relationships that operated in past societies. The papers in this volume have not employed formal network analysis methodologies or digital modelling techniques. In contrast to Roux and Manzo's (2018) special issue of the *Journal of Archaeological Method and Theory* focusing on how sociological theory and formal network methodologies can provide interpretive insights into ancient diffusion processes, the contributors to this volume have largely explored the interpretive and explanatory power of network thinking, and in some cases the issues that arise in using these approaches, on their specific research questions and case study data.

As archaeologists we seek to grapple with the bigger question of how we can approach this wave of enthusiasm in critical and constructive ways to map out both the potential and the limitations of available network methodologies and network thinking using the (normally) fragmented and partial evidence at our disposal. The first two papers in this collection address the wider intellectual frameworks with which network perspectives, theory and methodologies intersect. Foxhall considers the engagement between quantitative and qualitative network approaches and the body of current material cultural theory on the roles and agencies of objects in human societies. She builds on this to interrogate how effectively current network approaches address the pitfalls inherent in archaeological data sets and whether the intensity of archaeological focus on the primacy of the agency of objects and the material realm in human social interaction is altogether helpful or justified for building network narratives. Hakenbeck *et al.* set out a lateral approach to networks of knowledge coming out of Germanic archaeological thought and practice. They explore in new ways the utility of the concept of *Zeitgeist* as an intellectual framework for understanding the large scale adoption of practices and ideas in cases where traditional notions of diffusion, adoption and adaption, and in some cases networks, seem to be inadequate to explain them. The authors argue that the phenomena on which they focus are broad and widespread cultural trends characteristic of a particular period with no obvious point of origin or centre and pathway of dispersal which cannot easily be explained by current models of diffusion, cultural evolution or networks; rather they are founded in a larger, shared worldview specific to an era.

Legarra Herrero demonstrates how network thinking as an approach can be applied to change significantly the interpretation of the political hierarchies and landscape organisation of the Bronze Age (c. 2200–1500 BC) El Argar culture of southeastern Iberia. He cautions, however that the variability and fluidity of El Argar settlements and cultural behaviours, as well as the limitations of the data, present considerable challenges for network analysis. At a different scale, Sofaer hypotheses a complex social network of apprenticeship, including expert specialisation of certain parts of the manufacturing process such as firing, which underpins the maintenance and transmission of ceramic manufacturing skills and knowledge during the Middle Bronze Age in the Carpathian Basin. She argues that the breakdown of these networks towards the end of the period, manifest in the increasing decline in the level of the most technically sophisticated elements of potters' skills and the decreasing transmission of high levels of skill, appears to reflect a disruption in the top-down transmission of knowledge from masters to apprentices, potentially indicating adjustments to wider social relationships and networks.

Harding considers the impact of a network perspective on our interpretations of long-range connectivity in the Mediterranean and European Bronze Age, considering its potential for deepening our understanding of the complexities of the cultural and social interactions involved. While most attempts to explore these large-scale networks have operated at site level, network perspectives, he suggests, have the capacity to work at the level of individual objects such as amber and metal items in combination with site data, enabling new levels of interpretation. In contrast, Hruby questions the scholarly tendency to implicitly value networks of cultural exchange and integration as positive. She argues that engagement with large-scale, cross-cultural cultural networks might at times offer economic challenges or political threats to local societies. Through a case study of miniature ceramic vessels from Late Bronze Age Pylos and Messenia, she explores evidence for resistance against incorporation into some kinds of networks, and importantly, questions the assumption that networks in past societies were by default considered to be positive or desirable by contemporary people and societies.

Antonaccio explores network perspectives in the context of post-colonial approaches to archaic Greek overseas settlement, explicitly the relationships between Greek and indigenous communities, however these might be defined. She identifies as a strength in network perspectives the potential to overcome the linear and evolutionary thrust of traditional culture history models of diffusion, while observing that there is a danger that network perspectives can be seen as a panacea for untangling cultural interaction and connectivity, thereby encouraging scholars to apply network methodologies to every situation somewhat indiscriminately. She links a network perspective to assemblage theory to investigate the heterogeneity of material assemblages at Morgantina, Sicily, revealing the challenges of extrapolating clear social identities in this complex and diverse world.

All of the contributors to this volume have acknowledged the importance of networks and network thinking as perspectives for understanding past societies at many different levels. However, they have additionally presented a range of important challenges and ideas for how we might interrogate network methodologies from different angles, address some of the issues these new perspectives raise, and deploy most effectively the data we have to investigate and interpret the enormously complex assemblage of relationships and connections linking people and things in the ancient past.

References

Roux, V. and Manzo, G. (2018) Social boundaries and networks in the diffusion of innovations: a short introduction. *Journal of Archaeological Method and Theory* 25, 967–73.

Chapter 1

Materiality, methodologies and the agency of things in archaeological networks

Lin Foxhall

This chapter considers how archaeologists and ancient historians have utilised network methodologies, largely derived from other disciplines, especially social sciences, and highlights issues that arise with datasets pertaining to past societies that are partial and fragmentary. The extent to which formal Social Network Analysis (SNA) and Agent-based Computational Modelling (ABCM) can presently produce effective representations of ancient networks, given the ways in which underpinning parameters are constructed as well as the relatively small size and the variegated and incomplete nature of most datasets, is questioned. The rigorous use of proxy data, and what it may or may not tell us, especially for archaeological studies, is critically explored. This is closely related to how and the degree to which objects may be attributed agency in human social interactions. The development of more nuanced methodologies for representing the complexities of even limited social interactions is advocated.

Key words: network methodologies, material culture, agency

1. Network thinking

The concept of networks has been applied to a wide range of archaeological and historical situations, contexts and datasets in a variety of ways from the impressionistic to the high-tech. In tandem, there has been a particular surge of interest in mathematical methodologies such as Social Network Analysis (SNA) and agent-based computational modelling (ABCM), as toolsets for the representation and analysis of relationships, connections, interactions and networks in the past (Cegieski and Rogers 2016). However, the application to archaeological datasets of these methodologies at their current state of development raises many issues for the robust deployment and interpretation of our evidence. My purpose in this chapter is to consider the effectiveness of current network thinking and network methodologies as applied to archaeological and related data, and to flag some of the obstacles we will need to overcome to make them more effective.

Knappett (2011, 37–8) in his thoughtful monograph on the uses and utility of network approaches in archaeology, has highlighted three areas in which the rigorous deployment of network methodologies can advance archaeological investigations of interaction:

- networks can represent purely relational links or they or can be set in actual physical space;
- networks can potentially overcome problems associated with scale, since many archaeological and historical data sets include components evidencing interactions at different scales;
- networks can be heterogenous, incorporating different kinds of nodes and links.

While Knappett is correct in identifying these advantages, some qualification might be added to each of these points. On the first, it might be noted that much network theory in computer science and in social sciences, especially Latour, emphasises the relational over the spatial, hence potentially glossing over a parameter that is almost always essential for archaeologists. On the second and third, while in principle these features are advantageous, in practice overcoming issues of comparability raised by heterogeneous data streams operating at different scales can be easier said than done.

The development of network theories and methodologies which archaeologists and historians have used originated largely in other disciplines, notably the social and biological sciences and more recently informatics and computer science (Brughmans 2013, 632–3). In particular, the social science network methodologies we have most often adopted and adapted, along with their theoretical infrastructures, have been designed primarily for representing relationships and connections in modern societies with living actors and participants (Roux and Manzo 2018, 967). Generally researchers of contemporary societies possess a relatively full understanding of the contexts, content and character of the relationships and interactions under investigation, and there are opportunities for the more-or-less direct interrogation of actors and agents through direct contact in one form or another (*e.g.*, ethnographic research, interviews, questionnaires, etc.). Where research focuses on the contemporary, modern societies of the researchers themselves, the underlying motivations, character and contexts of relationships or connections may often be considered as 'self-evident' (even when it might not be), and the fullness and complexity of them is reasonably well-known.

For studying many aspects of past societies, however, none of this is the case, creating a gap between established, and even developing, methodologies and the uses to which we need to put them. This raises many intellectual and practical difficulties precisely because our data can rarely provide this deeper, underlying infrastructural knowledge and its nuances (cf. Brughmans 2013, 641, 649). Simultaneously, the use of SNA and ABCM are expanding and developing as methodologies for representing and visualising network patterns in specific bodies of data, particularly as digital techniques and software packages develop in sophistication and become more widely accessible. Hence, the application of network thinking, theory and methodology to past societies is far from straightforward (Hodder and Mol 2016, 1067; Flache 2018, 1019). And, even the most ardent advocates of network methodologies recognise that they are most effectively used in conjunction with other kinds of analytical and interpretative approaches (Brughmans 2013; Collar *et al.* 2015, 16; Brughmans *et al.* 2015, 93). Many challenges must still be overcome if we are to boost their utility for interpreting archaeological data. Some of these challenges emerge from how archaeologists have theorised social relationships and interactions through the lens of the material world, and how this has shaped the uses of network theory and methodology.

Here I will argue that current archaeological theories of material culture and materiality, set out in section 2, have developed in ways that prioritise and, in my view, sometimes overstate the roles and agency of material things in human social relationships and societies. This has influenced how many archaeologists incorporate network thinking and network methodologies into their analysis and interpretation of archaeological data, particularly with regard to Actor-Network Theory (Latour 2005), as set out in section 3.

There are at present considerable methodological obstacles in the application of formal quantitative methodologies for modelling process in its many different forms using archaeological data. In part this arises because of the messy character of the datasets themselves. One consequence of the fragmentary and heterogenous character of our data is that although we are aware that the relationships we infer from our objects were complex and our view of them is partial, it is difficult to represent the range of alternative narratives that might be plausible, test against null hypotheses (Östborn and Gerding 2014, 78, 83), or to represent this complexity, incompleteness and uncertainty at many levels, in our models and narratives, both formal and qualitative. But in addition, I will argue, formal methodologies, although quantitative in one sense at the front end, depend on underpinning assumptions, which are to a large extent qualitative, for example, in terms of what constitutes a relationship or connection, who/what the actors were, and what were their motivations (cf. Östborn and Gerding 2014, 79, 83–4). In section 4 I will probe this argument by working through two specific examples of the application of network methodologies to two studies of the distribution of Roman Sigillata finewares each using different approaches. In section 5 I will consider ways of rethinking how and under what conditions objects exert agency in human social relationships. Following this, in section 6 I will explore the life story of a single object. I use this to demonstrate the problems with the limits of our data for extrapolating the networks in which it was embedded over the course of its life, and thus with our secure knowledge of the human relationships of which it was a part.

2. Material networks: things and people

For archaeologists, networks are often an intuitively obvious way of conceptualising and visualising the kinds of data we have in order to address many of the kinds of questions we ask about past societies, for example, around the distribution over time of specific types of objects, or investigating the movement of people, ideas or technologies across regions and cultures. Obviously, a focus of particular interest is the roles of material objects/things and their agency in social networks, since surviving material remains are the key proxies from which we are generally compelled to derive our knowledge and understanding of networks that include human agents in one form or another.

Several lines of current archaeological theory have developed which forefront the centrality of material objects in relationships between people. Increasingly, arguments have been made that that all human relationships involve things (Hodder and Lucas 2017, 119–20). Similarly, Gosden (2008; 2004) has argued that 'all relations between people are also material in their form and content'. He has proposed the notion of 'genealogies' (Gosden 2005, 198–9, 203–7) as a concept for understanding the complex histories of types of artefacts and their modification and descent, as well as how changes in form are entwined with changes in practice. More recently, Gosden and Malafouris (2015) have proposed that a far more encompassing concept and philosophy of 'process' as 'becoming' is necessary in archaeology to overcome perceptions of ontological discontinuity between humans, things and the environment in which they live. Recent discussion in *Archaeological Dialogues* (2017) between Ian Hodder and Gavin Lucas explores symmetries and asymmetries in human-thing relations, using the notion of material agency as a starting point. Such arguments perhaps go too far in implying that human relationships without, or beyond, the material do not exist, or are at best insignificant.

However, the specific ways in which the material realm is an inseparable part of human relationships has been explored in a range of interesting and often helpful ways. Van Oyen (2016, 131–4; 2017a), inspired by Latour, has focused on trajectories as a way of expressing the kind of agency that objects have in both human networks and in the building of historical narratives. She argues that 'a trajectory plots the generic possibilities of a thing'. Although things do not possess intentionality, they have 'a loose sense of directionality' (Van Oyen 2016, 132). That is, 'things with a certain kind of material agency are preferentially directed to certain kinds of actions' and are an intrinsic part of the descriptive trajectories that construct historical logic and contingent phenomena such as empire; they are not external to it. However, as discussed in more depth below, this formulation is still too bounded in terms of how the material and historical 'agency' of terra sigillata operated more widely. Van Oyen's trajectories also share features with affordances in that they provide directionality rather than genuine agency (Van Oyen 2016, 131).

For Hodder (2012; Hodder and Mol 2016, 1067) material relationships have been elaborated as 'entanglement', the collective set of dependencies between humans and things. This consists of two types of relationships: *dependence*, the reliance of human and things on each other and *dependency*, the constraints that humans and things put on each other. Hodder himself (Hodder and Mol 2016; Hodder and Lucas 2017) has explicitly attempted to use SNA and ANT (Latour 2005) to explore and represent entanglement in greater depth and more effectively. In contrast Ingold (2011, 63–4) specifically distances his concept of complex meshworks of interwoven lines where 'action emerges from the interplay of forces along the lines of the meshwork' (potentiality encompassing temporality?) from ANT networks of connected points. These concepts too are clearly not entirely unrelated to the notion of affordances. Indeed, in my view, the notion of affordances provides a vital theoretical link between agency and process, since these two trajectories at times appear to pull in opposite interpretational directions in terms of understanding how the interactions of humans with each other in societies, and with the material world in which those societies are embedded, operate.

Unquestionably, the theorisation and understanding of operational processes, pathways and directionality (*e.g.* Gosden and Malafouris 2015; Hodder and Mol 2016, 1079) is central to archaeological conceptualisations of human/material 'networks', *sensu lato*. Many of the relationships that archaeologists study between things and humans are concerned with the ways in which people transform stuff into other stuff. This has long been a widespread core concept incorporated in archaeology as the *chaîne opératoire* (Sellet 1993): the mapping of all of the steps by which an object is made from the procurement of raw materials, their combination, the steps of processing, producing the finished item, its distribution, use-life, repurposing/recycling and disposal. An important theoretical extension of this has been the notion of the cultural biography of an object, the lifecycle of an object and the accumulation of changing meanings and roles attributed to it over its lifespan (Appadurai 1986; Kopytoff 1986; Gosden and Marshall 1999). The notions of *chaîne opératoire* and cultural biography are linked in terms of the dissemination of craft knowledge to the key concept of cross-craft exchange (Brysbaert 2007), the idea that skills and knowledge in one craft domain can be transferred across to different domains, for example the pyrotechnological links between metallurgy and the manufacture of glass or faience. For the kinds of networks archaeologists often need to map, therefore, relationships (links between nodes) are not simply dyadic, but part of complex intersecting pathways, which often (though not always) can proceed in some directions but not others. So, for example, clay can be collected to make bricks, daub/plaster, roof tiles or pots. But, once that clay has been processed in a specific way, often with particular ingredients added to it, it has already developed a directionality towards some uses but not others. Once it has been made into a vessel and fired it cannot be 'unmade' to become raw clay again. Its specific form, for example an amphora, launches it in a particular direction (*i.e.* as a vessel for storage or transport), and once it is broken, chunks of it might be used to fix holes in a road, or its mouth might be repurposed as a drainpipe. Hence the adoption and adaption of network methodologies must take into account directionality, including in the realm of technological processes.

3. Translating methodologies

It is easy to see why Latour's (2005) qualitative, social theoretical approach to networks, developed as Actor-Network Theory (ANT), has proven attractive to archaeologists and historians. Latour advocates that instead of starting with fixed groups, entities and agents, we should view these as contingent, in a continual process of formation. Hence our focus should be on the acting not the actors, and in traditional network parlance we should be looking more closely at the edges or links, *i.e.* the associations, rather than at the nodes (which are no longer stable entities) in a network. One feature of ANT that has particularly resonated with archaeologists (Robb 2010; Knappett 2011, 104; Hodder 2012, 92–3, 215–16; Hodder and Mol 2016) and their core concerns with material cultural theory is the extension of the range of actors advocated by Latour (2005, 63–86) to include objects. This aspect potentially harmonises with a number of other lines of current archaeological theory.

Latour (2005, 72) observes that because there is a spectrum between active and passive, *i.e.* 'full causality and sheer inexistence', there are many different ways in which things might act as agents in relationships between humans, without possessing agency or intentionality in exactly the same ways that human often do. So, if there is a huge rock blocking one path, one might choose to take a different path rather than climb over the rock: here the rock shapes the choice and action of the human actor. Latour's (2005, 72, n. 83) thinking here refers directly back to Gibson's (1986, 127–38) seminal development of the theory of affordances. At its most basic this is the idea that the perceived character and properties of things in the environment play a major part in shaping how people (and animals) use them. So, one might select a smooth rock situated at knee height to use as a seat, but one is less likely to choose a rock with a jagged surface, at least without modifying it. Similarly, with materials, one is less likely to make a cloak than a house with wood, although the bark of a tree might be perceived as more suitable for making fabric than for making a bench. Spuybroek's (2015, 211–12) critique of Deleuze's idea of exteriority in the context of the theory of design, in terms of how objects relate to each other, follows a similar logic, not far from a notion of affordances. A glass sits on a table not because of any exterior quality of the objects, he argues, but because they share the property of flatness, which is a deliberate element of the design of both objects (cf. Hodder 2012, 49).

While the appeal of ANT for archaeologists is therefore easy to understand, the difficulty is that although Latour describes ANT as a methodology rather than a theory, he does not propose concrete ways of implementing it in practice, or applying it systematically to the analysis or representation of a specific case study or body of data (Vadala and Duffy 2020, 4). Van Oyen (2016) has taken up the challenge of applying ANT qualitatively to the manufacture and distribution of Gaulish terra sig-illata pottery and Rhenish ware of the Roman west (see below section 4). Hodder and Mol (2016) also represents an interesting attempt to combine some of the principles of ANT with established SNA methodologies to represent the entanglement of clay across the whole span of activities and interactions at Çatalhöyük. Vadala and Duffy 2020 have applied ANT to the investigation of the rituals, relationships and networks that produced ancient Mayan caches, deliberately deposited assemblages of objects associated with the lifecycles of architectural structures. However, the application of ANT in this case is informative and robust in large part because the results can be val-idated to some extent by modern ethnographic data, on the basis of past and present shared knowledge (see below, section 5). But these are first steps in the development of concrete methodologies suited to archaeological evidence, and many underlying methodological issues remain.

4. Methodological obstacles

The difficulties of implementing systematic network approaches with our datasets and questions are particularly evident for the adaptation of formal, quantitative digital methodologies of SNA (Knappett 2011; Brughmans 2013) and the incorporation of ABCM into the construction of archaeological networks (Brughmans and Poblome 2016; Van Oyen 2017b; Amati *et al.* 2018; 2020; Flache 2018). In large part this is a direct outcome of the nature of our datasets, and the kinds of question that we can, and want, to ask of them.

It is a truism that the character of our fragmented, incomplete, heterogenous, multiscalar and often temporally fuzzy datasets offers the first hurdle. Although archaeologists are sometimes fortunate enough to have 'big data', this is usually 'bad data' compared to that available to contemporary social science. For example, in Brughmans and Poblome's (2016) study of the distribution of Hellenistic-Roman Eastern Sigillata tableware across the eastern Mediterranean, 5121 sherds dating to between 25 BC and AD 150 from 222 sites were extracted from the ICRATES dataset of 33,000 sherds from published sites. This is still a comparatively small data set in comparison to 'big data' in research on contemporary societies. Moreover, because of factors inherent in the collection, publication and typologising of the original data and unevenness in the distribution of published excavations across the study area, the authors have stated that only broad trends and patterns in the data are robust and that more detailed comparisons and analyses at the level of individual sites or assemblages were not possible. Inevitably the need to take such a high-level, broad-brush approach even with a comparatively large archaeological dataset limits the interpretative potential of the ABCM developed for constructing networks (Brughmans and Poblome 2016, 400).

The mismatches between our data and the kinds of datasets for which most network and ABCM methodologies were designed is widely acknowledged but far from overcome. For example, Flache (2018, 1019) observes that that there are significant challenges for the use of quantitative ABCM methodologies to model the movement of objects and technological knowledge over space and through social networks in the past, notably in terms of the calibration of the behavioural and structural assumptions underpinning models with the available data, and the resolution of the archaeological timescales over which change is observable with the operation of influence events in many models. While any modelling (or indeed typological) methodology of course produces a simplification of reality, the simplified networks we can construct are still quite rudimentary because there are usually so many missing pieces that it is difficult to establish the certainty or depth of many constituent links and relationships

(Östborn and Gerding 2014, 82; Cegieski and Rogers 2016, 286). Although a range of different ABCM methodologies are available (Cegieski and Rogers 2016; Flache 2018; Amati 2020) and undergoing development, so far, we have not yet developed sufficiently sophisticated tools specifically designed to work with our 'flawed' data. One interesting attempt in this regard is the work of Amati *et al.* (2018; 2020), who have experimented with Exponential Random Graph Models (ERGM) (cf. Brughmans 2015), a probabilistic methodology, to try to address the problem with current network methodologies based on an underpinning assumption of independent dyadic ties between nodes (maximum distance networks, proximal point analysis, gravity models). Such models, they suggest, cannot effectively represent the complexity of relationships between entities (*e.g.* sites, households, communities) which go beyond the dyadic to demonstrate tie dependence, for example in the case of indirect exchange, where site *a* might depend on sites *c* and *d* to obtain goods from site *e*. Because the methodology is probabilistic rather than deterministic it can partially control for incomplete information (Amati *et al.* 2020, 213). However, like all methodologies for interrogating networks, this too has its limitations. ERGM can compute the probability of a relationship under specific conditions, not the certainty. It records ties only as present or absent with no indication of their strength. It cannot represent changes over time, and so produces a static picture of relationships between entities. This last factor poses problems for datasets with a wide chronological bandwidth, where for example the methodology must tacitly assume that over a period of hundreds of years levels of activity at any particular site and its significance and degree of engagement in a network remain the same throughout the period. It also highlights the issue that most network analyses and models are horizontal and largely synchronous, while the analysis of archaeological datasets regularly demands the construction of networks which are both vertical (often stretching over long time periods) and horizontal (in both spatial and relational terms). As with virtually all other quantitative network and modelling methodologies, the interpretative utility of ERGM is affected by uncertain and missing data, flagged by the authors as a significant problem with archaeological datasets because of their high level of uncertainty and incompleteness, which could be addressed only by reference to additional archaeological data and evidence outside the scope of the model (Amati *et al.* 2020, 214). The use of network analysis and modelling methodologies refined with the use of additional statistical methodologies offers one kind of solution, but these techniques are still in the relatively early stages of development (Östborn and Gerding 2014; Amati 2020, 214).

The two studies of Roman Sigillata fineware pottery in different parts of the Roman Empire by Brughmans and Poblome (2016) and Van Oyen (2016; 2017b) already mentioned provide good examples of divergent approaches to some of these methodological obstacles that have not yet been overcome. Brughmans and Poblome used ACBM to simulate the distribution of Roman Eastern Sigillata ware with the aim of testing two alternative ideas about how the Roman economy worked, both dependent on the nature of the social networks of traders: were markets weakly integrated with traders having little information about prices and the availability of goods, so that opportunism and protectionist behaviour hampered the flow of goods and commercial information, or were markets more strongly integrated so that commercial informa-tion from one market was more easily accessible in other markets? The simulation used an algorithm developed for modern economic 'small world' network behaviours (Brughmans and Poblome 2016, 400) but the motivations of and behaviours of traders were based on modern economic concerns around supply and demand. As noted above, because of issues with the quality and unevenness of the data, only relatively broad-brush results of the simulation were considered reliable (Brughmans and Poblome 2016, 396, 403). Simulated distributions that premised unequal numbers of traders at different production centres catering for high local demand, but with high proportions of inter-site links suggesting well-integrated markets, best fitted the archaeological data (Brughmans and Poblome 2016, 402–3). The authors concluded that: 'in general, a large urban centre close to tableware production centres would have served as a primary market with a high demand, and therefore offered an impetus to produce large amounts of tableware' (Brughmans and Poblome 2016, 403). It is difficult to see how this analysis adds significant new knowledge on the production, distribution and consumption of Roman tableware, or how it adds new insights on the social networks of Roman 'traders' (if that is the group whose actions and interactions we are really seeing in the distributions of these wares in any case), let alone the wider Roman economy. In light of our wider contextual information about the Roman economy and our lack of specific knowledge of how the pottery trade worked in the eastern Mediterranean, there are simply too many untested assumptions in the model about through whose hands this pottery moved and what motivated the movement.

Astrid Van Oyen (2017b) in her response to Brughmans and Poblome (2016) has gone straight to the heart of the methodological flaws with this paper. She points out that while agent-based modelling has the strength of forcing us to articulate concepts and assumptions clearly, the methodology as currently practised makes it difficult to incorporate the complexity, messiness and fluidity of relationships and social networks in ancient societies where the realm of the social and the economic may often not be clearly separated, inclining the investigator instead to rely on modernist motiva-tions such as maximising profit (Van Oyen 2017b, 1357). In this particular exercise, she also identifies the problem of treating the pottery used as the proxy for Roman economic activity simply as a 'commodity': while it might be a commodity in some contexts, it served many other roles in Roman society and in Roman social networks (Van Oyen 2017b, 1359–60). In short, Brughman and Poblome's study presents a good example of how, even in the case of a society where we have a great deal of additional contextual information, the attempt to recreate social networks (which in this case attempt to explain how the economy worked) from archaeological data has produced disappointing results.

This example raises key methodological problems in trying to construct and deploy quantitative network methodologies from archaeological data and use them analytically. One is how we ensure that the assumptions on which we premise our models are appropriate to the cultures that we are investigating (Östborn and Gerding 2014, 79), especially when our data usually do not provide us with sufficient information to be certain what the most appropriate assumptions should be. Here is where the experimental capacity of using multiple modelling methodologies for testing different underpinning assumptions could enable us to gain new insights that would allow us to test the efficacy of different foundational premises, going beyond adjusting the parameters to run different scenarios within a single model (cf. Östborn and Gerding 2014).

A second, related problem, particularly evident in a case study focused on a complex historical entity like the Roman Empire, is to develop more robust modelling methodologies to incorporate and represent more of that complexity without over-complicating the clarity of the resulting modelling. This emerges in Van Oyen's (2016; 2017b) own study of Gaulish terra sigillata, which presents a sophisticated and nuanced vision of the ways in which this class of pottery was entangled in the interactions of Roman social networks. At a higher level, this study attempts to encourage better use of archaeology in historical narratives by considering the entanglement of terra sigillata as a trajectory 'rooted deeply in possibilities for action' so that 'empire formed as terra sigillata was made', viewing terra sigillata as an active agent in the process, rather than as a retrospective model which is dependent on external actors. In her view, 'a trajectory plots the generic possibilities of a thing' and serves as the vehicle through which objects exert agency (Van Oyen 2016, 131–4). This idea, in fact, shares similarities with Hakenbeck *et al.*'s (this volume) idea of the operation of *Zeitgeist*.

However, an important element of 'trajectory' in this case is the tension between the affordance of a terra sigillata vessel itself and the extent, depth and quality of shared knowledge associated with the object. In some places and contexts where that object might end up, knowledge is shared to varying degrees and not always in the same way. So, for example, the trajectory of empire and the trajectory and affordances of terra sigillata are linked to many other features of Roman lifeways. Terra sigillata is shaped for particular kinds of foods and dining habits (themselves contingent and dynamic), so its attributed agency strengthens with increased availability of particular kinds of desirable food and drink, and this itself is potentially also related to the trajectory of and imperial 'environment' and the affordances it offers in particular directions. But, in the different communities and contexts in which it is found, the degree to which knowledge of Roman food, dining habits, etc. were shared or accepted clearly varied, and imaginative new uses also emerged, so that the trajectory of terra sigillata was not uniform in the way that other elements of empire might have been, precisely because 'agency' (as perceived by modern scholars), or at least significance (in emic terms), was attributed to these objects in different ways and to different degrees in different places by ancient communities. And this could be multiplied many times over, with the multiple links and connections between other categories of material (and non-material) things. This study effectively demonstrates the acute need to capture at least some elements of that complexity of 'trajectory' in the construction of computational models and the algorithms underpinning them.

In most archaeological contexts and data sets we have access to the things but not to the people, that is, we have more understanding of the material objects and their settings than of the actual individuals who made or engaged with them. This raises a third interpretive issue which needs more careful thought in (re)constructing past networks and modelling them: the use of proxy data.

In archaeology we cannot observe or model human behaviour directly. Instead we usually observe things or sites (*e.g.* graves, settlements, structures, activity areas, etc.) along with contextual and other (*e.g.* environmental, textual) evidence to help us to understand what motivated human choices, behaviours and actions. Such evidence, however, will provide us with only a limited grasp of the full range of possible motivations or how people might have construed, considered or enacted their range of choices. Hence, when we are trying to understand the shape, operation and dynamism of a set of relationships or interactions by formulating them as a network, we need to think very hard about how we infer, reconstruct and represent a set of relationships between people. This is especially the case if we do so in ways that present these relationships as if they were clear-cut and fixed, when they have been inferred directly from the relationships we perceive between things (even those that are humanly made or modified). For a start, there is an obvious danger of circularity. Moreover, in contexts where there is a wide range of potential motivations behind human choices and actions, and considerable uncertainty about how and why particular choices were made, a network representation that does not take such potential for motivational complexity into account is bound to oversimplify and perhaps misrepresent, when it attempts to translate relationships between things, as we can perceive them, directly back into relationships between humans (or even between humans and things) (Van Oyen 2016). In effect, we need to find a way to ensure that the proxies we choose to model actually will allow us to infer in a rigorous way the behaviour of the agents that we think they represent. In some cases this is straightforward, in others it is not. For example, in the case of fineware pottery that moves over long distances, does modelling the movement of pots allow us to infer the actions and decisions of manufacturers, traders, consumers, travellers, state authorities, or some kind of messy aggregate of all of these and possibly more? However, what we think things as proxies represent in past human networks is also affected by what roles we think those things played.

5. Rethinking the agency of things

As discussed in section 2, current archaeological thinking attributes a prominent role to material objects in human relationships and networks, for example in Hodder's recent arguments that things can have primary agency in the dependences and dependencies of human-thing entanglement, or Gosden and Malafouris' (2015, 703, 709–10) question about whether the notion of sentience extends to everything (including objects?). As archaeologists, prioritising the realm of the material comes naturally, and although the material world and environment that we are continually creating and in which we simultaneously exist is plainly entangled in relationships and networks, we are sometimes in danger of overestimating the power of things to enact autonomous agency. I would argue that although things, like other kinds of entities, can be *actors*, they are not usually *agents* in any pure sense because their agency is virtually always ultimately contingent on human actions and choices. So, while we absolutely should understand and represent things and other elements of the material world as actors, they are not autonomous agents. Hodder (2012, 215–16), like many other scholars, uses the terms 'actor' and 'agent' synonymously. This may sound like semantic pedantry, but this is a critical distinction that is often blurred, and perhaps it is more helpful to make the distinction clearer by using another, different word such as *actant* (a word that Latour, in fact, uses for non-human actors).

The difficulties become more evident if we go back to basics to reconsider the most fundamental ways in which humans engage with the material world, and the roles that things themselves play in these engagements. Here I offer three suggestions for reconsidering the role of object agency.

1. **Things perform as actors when agency is attributed to them by humans**. This is not a new idea – in a different form it goes right back to Gell (1998; cf. Robb 2010, 504–5) for whom this was 'secondary agency', and it has been widely adopted by others in one form or another. I would prefer the term 'attributed agency' for two reasons. First, this term enables us to distinguish between agent and actor (or actant) – in my view 'attributed agency' enables a non-sentient or non-human entity to perform as an actor, but does not assume it exerts independent agency or autonomy (I would consider animals as sentient, though not always in the same way as each other, or as humans). For Latour, and to some extent Hodder, the agency resides in the enactment of the relationship, or for Gosden and Malafouris (2015, 702–3) in 'becoming', not as an essential quality of the actors. But this still implies that agency is something that non-sentient entities can actually initiate. Second, 'attributed agency' can also be applied to a wide range of non-human or non-sentient entities, including deities and other natural or supernatural forces and beings, which need not be material (*e.g.* climate change), some of which we would not necessarily consider 'real', even if people in the societies we study clearly did and adjusted their behaviour accordingly.

2. **Things also become actors/actants when humans share beliefs or knowledge about that thing which transcends time and/or space, and such a thing takes on agency because of these beliefs or knowledge**. Agency attributed to a material thing often depends on humans' shared beliefs or knowledge. A thing or feature can elicit a specific response because knowledge about its meaning, use, significance is shared in a particular context. So, for example, most drivers can distinguish a

speed bump, even one without markings, intended to restrict the speed of motor vehicles, from a random lump in the road because of shared knowledge of their purpose and of where speed bumps are likely to be situated (*e.g.* residential areas). If the key shared human knowledge vanishes, or a link in the knowledge chain is broken, the capacity for it to serve as an actor is lost. Hence, it is humans (or perhaps more accurately humans' engagement with a particular thing or type of thing) that are exerting the agency, not the material thing, even though it may be in some sense an actor because it precipitates a particular human choice or action. Vadala and Duffy's (2020) study of Maya caches depends heavily for its interpretations of the ancient past on knowledge shared (at least partially) with present day descendant communities about the use, placement and significance of specific things. Another good example can be found in Forbes' (2007, 352–4) study of the Methana peninsula, where the modern villages were constructed by a new population arriving during the Greek War of Independence (1821–32), before which the peninsula had been deserted for several centuries. All except two of these villages were built around a pre-existing Byzantine church, some of which were restored from ruins when the villages were built. Although there was no direct historical link between the nineteenth-century incomers and the earlier Byzantine inhabitants, their shared knowledge of Greek Orthodox Christianity ensured that the newcomers recognised and understood the sacred landscape in which they had arrived and made their choices of settlement location accordingly, even when the church buildings themselves were in a ruinous condition.

3. **Things can have specific physical qualities or properties as perceived by humans that evoke particular ideas or responses to them in particular circumstances or contexts.** This is the notion of affordances, going right back to Gibson (1986). Sometimes these circumstances are historically or culturally grounded and limited; but in many cases, as has been regularly observed, affordances have a very wide currency even if they are not quite universal, for example the properties of different kinds of materials. Sometimes this is simply obstructive as in the big rock that might block one path and encourage people to choose another path. However, sometimes this is suggestive, providing directionality in terms of the desirability of one choice or course of action over another. But suggestiveness also depends on human experiences, knowledge, imagination and ultimately agency. In these cases, too, the thing is an actor in that its specific properties feature in the decision, but it is not an agent because it does not make the decision: it precipitates or encourages a choice or action, but does not devise or implement it.

If these suggestions reflect pragmatic social realities to any extent, we must add another set of considerations to transcend from networks of things to networks of people in which those things were entangled. When we only have the things, and even then, only some of them, to what extent can we infer the human relationships, decisions, behaviours and beliefs for which the networks we construct stand as proxies? We can only construct narratives of how the ancient networks we detect operated to a limited extent or with any certainty. But what network methodologies should offer, if used critically and judiciously, is the possibility of asking new questions, building in uncertainties and testing the answers we get.

6. One object and its potential networks

To exemplify this problem of building in uncertainty to our interpretations, I want to focus on a single object and the range of ways it could have fitted into social networks. This is an object about which there is a considerable amount of information but with varying degrees of certainty about different elements of that information. It is a pyramidal loom weight found on the floor of a carefully excavated, small, rural house (Fattoria Fabrizio) in the Metaponto countryside in southern Italy (Figs 1.1 and 1.2).

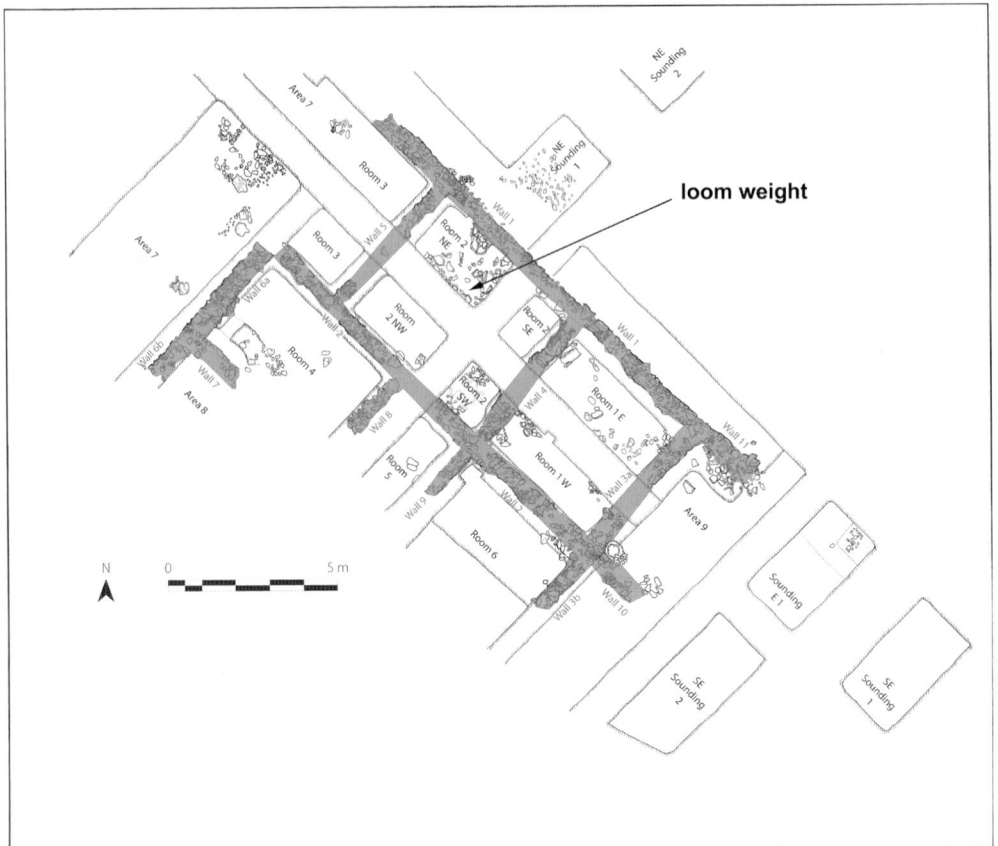

Figure 1.1 Plan of the Fattoria Fabrizio site, Metaponto (Courtesy of University of Texas Press).

Figure 1.2 Pyramidal loom weight from the Fattoria Fabrizio site (author's photograph).

The structure was built very late in the fifth or at the beginning of the fourth century BC and was abandoned around 300 BC or very shortly afterwards (Lanza Catti and Swift 2014, 7–8). This object was part of the debris of the final stages of occupation, probably stored on a shelf with the late fourth-century pottery and household items found with it.

This type of loom weight in this locality was mostly used in the sixth and fifth centuries BC as part of a warp-weighted loom. This one is suitable for making relatively fine cloth. The graffito on it, probably incised when it was leather hard, confirms a rough date, since it uses an alphabet that went out of use very early in the early fifth century BC. Its form of wiggly iota is not a regular feature of the local alphabets; it is more characteristic of communities much further south in Italy, such as Rhegion (Jeffery 1990, 254). So, we can be fairly sure that the person who inscribed this graffito learned to write elsewhere. This is unlikely to be a manufacturer's or potter's mark, since, again, it is clear from looking at many other examples of similar loom weights in the area that in these societies women personally marked some loom weights before firing. Where professional manufacturers' marks occur, they (and the patterns of their distribution) are clearly distinguishable from personal marks. So, the chances are that the mark was made by a literate woman from a different part of southern Italy.

There is a good chance that in its archaeological context with other domestic pottery that was probably stored in the same room, this object was an heirloom, made at least 180 years (around five or six generations) earlier than the late fourth-/early third-century BC context, space and material with which it was discovered. There remains a chance that it could be residual because the sites of these farmhouses tend to be occupied and used in short, discontinuous phases for a wide variety of purposes (Foxhall 2020). There is ceramic evidence of the use of this particular site earlier in the second half of the fifth century and in the late sixth–early fifth century, but no discernible structures (Lanza Catti and Swift 2014, 10–13). The use of the site in these earlier phases may not have been residential, and non-residential rural sites (*e.g.* for agricultural processing and storage or industrial purposes) do not normally include loom weights or other textile tools. Although loom weights do show up in pottery kilns, sometimes repurposed as kiln separators, there is no evidence of a kiln in the earlier phases here. However, if the earlier occupation was domestic in character (which is genuinely uncertain), it is possible that someone living in the later house found it and kept it or put it back into use. So, despite the uncertainty, the balance of probability suggests it was an heirloom in one sense or another.

There is a large body of supporting evidence that in this society over a very long period textile manufacture was extremely strongly associated with women, both conceptually as a fundamental element of femininity, and in practical terms; it was largely women who used textile tools in their primary functions, *e.g.* as loom weights, although interestingly this is probably not true for some of their reuses (Foxhall 2013, 95–101). Loom weights also appear as votives in shrines associated with women, and there is a local example, the Pantanello sanctuary, where over 400 votive loom weights have been found (Foxhall 2018).

We can therefore identify the existence of at least two women who had a relationship with this object (though of course we do not who they were): the woman who made or inscribed it around 500 BC and the woman who stored and/or used it around 300 BC. We cannot be certain that these women had any relationship, connection or interaction with each other, directly or indirectly. If the earlier woman came to the Metaponto countryside from elsewhere, we cannot be certain about the circumstances of how she arrived or what her status was. The balance of probability based on what we know from other evidence about how this society worked is that she came either as a wife or as a slave, but these are not the only possibilities. Although it seems probable that other women in the intervening time span also had a relationship to this object and may have interacted with one or both of the women who definitely engaged with it, we cannot be certain of this. If this object was found by the later woman and kept or reused, it is an excellent example of shared knowledge leading to attributed agency: the object itself would have been meaningful and potentially significant for the later woman because the two women in different periods would have shared knowledge of textile manufacture, warp weighted looms and beliefs about the cultural significance of weaving and weaving tools.

However, it is equally possible that this was handed down through family, and if so, probably through a line of women. There is additional, independent evidence from archaeological survey in Metaponto (Foxhall 2011) and elsewhere suggesting that this happened and can sometimes be detected or suspected in the archaeological record. Normally excavated Greek houses, both urban and rural, do not have enough loom weights for a loom, with only very few exceptions. This is almost certainly because when a house was abandoned, women took their loom weights with them (Foxhall 2012). So, why was this one not taken away when the house was abandoned, especially if it was an heirloom, and therefore 'special'? One possibility is that by the time the house was abandoned it had lost its significance as well as its practical value as a textile tool. By the end of the fourth century BC pyramidal loom weights were no longer the predominant type used for weaving and flat, disc-shaped loom weights were more often used instead. The only two loom weights discovered in this house were both pyramidal. During the period when it was occupied, any sets of loom weights actually in use in the house would more likely have been disc-shaped rather than pyramidal, so it is likely that these two did not match and could not be used with other loom weights or sets of loom weights in use in the house (thickness is a crucial variable for the density of the woven cloth, and denser cloth may have been preferred in the later period). If these pyramidal loom weights had little or no practical value and had lost their significance, this could be one possible explanation for why they were left behind. If so, that suggests that even if there had been a link between the 500 BC woman and the 300 BC woman, however indirectly (whether through a line of other women invisible to us who engaged with this object and perhaps had relationships or links with more or other women in the line, *e.g.* through kinship), then somehow, that link had been forgotten or broken. In that case, some crucial part of the specific relevance, meaning and significance of the object had been lost. Five or six generations is a long time for Greek families to maintain continuity – normally Greeks forgot whom they were related to after three or four generations, and women regularly moved from their natal house to that of their husband or husband's family on marriage. All that would have been needed was for one of the women in the line to have no daughters for this loom weight to have ended up as a useless object on a shelf, whose meaning was forgotten. Effectively, it could have dropped out of the network, and while a network of relationships among women might have continued to exist, albeit morphed into another form, this particular object was no longer part of it or meaningful to it. So, its presence in this particular context could indicate the lack of a contemporary network of social relationships (or at least the lack of one that included this object); equally it could be the ghost of social networks that no longer existed.

What this example shows is that we can interpret this loom weight as a proxy for human relationships (probably mostly between women), but we cannot capture or validate most of the links, people or other objects that constituted the networks of which it was a part over time. The potential relationships and network narratives hypothesised could not easily be represented or modelled using the available methodological tools at their current stage of development, nor would it be possible to suggest which narratives are more or less likely. This object operated in a network that was spread vertically across generations, although there are horizontal spatial and geographical elements as well, especially when it is contextualised with other similar objects in the region. It is also a clear example of an object that does not exhibit autonomous agency, but which does appear to demonstrate attributed agency, in this case based on a shared body of knowledge (about weaving technology), and perhaps also on some knowledge of its lineage as an heirloom, passed through human generations.

7. Building better networks

I have tried to show that while we are good at demonstrating the existence of connections or relationships using material objects, it is much harder to understand the deep complexities of their social content, and the underlying motivations behind relationships, interactions and connections, especially when we are trying to look at many of them simultaneously, often over long time periods. This is why it is critical to pin down both the ways and the extent to which material objects themselves perform as actors in such networks, and how they might serve as proxy data for representing and analysing them, if we are to develop robust and sufficiently sophisticated formal quantitative, and qualitative, methodologies for understanding how complex clusters of relationships functioned in the past. By building our models and networks on assumptions that are not adequate for representing sufficient complexity of behaviours or motivations (*e.g.* risk or uncertainty), assumptions that are anachronistically modern (*e.g.* assuming optimization is always a top priority) and by not explicitly considering and clarifying what we think our proxy data is proxy for, the outcomes will in many cases have limited interpretative utility. At present quantitative methodologies are most effectively deployed to test a straightforward and carefully constrained hypothesis about a body of data, for example Broodbank's (2000) use of Primal Point Analysis to test the centrality of specific Early Bronze Age island sites in the Aegean, or to choose the best fit to data from among several hypotheses, as in Brughmans and Poblome's (2016) study of the economy of the early Roman eastern Mediterranean region, discussed above. Often the outcomes simply confirm previous views (*e.g.* Östborn and Gerding 2014, 78; Amati *et al.* 2020, 201–15).

By exaggerating or misrepresenting the agency of material objects we are in danger of distorting their key roles in social networks, both in relation to human agency, as well as in relation to other objects that we no longer have. We need to be more explicit about the limits of our evidence and data and their capacity to serve as proxies. We need to consider in more depth the full range of relationships that our chosen data for modelling might be proxies for; in addition we need to test at least some of this range of possibilities and to set out explicitly how these limits might encourage us to reimagine those ancient networks and connections more openly and flexibly.

On the other hand, we need to develop our own quantitative and qualitative methodologies that are specifically designed for the character and kinds of data that we have, for example to design, represent and visualise networks that are simultaneously vertical and horizontal. To achieve this, we must move beyond the application of methodologies designed for data of different quality, density and resolution. Much exciting research is underway to improve the sophistication and broaden the scope of both quantitative approaches such as SNA and ABCM, as well as more qualitative and theoretical approaches to networks of people and things. To expand their utility we need to ensure that as improved and new methodologies emerge we find better ways to build in more sophisticated underlying assumptions, appropriate to the particular kinds of societies we are investigating, and that we develop more effective and sophisticated techniques for modelling complexity, dynamism and time depth. No model can capture the full depth and richness of the ancient networks we study on the basis of the evidence we have, nor should we expect them to; that is not their purpose. But we can improve the interpretive utility of network perspectives and models and their fit to our data sets if we control more carefully the simplification of relationships for modelling purposes, and we do not over-claim the power of the things we have.

References

Amati, V., Shafie, T. and Brandes, U. (2018) Reconstructing archaeological networks with structural holes. *Journal of Archaeological Method and Theory* 25, 226–53.

Amati, V., Mol, A., Shafie, T., Hofman, C. and Brandes, U. (2020) A framework for reconstructing archaeological networks using exponential random graph models. *Journal of Archaeological Method and Theory* 27, 192–219.

Appadurai, A. (ed.) (1986) *The Social Life of Things*. Cambridge, Cambridge University Press.

Brughmans, T. (2013) Thinking through networks: a review of formal network methods in archaeology. *Journal of Archaeological Method and Theory* 20, 623–62.

Brughmans, T., Keay, S. and Earl, G. (2015) Understanding inter-settlement visibility in Iron Age and Roman southern Spain with exponential random graph models for visibility networks. *Journal of Archaeological Method and Theory* 22, 58–143.

Brughmans, T. and Poblome, J. (2016) Roman bazaar or market economy? Explaining tableware distributions through computational modelling. *Antiquity* 90, 393–408.

Brysbaert, A. (2007) Cross-craft and cross-cultural interactions during the Aegean and eastern Mediterranean Late Bronze Age. In S. Antoniadou and A. Pace (eds) *Mediterranean Crossroads*, 325–59. Athens, Pierides Foundation.

Cegieski, W.H. and Rogers, J.D. (2016) Rethinking the role of agent-based modelling in archaeology. *Journal of Anthropological Archaeology* 41, 283–98.

Collar, A., Coward, F., Brughmans, T. and Mills, B. (2015) Networks in archaeology: phenomena, abstraction, representation. *Journal of Archaeological Method and Theory* 22, 1–32.

Flache, A. (2018) Between monoculture and cultural polarization: agent-based models of the interplay of social influence and cultural diversity. *Journal of Archaeological Method and Theory* 25, 996–1023.

Forbes, H.A. (2007) *Meaning and Identity in a Greek Landscape. An archaeological ethnography*. Cambridge, Cambridge University Press.

Foxhall, L. (2011) Loom weights. In J.C. Carter and A. Prieto (eds) *The Chora of Metaponto 3. The Survey I. Bradano to Basento*, 539–54. Austin, TX, University of Texas Press.

Foxhall, L. (2012) Family time: temporality, materiality and women's networks in ancient Greece. In J. Marincola, L. Llewellyn-Jones and C. Maciver (eds) *Greek Notions of the Past in the Archaic and Classical Eras. History without historians*, 183–206. Edinburgh, Edinburgh University Press.

Foxhall, L. (2013) *Studying Gender in Classical Antiquity*. Cambridge, Cambridge University Press.

Foxhall, L (2018) Loom weights. In J.C. Carter and K. Swift (eds) *The Chora of Metaponto 7. The Pantanello Sanctuary*, 1027–86. Austin, TX, University of Texas Press.

Foxhall, L. (2020) The village beyond the village: communities in rural landscapes in ancient Greek countrysides. *Journal of Modern Greek Studies* 38.1, 1–20.

Gell, A. (1998) *Art and Agency: an anthropological theory*. Oxford, Oxford University Press.

Gibson, J. (1986) *The Ecological Approach to Visual Perception*. London, Routledge.

Gosden, C. (2005) What do objects want? *Journal of Archaeological Method and Theory* 12, 193–211.

Gosden, C. (2008) Social ontologies. *Philosophical Transactions of the Royal Society* 363, 2003–10.

Gosden. C. and Malafouris, L. (2015) Process archaeology (P-Arch). *World Archaeology* 47.5, 701–17.

Gosden, C. and Marshall, Y. (1999) The cultural biography of objects. *World Archaeology* 31, 169–78.

Hodder, I. (2012) *Entangled: an archaeology of the relationships between humans and things*. Cambridge, Cambridge University Press.

Hodder, I. and Lucas, G. (2017) The symmetries and asymmetries of human-thing relations. A dialogue. *Archaeological Dialogues* 24, 119–37.

Hodder, I. and Mol, A. (2016) Network analysis and entanglement. *Journal of Archaeological Method and Theory* 23, 1066–94.

Ingold, T. (2011) *Redrawing Anthropology: materials, movements, lines*. Aldershot, Ashgate.

Jeffery, L.H. (1990) *The Local Scripts of Archaic Greece*. Rev. with suppl. by A.W. Johnston. Oxford, Clarendon Press.

Knappett, C. (2011) *An Archaeology of Interaction*. Oxford, Oxford University Press.

Kopytoff, I. (1986) The cultural biography of things: commoditization as process. In A. Appadurai (ed.) *The Social Life of Things*, 64–92. Cambridge, Cambridge University Press.

Lanza Catti, E. and Swift, K. (2014) *The Chora of Metaponto 5: a Greek farmhouse at Ponte Fabrizio*. Austin, TX, University of Texas Press.

Latour, B. (2005) *Reassembling the Social: an introduction to actor-network theory*. Oxford, Oxford University Press.

Östborn, P. and Gerding, H. (2014) Network analysis of archaeological data: a systematic approach. *Journal of Archaeological Science* 46, 75–88.

Robb, J. (2010) Beyond agency. *World Archaeology* 42, 493–520.

Roux, V. and Manzo, G. (2018) Social boundaries and networks in the diffusion of innovations: a short introduction. *Journal of Archaeological Method and Theory* 25, 967–73.

Sellett, F. (1993) Châine opératoire: the concept and its applications. *Lithic Technology* 18.1–2, 106–12.

Spuybroek, L. (2015) *The Sympathy of Things: Ruskin and the ecology of design*. London, Bloomsbury.

Vadala, J. and Duffy, L. (2020) Using Actor-Network Theory to characterize the production of ancient Maya caching events at Cerro Maya (Cerros, Belize). *Journal of Archaeological Method and Theory* [early view]. doi: https://doi.org/10.1007/s10816-020-09485-4.

Van Oyen, A. (2016) *How Things Make History: the Roman Empire and its terra sigillata pottery*. Amsterdam, Amsterdam University Press.

Van Oyen, A. (2017a) Finding the material in 'material culture'. Form and matter in Roman concrete. In A. Van Oyen and M. Pitts (eds) *Materialising Roman Histories*, 133–99. Oxford, Oxbow Books.

Van Oyen, A. (2017b) Agents and Commodities: a response to Brughmans and Poblome (2016) on modelling the Roman economy. *Antiquity* 91, 1356–63.

Chapter 2

Zeitgeist: materialised worldviews in archaeology

Susanne Hakenbeck, Katharina Rebay-Salisbury and Roderick B. Salisbury

Wagner
Verzeiht! Es ist ein groß Ergötzen,
Sich in den Geist der Zeiten zu versetzen,
Zu schauen, wie vor uns ein weiser Mann gedacht,
Und wie wir's dann zuletzt so herrlich weit gebracht.

Faust
O ja, bis an die Sterne weit!
Mein Freund, die Zeiten der Vergangenheit
Sind uns ein Buch mit sieben Siegeln.
Was Ihr den Geist der Zeiten heißt,
Das ist im Grund der Herren eigner Geist,
In dem die Zeiten sich bespiegeln.

J.W. von Goethe, *Faust. Erster Teil*, 1808

This article investigates large-scale, broadly contemporaneous patterns of archaeological evidence that are shared beyond cultural or regional boundaries and have no obvious point of origin. *Zeitgeist* offers a conceptual framework that allows us to discuss these phenomena. It champions an investigation of the large scale while retaining a direct link with people's subjective and personal experience of the world. Three case studies examine the concept of material worldviews for different periods: 1. the emergence of Kreisgrabenanlagen in the Carpathian basin at the end of the Neolithic, 2. the reappearance of human representations at the Bronze Age/Iron Age transition and 3. the rise of a new burial practice and a new use of metalwork in the early Middle Ages. A shared *Zeitgeist* seems to be of particular importance during periods of great social upheaval when it appears to provide a sense of stability and a rootedness in a particular time.

Key words: *Zeitgeist*, Neolithic, Bronze Age, Iron Age, Middle Ages, worldview, materiality

1. Introduction

In all regions and periods, we come across large-scale, broadly contemporaneous phenomena shared beyond cultural or regional boundaries. *Zeitgeist*, the dominant intellectual, cultural, ethical and political climate of an era, or the spirit of the age, describes such trends. We propose that the concept of *Zeitgeist* may provide archaeology with a new way of understanding these complex phenomena, distinct from other theoretical models of shared cultural traits that are based on evolutionary change, the spread of peoples or culture groups, or the direct transmission of ideas. We see *Zeitgeist* phenomena as not fitting into any of these models.

Crucially, *Zeitgeist* phenomena have no obvious single point of origin. Differently from, for instance, the spread of agriculture or metallurgy for which a direct transmission of knowledge is required, such *Zeitgeist* phenomena do not have an obvious point of origin and do not appear to be transmitted in a linear way. Yet they are shared across long distances. They appear to be expressions of deeply running ideological currents – the *Zeitgeist* of an era.

Theoretical engagements with time as an important concept in archaeology have regained popularity recently (*e.g.* Lucas 2005; Robb and Pauketat 2008), as archaeologists direct their attention back to the observation and explanation of long-term change and large-scale phenomena (*e.g.* Bintliff 1991; Clark 1999; Robb and Harris 2013; Shennan 2013). In this article, which emerged from a session at the annual meeting of the European Association of Archaeologists in Riva del Garda 2009 (Rebay-Salisbury and Hakenbeck 2009), we will discuss some issues such as long-distance communication, collective experience, chronological and geographical networks and material expressions of ideas that are captured by the concept of *Zeitgeist*.

2. *Zeitgeist* in its time

Zeitgeist broadly means the spirit that marks the thought or feeling of an era, describing its intellectual, cultural, ethical and political climate. The concept emerges in the second half of the eighteenth century as a response to the perceived loss of truths that had been considered certain and timeless before the Enlightenment (Konersmann 2006). Knowledge is now for the first time understood to be specific to a particular era. The word *Zeitgeist* can be traced to a debate between Christian Adolph Klotz and Johann Gottfried Herder in the 1760s about the merits of using coins to determine the national character of the ancient Greeks and later peoples (Hiery 2001). Klotz aimed to draw out the unique aspects of an epoch – the *genius saeculi* – through what we now call material culture (Klotz 1767). Herder translated the term into German and thus coined *Zeitgeist* (Otto 1769 [1990], 396). He defines it as 'the collection of thoughts, attitudes, efforts, desires and living forces, which become manifest in a particular course of events with given causes and effects' (Suphan 1877, 80, our translation). In Herder's writings, *Zeitgeist* represents the 'spirit of the age' as much as the 'spirit of our age'. Ultimately, it is an expression of the 'genius of humanity' common to all peoples across all epochs (Konersmann 2004).

Influenced by the fall-out from the French revolution, *Zeitgeist* takes on two distinct meanings in the early nineteenth century (Konersmann 2004). On the one hand, it directly refers to current events, where it is used to describe the collective energy that influences political convictions, for better or worse. In this sense, Johann Wolfgang Goethe's Faust questions the contemporary popular enthusiasm with *Zeitgeist* as a progressive force. On the other hand, *Zeitgeist* becomes a concept within the history of philosophy, developed in particular by Georg Friedrich Wilhelm Hegel, according to whom the aim of philosophy is to understand an era by its thoughts:

> As for the individual, everyone is a son of his time; so philosophy also is its time apprehended in thoughts. It is just as foolish to fancy that any philosophy can transcend its present world, as that an individual could leap out of his time or jump over Rhodes. (Hegel 1821 [2001], 19)

Philosophy has to transcend the specifics of the *Zeitgeist* but also to engage with the social and political issues of a particular era (Bollenbeck 2007, 123f.). In Hegel's writings, the notion of *Zeitgeist* was closely linked to the idea of the *Volksgeist*, the spirit of a people. Just as a period in time was characterised by a certain intellectual spirit, so a people was defined through its ethnic spirit, or fundamental national characteristics.

Both concepts became popular among revolutionary Romantics in the period between the French Revolution and the revolutions of 1848, because they felt themselves to have been directly caught up in the 'revolutionary spirit'. Hegel's followers see *Zeitgeist* as a historical subject worthy of investigation and one that ought consciously to be enacted. While Herder had aimed to define the multiple expressions of an era into a coherent *Zeitgeist*, Hegelians now reverse effect and cause: *Zeitgeist* is not an expression of an era, but its driving force (Konersmann 2006). Nationalism and political unification were the central political projects of the nineteenth century, and the purpose of the *Zeitgeist* was therefore seen as bringing them to life. By the end of the nineteenth and the early twentieth century, the two meanings of *Zeitgeist* converge again. *Zeitgeist* (along with its related concept *Volksgeist*) is reified as a social and political force. As such it is used by critics and proponents of nationalism and later Nazi ideology alike (Konersmann 2004).

Nevertheless, it remained popular throughout the twentieth century. This is illustrated, for instance, by Michel Foucault's reworking of the concept. Foucault criticises the Hegelian transcendental aspect of *Zeitgeist*, focusing instead on the 'total set of relations that unite, at a given period, the discursive practices that give rise to epistemological figures, sciences, and possibly formalised systems' (Foucault 1969 [2005], 211). This so-called *episteme*, however, rings familiar:

> This *episteme* may be suspected of being something like a world-view, a slice of history common to all branches of knowledge, which imposes on each one the same norms and postulates, a general stage of reason, a certain structure of thought that the men of a particular period cannot escape – a great body of legislation written once and for all by some anonymous hand. (Foucault 1969 [2005], 211)

3. *Zeitgeist* and archaeology

Zeitgeist and *Volksgeist* were powerful concepts in the philosophy of history in the nineteenth century, and they provided the foundation of thinking about archaeological remains. As early as 1767, Klotz had tried to draw out the characteristics peculiar to a particular time and people from a study of ancient coins (Klotz 1767). *Volksgeist* provided a link between past peoples and their technology and material culture (Brather 2000, 149ff.; Gramsch 2006). The development of a certain technology in the past was considered the expression of sprit of a people. This was codified in the writings of Gustaf Kossinna, who made a link between ethnic groups and archaeological material when he spoke of 'ethnographically sharply defined cultures' (Kossinna 1896, 2). In 1911, he clarified this further, creating the axiom that 'sharply defined archaeological provinces at all times coincide with specific peoples or tribes of peoples' (Kossinna 1911, 3).

Kossinna's thinking directly fed into the political instrumentalisation of prehistory during the Nazi period. Intellectual engagement with the role of archaeologists during the Nazi period began soon after 1945 (Hakelberg 2001, 274ff.). Kossinna, who had already been criticised by his contemporaries, was presented as a convenient scapegoat: he not only carried all guilt for the ideological misuse of archaeology, but also exonerated his critics. In the following decades the so-called 'Kossinna-syndrome' (Smolla 1979/1980) brought about a retreat from grand narratives and large-scale theorising in German archaeology in favour of writing individual site histories and a more descriptive approach to life in the past (Härke 1991; 1995).

Anglophone archaeology continued to champion interpretations at the large scale into the 1980s. Gordon Childe (1925; 1950), Grahame Clark (1952), Glyn Daniel (1963) and Lewis Binford (1983), amongst many others, frequently operated at super-regional levels, propounding theories about long-term cultural change. Influenced by a postmodern loss of certainty, post-processual archaeological theories in the 1980s criticised earlier large-scale syntheses and grand narratives, because they did not place enough emphasis on individual agency. Post-processual theories represented a philosophical shift from a view of the world as objectively observable to an internal perspective that emphasised the subjective and personal experience of the world (Hodder 1987). Throughout the 1990s, the focus lay almost exclusively on the individual, his or her experience of the world, and on the subjective and multiple meanings of material culture. Research interests shifted from large-scale regional overviews to the histories of specific sites or landscapes. Social change was explained primarily with indigenous developments and, more specifically, with the notion that shifting ideas and identities bring about change in material culture.

This rejection of the large-scale effectively threw the baby out with the bathwater. Post-processual critique equated the large-scale with social, economic or environmental determinism, because many earlier studies had drawn on systems and structures for their interpretations. Instead, post-processual interpretations were committed to building interpretations from the local, individual or single artefact. Local developments were tied loosely into larger-scale patterns, but rarely sought to contribute to their better understanding. While such bottom-up approaches certainly challenged established grand narratives of migration, diffusion and evolution, this seldom resulted in different explanations at the top. However, interpretations operating at different scales of resolution do not necessarily have to fall into different theoretical camps. Indeed, the necessity for integrating interpretations of archaeological patterns at multiple scales of resolution is increasingly recognised (*e.g.* Robb 2008; Hakenbeck 2011; Parkinson and Gyucha 2012; Robb and Harris 2013).

Our chapter is intended as a further contribution to this issue. In contrast to large-scale studies that address both large areas and long time spans, primarily with the aim of explaining cultural change, this study is concerned with large-scale, broadly contemporaneous patterns in the archaeological record which cross-cut traditional notions of regions, cultures and trajectories. These we see as material manifestations of the *Zeitgeist*, 'time-slices', so to speak; phenomena that express temporal identity, but cannot be understood in terms of a point of origin, diffusion or cultural change. The following three case studies will exemplify the notion of *Zeitgeist* in the archaeological record in three very different settings.

Capitalising on the malleability of the concept since its first use in the late eighteenth century, we move away from Hegel's *Zeitgeist* as an external force towards a contemporary reinterpretation. In his work on cultural philosophy, Ralf Konersmann (2006, 263) has suggested that *Zeitgeist* is experienced as 'home in time', that is a sense of belonging to or rootedness in a particular time. Konersmann draws a parallel to people's sense of belonging in geographical space: 'What is experienced and appreciated as home in geographical space, is *Zeitgeist* in temporal space' (Konersmann 2006, 248, our translation). In a world where events and the passing of time are experienced as contingent, a feeling of belonging to the *Zeitgeist* provides orientation and stability (Konersmann 2006, 262ff.). As such, *Zeitgeist* represents a particular worldview rooted in time. This rootedness is integral to Foucault's (1969 [2005], 211) notion of the *episteme* (his interpretation of *Zeitgeist*) as the 'total set of relations' between different forms of practice. *Zeitgeist* is not an idea that is external and detached from the world, but is grounded in people's practices. Archaeological patterns that we would call *Zeitgeist* phenomena therefore represent a materialised worldview and this may be shared over large geographical areas.

4. *Zeitgeist* in today's world

The term *Zeitgeist* has entered our everyday vocabulary in both German and English (Fig. 2.1), and it is also popular in many other languages. In a globalised world, it seems to satisfy the need for a sense of belonging, shifting the sense of identity from the national and ethnic to the temporal. Its philosophical baggage has largely been lost in contemporary usage, and *Zeitgeist* now is a popular concept in architecture, design, music and other branches of art. *Zeitgeist* might be tied to a worldview in which the individual understands him- or herself in terms of a global community. An example of this is 'The Zeitgeist Movement'. Inspired by a film from 2007 (Zeitgeist 2007), it advocates a broad social change of global society from a monetary-based economy to a resource-based economy. It aims at unifying the world through a common ideology based on the fundamentals of life and nature to solve all the world's problems, ignoring conventional politics, religion and traditions.

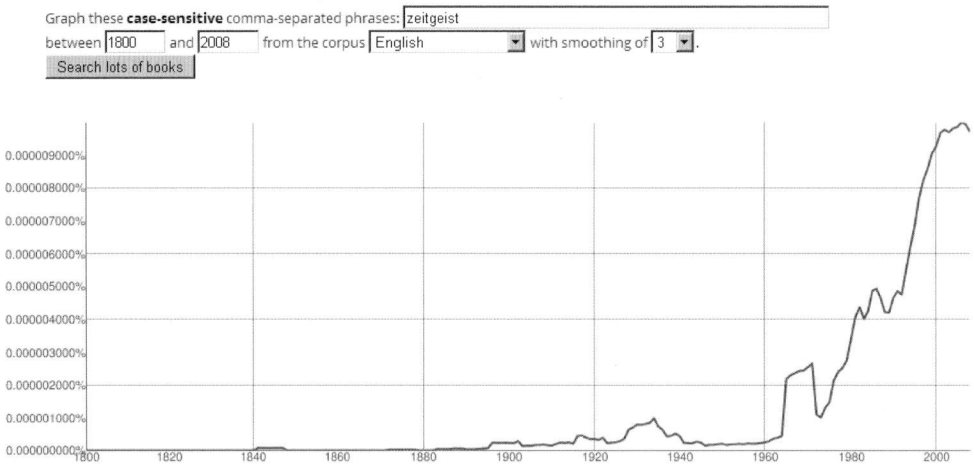

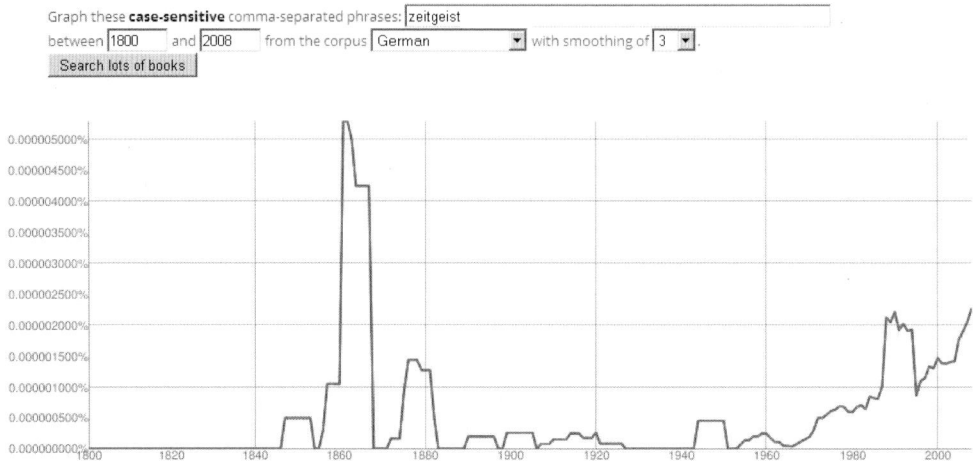

Figure 2.1 The frequency of the use of the word 'Zeitgeist' in English and German books between 1800 and 2008, normalised by the number of books published in each year (data source and graph generated by Google Books Ngram Viewer, http://books.google.com/ngrams, accessed 31 January 2012).

The internet platform Google offered 'Google Zeitgeist' (http://www.google.com/zeitgeist/, accessed 31 January 2012), an insight into millions of search queries on the internet every day tracked by one of the most popular search engines. Google Zeitgeist covered the years 2001 to 2011 and was then replaced by Google Trends. With Google Zeitgeist, the spirit of the age is captured through a statistical analysis of popular search-terms, revealing what 'captured the world's attention'. Archives go back as early as 2001 – surely a lifetime in internet terms. Interest in news items, celebrity names, sports and passions are ranked and can be browsed by countries, regions, languages and time spans, zooming in on weeks, months and years. As queries become more and more complex, so do associated statistics. These data not only reveal a general sense of what people were interested in at any given time, but can be extremely useful in a practical sense, for instance when monitoring outbreaks of pandemics like dengue or flu (Ginsberg *et al.* 2009) or responding to natural disasters and humanitarian crises by analysing information flow (http://www.google.org/crisisresponse/, accessed 31 January 2012).

In 2012, many information providers such as the BBC and the Guardian offered services, now defunct, showing readers what might be most interesting to them based on what other readers read (or clicked on). With Google Trends (http://www.trends.google.com, accessed 4 January 2021), average worldwide traffic of search terms and occurrence of particular words on websites can be numerically investigated: entering the term *Zeitgeist* revealed that it was particularly popular in 2007, when The Smashing Pumpkins released their album 'Zeitgeist', when Google *Zeitgeist* was first launched, and then at the end of each year when Google's end of the year *Zeitgeist* list was revealed. By 2014, searches for the word flat lined. Tools and applications like these give an instant sense of what is important to many people around the globe, and they reveal trends in real time, such as the seven-year history of *Zeitgeist* as a trivia topic – but can we identify trends, interests and ideologies in retrospect, without the help of digital technology or documentary evidence? How might we identify *Zeitgeist* in archaeological data and deep time spans? We have picked three case studies from different periods in European pre- and proto-history to illustrate what we mean by *Zeitgeist* phenomena.

5. Case study: circular enclosures (*Kreisgräben*)

We often impose our ideas on the past, as explanations that reflect how we think the past should have been, and the explanations change as the social paradigms of the interpreters change. For example, we explain ditches and fences surrounding settlements as defensive structures, because we are heavily focused on conflict today and because enclosures then have a readily identifiable function. If people stop building enclosures, then conflict must have ceased as well. In some cases this link between form and function may be partially true; the Iroquois Nations of New York State constructed timber palisades around their settlements for purposes that included defence, and the size and complexity of these increased when pressure from European expansion and demand for furs caused increased conflict with other tribes (Coyne 1903; Barr 2006).

In other cases, such as the Neolithic ditch enclosures – *Kreisgrabenanlagen* or rondels – of the fifth-millennium BC in Central Europe, conflict or crisis does not seem to have been the reason for their construction. Their distribution, relatively narrow period of construction and the limited evidence regarding their function make them an inter-esting candidate for thinking about *Zeitgeist*.

Sites enclosed by ditches are not peculiar to either the time or the space of the archetypal *Kreisgrabenanlagen*. Causewayed enclosures are known from Neolithic England, France and Denmark (Andersen 1993; Darvill and Thomas 2001; Oswald *et al.* 2001), Neolithic ditched enclosures occur in southeast Italy (Skeates 2002), Copper Age ditched enclosures of varying size and complexity are found across the Iberian peninsula (Diaz-Del-Rio 2004), and earthwork enclosures such as Poverty Point are known from the Archaic period in the southeastern United States (Sassaman 2005). Summarised in Parkinson and Duffy, prehistoric enclosure types and the terminology used to describe them vary widely (Parkinson and Duffy 2007, 102, table 1), and they are found throughout Europe (Parkinson and Duffy 2007, 99, fig. 2).

Kreisgrabenanlagen are common at the macro-regional scale, occurring across north-ern Austria, western Hungary and parts of southern Slovakia, the Czech Republic and southeast Germany. Temporally, they cover the period between 4800 and 4500 BC, the period of the Lengyel and late *Stichbandkeramik* groups (Petrasch 1990; Trnka 1991; Daim and Neubauer 2005). Most *Kreisgrabenanlagen* are known from aerial reconnais-sance and geophysical prospection. In hilly regions, they have been exposed to severe erosion, and remains of interior features are rare. There is therefore little evidence for their function, and the few radiocarbon dates that exist mostly come from within the ditches. Thus, relatively little is known about them except for their distribution and general physical form. We do not know why they were constructed, what people did at them, and how they fit within the larger social networks. We propose that there were practical reasons for the development of enclosed sites during the Neolithic, that enclosures in Central and southeast Europe broadly, and the Carpathian Basin more specifically, were functional aspects of settlement design. Over time, they became formalised in design as they began to reflect a *Zeitgeist* that has little to do with what we may think of as 'practical' or 'pragmatic' function.

During the sixth millennium BC, *Linearbandkeramik* farmers in Central Europe began constructing various combinations of ditches, palisades and earthworks around some settlements. Ditches are typically V-shaped cuts running parallel to one another, generally enclosing less than 2 ha, with irregular forms varying from round to oblong to nearly rectangular (Petrasch 1990). *Linearbandkeramik* enclosures like Herxheim, Weinstein and Asparn were most likely constructed as fortifications, based on osteological evidence of violence (Orschiedt and Haidle 2006). Enclosures from the *Linearbandkeramik* period in the eastern Carpathian Basin appear to be less widespread, with the eastern *Linearbandkeramik* site of Csanytelek-Újhalastó (Hegedűs 1981) being the best known.

Populations in eastern Hungary had nucleated by the end of the sixth millennium. Large horizontal sites and vertical settlement mounds, or tells, came to dominate the settlement pattern in eastern Hungary, and many sites from this period were surrounded at least partially by ditches. For example, there are ditches around Tisza culture sites such as Vésztő-Mágor (Sarris *et al.* 2013) and the latest occupation phase at Gorzsa (Horváth 1987), as well as at Herpály sites like Berettyóújfalu-Herpály (Kalicz and Raczky 1984). The specific function of these features is not certain. They have alternatively been interpreted as animal pens (Tringham 1971), defensive fortifications (Chapman 1981, 151; Kalicz and Raczky 1987), strategies for drainage and water control (Chapman 1981, 90–2), devices to define settlement perimeters or for purposes of inclusion and exclusion (Bailey 2000); probably they served several or all of these functions. Nucleated tell settlements in the southern Balkans, often surrounded by ditches, began earlier than those in Hungary, and the fortification of villages in Central Europe continued into the Bronze Age (Parkinson and Duffy 2007).

During the early fifth millennium BC, enclosures in Central Europe become more formalised in design and no longer necessarily surround settlements. These earthworks comprise very precise, concentric arrangements of banks, ditches and timber palisades, typically enclosing areas of 70–100 m, but varying from as small

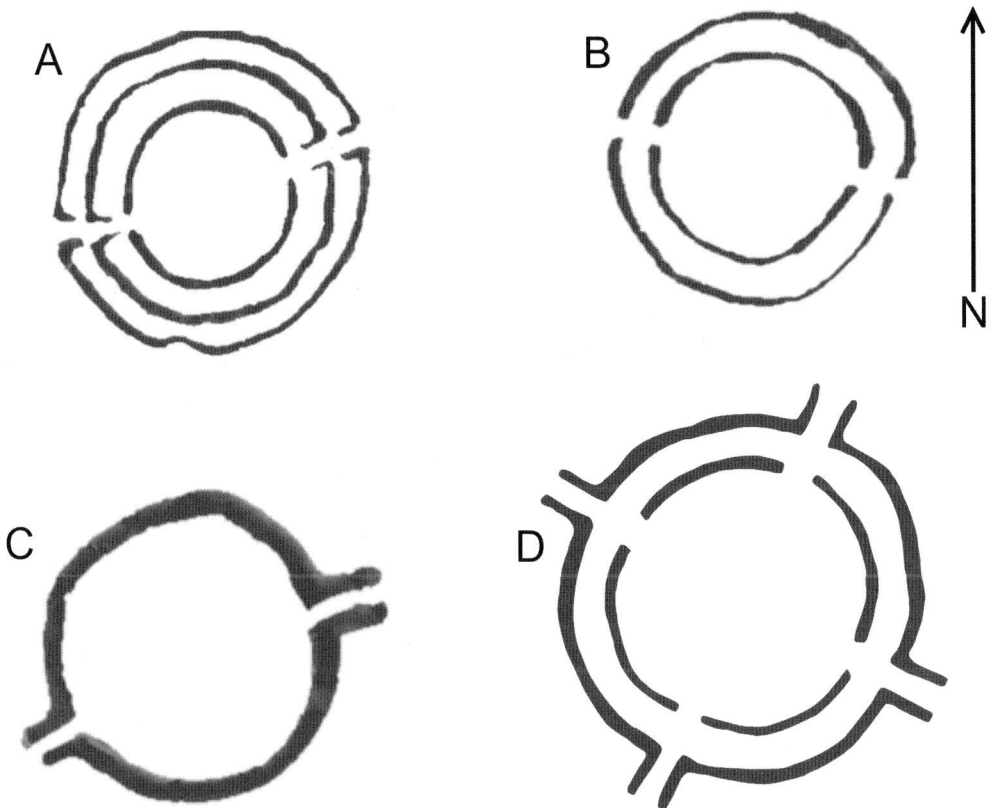

Figure 2.2 Circular ditch enclosures of Central Europe, Lengyel culture. (A) Hornsburg 1, Lower Austria. (B) Hornsburg 2, Lower Austria. (C) Schletz, Lower Austria. (D) Bučany, Slovakia. Not to scale.

as 30 m to as large as 300 m. In the classic form, best known from the Lengyel culture of western Hungary and adjacent regions, there are two or four narrow entrances set opposite to each other. Examples include the sites of Hornsburg 1 and 2 (Fig. 2.2 (A and B)) and Schletz (Fig. 2.2 (C)) in Lower Austria (Daim and Neubauer 2005), Bučany-Kopanice (Fig. 2.2 (D)) in Slovakia (Bujna and Romsauer 1986) and Szemely-Hegyes in southwest Hungary (Bertók and Gáti 2011). The ditches are roughly V-shaped in section, up to 5 m deep and 8 m wide. Sometimes they were re-cut: segments of ditches near the western entrance at Hornsburg 2 in Lower Austria showed signs of multiple cutting and infilling episodes. Often there are circular timber palisades within the rings of ditches. Although differing in detail from site to site, this very formal circular layout seems to adhere to a preconceived overall plan. This particular feature distinguishes the *Kreisgrabenanlagen* from other Neolithic enclosures.

At the same time, there were ring ditch systems in the eastern Carpathian Basin that did enclose settlements. Probably the best-known example from outside the Lengyel area is the circular enclosure within the large Neolithic settlement of Polgár-Csőszhalom, a site in northeast Hungary with a 4.5 m high tell surrounded by five concentric ditches – a combination of a *Lengyel*-type *Kreisgrabenanlage* and a Herpály-type tell – set within a larger horizontal settlement (Raczky *et al.* 2007). The settlement of Vésztő-Bikeri has a ditch and palisade system surrounding a small settlement with houses, pits and evidence for several rebuilding episodes (Parkinson *et al.* 2004). There are other Hungarian settlements with ditches, including the Tisza site of Csárdaszállás-26 (Salisbury *et al.* 2013) Tiszapolgár sites at Körösladány-Bikeri (Parkinson *et al.* 2010) and Bélmegyer (Goldman 1977), and the Bodrogkeresztúr settlement at Szarvas-38, which contains a large *Kreisgrabenanlage* reminiscent of Lengyel sites (Makkay 1983). These sites speak to how embedded the construction of enclosures had become in Neolithic cultures in this part of the world. Even when the overall settlement pattern in the Great Hungarian Plain changed from nucleated settlements to dispersed farmsteads in c. 4500 BC, the construction of ditches was continued, not for all settlements, but at least for some.

Kreisgrabenanlagen have been subject to nearly as many interpretations as other enclosures – they could be forts (Pavúk 1991), astronomical observatories (Pásztor *et al.* 2008; Zotti and Neubauer 2011), chronological devices (Gervautz and Neubauer 2005), or act as ceremonial gathering places (Whittle 1996, 190–1). The structure and topographic location of most suggests they would fail as defensive structures. Perhaps the other possibilities all played a role, functioning as a mechanism for creating temporal identity of a macro-community. However, an important caveat about simplistic interpretations of *Kreisgrabenanlagen* is that while they are all generally similar – we know one when we see one – they are also all slightly different. No two rondels are identical, and their variance is polythetic, meaning that no one attribute of a rondel is both essential and sufficient to establish the monument as a Middle Neolithic *Kreisgrabenanlagen* (Taylor 2012). Therefore, they were intended to be recognisable as what they were, yet also recognisable as unique to the community that built them. Equally important is that enclosures, all being slightly different in both topographic position and structure, could not all have played the role of calendar, nor all aligned with the same astronomical observations. Acknowledging that one or a few could have played these roles, with the others perhaps being poor copies that never worked, this leads us to search for an alternative interpretation.

A direct and fundamental connection between people and soil may be part of this alternative interpretation. Soil was, for several millennia, a primary category of material: a material that affords fertility, solidity and plasticity. Within the early agricultural communities of Central Europe, soil was the construction material of choice for houses, pots, dishes, statues, figurines and, of course, for enclosures and other earthworks. Through time, beliefs and traditions associated with soil would become more ingrained, and also altered and ritualised. This connection with the soil is coupled with a long tradition of digging ditches. We should consider the profound social and cosmological consequences that feeling, piercing and altering of soil could have in light of these deep-rooted traditions and practices (Owoc 2004; Salisbury 2012). Ideology, practice and aesthetics are combined when several communities come together to turn the soil, digging down beneath the agricultural levels to bring clean, yellow subsoil to the surface, working in circular patterns that imitate the movement of the cosmos and seasons. Evidence for multiple cleaning episodes seen in many cases where ditches have been excavated suggests that renewal through cleaning an expanse of soil and later filling the ditch, returning the soil, were likewise important experiences.

These ideas about soils, astronomical alignments and the construction of place were held by people who also shared a common economy and were engaged in wide-ranging networks of exchange and other interactions. Different culture groups in Central Europe faced landscapes that were different in important ways – *e.g.* flat marshlands versus rolling hills. They had in common soil as economically and cosmologically important, and they shared intersubjective experiences of working and living with soil. Therefore, enclosures could act in a sort of symbiosis through several functions to provide a mechanism for creating temporal identity of a macro-community. Following Taylor's suggestion that the polythetic variance observed in the structure of these enclosures was an important source of information in the past (Taylor 2012), part of the *Zeitgeist*, then could also be the desire to express membership in a local community and membership in a macro-regional community in one monument. We can interpret the *Kreisgrabenanlagen*, at least, as physical manifestations of a *Zeitgeist* centred in part on shared interactions with the soil, on aspects of environmental and cosmological renewal, and aspects of self-identity. The relatively short period of *Kreisgrabenanlagen* construction, and a geographical focus in the world of the Lengyel and their neighbours, compared with the much broader spatial and temporal range of other enclosures, supports this interpretation.

6. Case study: the return of human imagery in Early Iron Age Europe

The transition from the Late Bronze Age to the Early Iron Age in Europe is character-ised not only by a technological change; it is accompanied by a number of interesting social and ideological developments. One of them is the return of human imagery to the body of figurative art in a range of media, materials and contexts. Middle and Late Bronze Age iconography in Europe appears rigid, restricted and geometric in com-parison to later periods. Only a few figurative elements such as birds, ships and some celestial motifs can be recognised (e.g. Kossack 1954; Meller 2004; Wirth 2006). Bronze Age images rarely decorate pottery, most often they are found on metal objects such as sheet bronze vessels, defensive armour, swords and belt buckles or razors, objects that are often associated with high status and warrior elites. The journey of the sun is a central Bronze Age motif: the sun is depicted as it travels from east to west during the day, and as it travels back from west to east during the night, assisted by various animals such as horses and birds or means of transport such as chariots and ships (Kaul 2004; Bradley 2006). Through these images, a shared cosmological understanding of the world is expressed, reinforced and perpetuated; perhaps we can even interpret these images as an expression of a sun-based religion.

The absence of human representation in the archaeological record of the Middle and Late Bronze Age is noteworthy, although Scandinavian and Alpine rock art (e.g. Louis and Isetti 1964; Anati 1994; Coles 2005), stele from Iberia (Harrison 2004) and figurines from the lower Danube region (Palincaş 2010) prove regional exceptions to the rule. Representing the human form in art seems something of a taboo for the period. The human body also did not feature very prominently in the burial rite of the time. In most of Europe, cremation became the dominant form of burial by the Late Bronze Age, completely replacing inhumation (Sørensen and Rebay 2008). Furthermore, objects associated with the body and elaborate grave constructions such as burial mounds cease to be important; the ubiquitous cemetery form of the late Bronze Age is the 'urnfield' with hundreds, if not thousands, of inconspicuous deposits of cremated bones in small pits or urns with few or no grave goods.

The Late Bronze Age/Iron Age transition brought a significant change in how the human body was treated and understood. This, again, becomes apparent in the burial record as well as the way in which the human body is depicted in art. With the beginning of the Iron Age, graves become more elaborate and the bodies are buried with a range of grave goods indicative of gender, activities and status. They became the focus of display in graves, often placed in chambers resembling domestic struc-tures, whilst a range of objects is placed around them. In some, but not all regions, cremation is given up in favour of inhumation, or both cremation and inhumation are used. Late Hallstatt 'princely' burials such as Vix, France (Knüsel 2002), or Hochdorf, Germany (Biel 1985), are amongst the pinnacles of this development. Most often, this fundamental change has been interpreted in terms of increased social stratification and a reorganisation of the social order; but in conjunction with the reintroduction of the human image in art we may be able to pinpoint an important ideological change, a new *Zeitgeist*.

Figurative decoration gains importance in Greece in the Middle Geometric style (about 850–760 BC) and replaces abstract decoration with minimal figure work (Boardman 1998, 15). Animals such as horses, stags, goats or waterfowl become common motifs, and humans feature in scenes of warfare on water and on land as well as on funerary scenes. Images painted on Greek vases tend to become ever more naturalistic and realistic over the next decades, providing a glimpse into everyday Greek life as well as mythology. Gods, heroes and warriors featuring in stories that have later been recorded as texts can be identified.

In temperate Europe, in the Hallstatt and Lausitz areas, we see a similar development. Early Iron Age ceramics are characterised by an explosion of decorative techniques, patterns and colours, and the depiction of humans is no longer a taboo. The way the human form is re-introduced as an acceptable motif is very interesting: rather than just adding a human image to existing motifs, familiar shapes are transformed into explicit human images. This may be accomplished by just adding small feet, arms or heads to triangles or hourglass shapes to turn them into human beings, such as on vessels from Statzendorf, Austria (Fig. 2.3; Nebelsick 1992, 405; Rebay 2006), or Krennach, Austria (Dobiat 1982, 285). In many of these Early Iron Age images, an element of ambiguity is part of the picture – is this really a human image, or rather a geometrical pattern? The very careful play with the human form may be an indicator of the careful way the boundaries of the socially acceptable are tested and gradually broken. After centuries of complying with the taboo of human depiction, it is given up.

Depictions of single human images, often representations of a particular type of person such as the orant, the hunter, the warrior or the musician, later become combined with other images to form narrative scenes; a shared repertoire of standard scenes of drinking and dancing, making music, competing in boxing or racing, or making love develops (Huth 2003; Rebay-Salisbury 2016). The images might have helped to recognise and memorise myths and widely known tales (Zipf 2006), furthermore, they communicate a certain lifestyle and pursuits that were most likely exclusive to a small high-status group or elites. The images might have played a significant and active role (Gell 1998) in casting new understandings of identity and society. It is

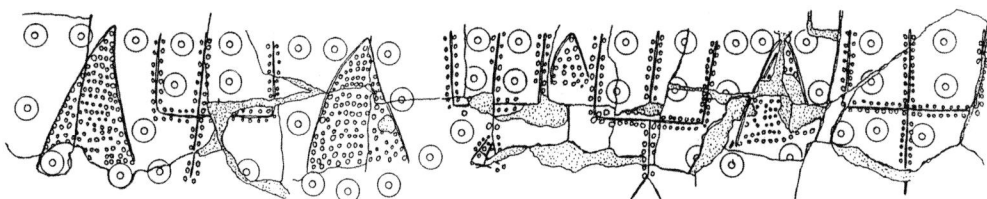

Figure 2.3 Small additions make a body. Statzendorf, Austria (Rebay 2006, 145).

difficult to decide whether it is better to interpret the scenes in terms of the profane or the religious – do they illustrate scenes of life or do they show how the afterlife might have been imagined? Are the people shown humans, heroes or gods, or all of the above as in the Mediterranean world?

The Mediterranean and Central Europe were bound up in a network of economic, diplomatic and social relationships that contributed to the transmission of technology and beliefs. Material traces of these contacts include 'imports', goods that have been produced outside the area of deposition, and were transmitted as trade goods or gifts. Copies, imitations and local varieties of goods, based on actual models and the memory of what has been seen might have been produced by travelling craftspeople. Similarities between images, motifs and narratives in both regions have long been noted (*e.g.* Kossack 1969; Siegfried-Weiss 1979; Kromer 1986; Hase 2005), but can we automatically assume a diffusion of ideas from the Mediterranean to the north or argue for independent, local developments? An alternative solution understands human images of the Early Iron Age as the expression of a new *Zeitgeist*, emerging out of a shared worldview or similar ideologies. Depicting humans is part of a large-scale, broadly contemporaneous phenomenon that is shared beyond cultural or regional boundaries and is enacted, at least initially, in local material culture and styles.

The Late Bronze Age/Iron Age transition can be understood as a broad ideological and cosmological shift, even part of new religious ideas. Whereas celestial motifs such as the sun do not completely lose their significance, they become just one of many figurative items in the endless canon of Early Iron Age imagery. It becomes acceptable to depict the human form, and a new human 'self-confidence' blurs the distinction between humans and gods; gods appear in human form and humans may be thought of as heroes or deities after death. Monumental funerary structures and excessive elaboration of grave goods for some, but not many, individuals materialise and further reinforce the idea that some individuals rise significantly over others. All these changes, including the reintroduction of human representations, might be symptoms as well as expressions of a new *Zeitgeist*.

7. Case study: shared funerary practices in early medieval Europe

With the demise of the western Roman Empire in the second half of the fifth century AD, a new burial practice gradually emerged in the frontier zones of the former Empire in Central and northern Europe. In these regions, burial practice had previously followed different traditions, such as cremation or the Roman practice that included a small number of personal adornments and frequently ceramic and glass vessels (*e.g.* Pearce *et al.* 2000).

The most characteristic archaeological feature of the early medieval period in north-central Europe, *vis-à-vis* the late Roman period, is the emergence of burials with grave goods that are directly associated with the deceased individual. Women were buried with a range of personal adornments that included large bow brooches, possibly a second set of smaller brooches, glass bead necklaces, belts and belt set attachments such as latch-lifters. For men, the burial often, but not everywhere, included a set of weapons, ornamental belt sets and personal grooming implements such as combs and tweezers (Steuer 1982, 309ff.; Bierbrauer 1994; Koch 1996; Siegmund 1996; Quast 1998). By the sixth century AD, this burial practice was prevalent in regions as far apart as Hungary and England (*e.g.* Barbiera 2005; Lucy 2000, 25ff.). A second, widespread shift in burial practice took place in the early seventh century. From Anglo-Saxon England to southern Germany, burial practice became socially more highly stratified: some graves included objects indicative of great wealth, while an increasing number was unfurnished or contained only a small number of grave goods (Böhme 1993; 1996; Geake 1997; Welch 2011). In the female burial practice, there was a move away from the use of several brooches towards the use of only one.

The introduction of furnished burial in the fifth century, and of weapon burial in particular, has long played a significant role in the central interpretive narrative of the period: that the demise of the Roman Empire was precipitated by the invasion of Germanic peoples into the territories of the empire. The introduction of a new form of burial into areas where heavily furnished graves were previously not common has been seen as evidence for the migration of Germanic groups (Werner 1973 [1950]; Böhme 1998a). Such interpretations were situated within the framework of a history of events derived from written sources. These sources spoke of a number of different Germanic tribes – Franks, Anglo-Saxons, Goths, Langobards and many others – that were the principal actors in this migration narrative (Goffart 1989). Based on their geographical distributions and assumed role in tribal dress, the various components of the burial assemblage therefore became associated with different ethnic groups (Fehr 2002, 188).

This assumed link between different kinds of artefacts or styles and the ethnicity of individuals has been criticised extensively as being inappropriate for understanding the role played by ethnicity and the way it was expressed materially during this period (Brather 2000; Lucy 2002, 72ff.; Von Rummel 2010, 63ff.; Hakenbeck 2011, 11ff.). Nevertheless, approaches to the archaeology of the early medieval period continue to emphasise variability and diversity over large-scale shared practices. Critiques of the grand narratives of the migrations of cohesive ethnic groups have drawn attention to the fragmented and multi-faceted nature of the evidence, emphasising small-scale, local and even individual identities expressed in burial (*e.g.* Lucy 1998; Theune 2004; Hakenbeck 2011). Such a nose-to-the-ground view of the evidence has numerous benefits, not least of being solidly grounded in data. However, at a high resolution other large-scale patterns that may be of equal significance may easily be missed.

If we take a step back from known historical events and the ever more detailed classifications of artefacts and look at the bigger picture, then we can see that, rather than being something that separated and distinguished people from each other, the way metalwork was produced and then used in burials was something that people had in common across large parts of Europe. From the Carpathian basin to northern

France, from England to northern Italy, grave good inventories were variations on a common theme. Manufacturing techniques and decorative styles were widely shared, combined and reworked, almost as if they were picked out from a common pattern book (cf. Martin 2020). These commonalities and the almost simultaneous changes – the emergence of the 'barbarian' burial practice in the later fifth century and the second big change in the seventh century – are representations of bigger shifts in the *Zeitgeist* of the period. They represent big social changes: new social relations at the end of the Roman Empire, and the consolidation of new forms of authority a century later. In the geographical homogeneity of burial practices and their concurrent changes, we can see materialised worldviews that were shared over wide geographical areas.

These changes in *Zeitgeist* are transmitted through many lines of communication and networks of shared practices. Metalwork is a fundamental component of grave inventories during the early medieval period, and in its creation and transmission, we can trace the transmission of *Zeitgeist*. Smiths were fundamental to this. Their social status, in particular their ability to move about freely, has long been debated (Henning 1991; von Carnap-Bornheim 2001; Pesch 2012b). Influenced by the story of Wayland the Smith in Germanic and Norse mythology, who was held captive by and forced to work for the king, the evidence for iron working at large sites such as Feddersen Wierde, northern Germany, and the Runde Berg, southwest Germany, was assumed to have been carried out by craftsmen in servitude (Haarnagel 1962; Koch 1984). A number of graves have been found that included gold and silver smithing tools and have therefore been identified as smiths' graves. Comparing grave inventories from the Iron Age through to the early medieval period, Henning (1991) noted an increase in weapons in smiths' graves, sometimes including helmets and even horse burials. Smiths therefore often seem to have been warriors as much as craftsmen. Gold and silver smithing may in fact have been elite pursuits, as much part of the accomplishments of high-status men as the ability to ride or handle weapons (Woolf 2011). Based on the variability of the evidence for smiths and metalworking it is likely that smiths were as socially heterogeneous, just as the products they were making. Highly skilled weapon smiths and gold- and silversmiths are more likely to have been itinerant or linked to high-status settlements, while the majority of blacksmiths were probably attached to rural settlements. Technological innovations followed the complex and varied paths of mobility during the late Roman and early medieval periods. Mobility could take the form of migrations of groups of people (for example, across the North Sea to East Anglia in the fifth century AD (Hills and Lucy 2013, 328ff.)), the movement of individuals to forge marriage links (Hakenbeck 2009; Hakenbeck *et al.* 2010), and travel for the purpose of trade, craft- or knowledge exchange (Werner 1961; 1970; Harris 2003, 41ff.). This created a dense network of different routes that often followed the great rivers and remains of the Roman infrastructure.

Artefacts provide insights into the creative processes of the smiths. Forms and decorations were frequently copied, referenced or reinterpreted. Ideas and designs were taken from a variety of sources, and then reshaped. Technology transfer from the Roman provinces to the areas outside the empire after the second century AD, in particular of some decorative techniques like wire inlay and fire gilding, may have been a conscious appropriation of some techniques in favour of others, reflecting local ideas about beauty and usefulness (Voß 2008). Bow brooches, the apparently quintessential barbarian artefacts, appear to have been developed from the crossbow brooches of Roman military dress. The Roman military belt, the *cingulum*, was also appropriated as part of female dress (Martin 1995). When the function of these objects changed, their meaning changed too, to express a new barbarian and a new gender identity.

The ability to transform materials may have given smiths themselves magical qualities, perhaps situating them outside or on the edge of society (Haaland 2004; Helms 2006; Birch 2011). They could be makers of powerful or dangerous objects such as swords (Theuws and Alkemade 2000) and had the ability to create new precious items from old ones (Behr 2012). Metalwork could thus also become a vehicle for the communication of complex transcendental ideas.

From the later sixth century onwards a distinct kind of interlaced animal style, Salin's Style II (Salin 1904), became ubiquitous on metalwork across wide stretches of northern and Central Europe, from Scandinavia to Pannonia and northern Italy. Its origins have been postulated as lying either in Scandinavia, where it was believed to have been developed from earlier animal ornament, or in Pannonia, influenced by Mediterranean interlace work (Haseloff 1984; Heinrich-Tamaska 2005). Yet no single point of origin can confidently be identified. Equally, the meaning of Style II imagery is unresolved. The appearance of Style II in Francia and southwest Germany has been considered to be Christian in origin with animal ornament being used to express an essentially Christian message (Arrhenius 1986), but it has also been interpreted as evidence for a unifying barbarian and pagan identity that was generated by a common understanding of pagan symbolism and myths (Hedeager 2000). Yet, it is clear that Style II was not in conflict with the Christian message, since in northern Italy and southwest Germany Style II was common on crosses made of gold foil (Fig. 2.4) that were presumably sewn onto shrouds (Böhme 1998b; Riemer 1999; Bierbrauer 2003).

More plausibly, as Pesch (2012a) suggested, Style II was a vehicle for communicating transcendental ideas that crossed religious boundaries. It was a style that was intelligible across large geographical distances, but only by those that were educated to read its complex and rule-bound symbolism. Style II appears most spectacularly on exclusive gold or gilt items such as the reliquary buckle from Sutton Hoo or high-quality brooches (Fig. 2.4). It required a shared ability, which may have been limited to the elites who were educated in its understanding.

The early medieval period was a time of great upheaval. The common experience of *Zeitgeist*, expressed through a shared understanding of material culture, provided stability in an unsettling time. Through their work, smiths communicated ideas about identity, status and authority, their place in the world and ideas about the supernatural – the *Zeitgeist* of their time. They did not operate in creative isolation, but were tied into the world in which they operated. The two big shifts in *Zeitgeist* in the early

Figure 2.4 Style II animal ornament on different artefacts from across Europe: (1) Gold-leaf cross from Immendingen, southwest Germany (seventh century); (2) gold belt buckle from Sutton Hoo, England (early seventh century); (3) gilded silver brooch from Tuscany (late sixth–early seventh century AD). Not to scale (© Trustees of the British Museum and Badisches Landesmuseum Karlsruhe).

medieval period – the emergence of barbarian polities along the former frontiers of the Roman Empire in the fifth century, and their consolidation in the seventh – were transmitted through a complex web of shared practices, joining producers and consumers, raw material, ideas, technologies and modes of transport.

8. Conclusion

Zeitgeist offers a conceptual framework that allows us to discuss the past at a large scale while retaining a direct link with people's subjective and personal experience of the world. *Zeitgeist* is generated locally, but it goes beyond cumulative variability at a local level because it represents a grand idea or particular worldview. This worldview is very specific to its time and provides what Konersmann (2006) has termed a 'home in time'. In all three case studies, *Zeitgeist* is evident in a shift in the material world, a widespread change of practice or particular aesthetic styles. The way in which *Zeitgeist* spreads and is communicated is central to understanding its role in engendering a temporal identity.

The interface between practice and style is often explained in terms of communities of practice (*e.g.* Wenger 1998; Sassaman and Rudolphi 2001; Kohring 2007), in which meanings, practices and engagement with materials are learned by daily experience. Recent work has emphasised the importance of networks for the exchange of ideas and skills in the past. Networks are not restricted to social contacts between people, they include things, architecture and the environment (cf. Latour 2005), which may act as repositories of ideas. Seeing a longhouse, for example, shapes the idea of what a house should look like and feeds into the way in which further houses are built. Even if most interaction takes place on a local scale, communities are connected by a number of external links to the outside – these may be people like itinerant smiths or things like diplomatic gifts. Communities thus linked together form a network (Watts 1999; Buchanan 2002), in which a small number of links suffice to let information flow. This 'small world phenomenon' (Granovetter 1973; 1983) is known in popular terms as the 'six degrees of separation' by which we are all connected to every other person in the world. The strong social links we may maintain on an everyday basis living in a community are vital for learning practices and forming traditions. In contrast, weak ties with people further away enable the rapid spread of information through which innovation can occur (Conway and Steward 2009). We need to bear in mind that in a world without electronic technology and written media, shared beliefs about the world only extend as far as regularly used exchange networks.

Kreisgrabenanlagen, for example, are not simply an expression of the Lengyel-era Neolithic, but might also have been a driving force in it. The communal construction of *Kreisgrabenanlagen* was, perhaps, an essential part of becoming a community, and symbolic of social capital (and perhaps political or economic capital as well). Developing out of necessity, these became monuments symptomatic of a drive for security and a broader *Zeitgeist* of enclosure. Moreover, the spatial distribution beyond the Lengyel heartland suggests that this particular expression of the enclosing *Zeitgeist* was shared via existing economic and social networks. At the same time, construction of monuments displaying a common worldview may have facilitated and secured these networks. In this way, the *Kreisgrabenanlagen* served to generate a shared identity at several scales of interaction.

The reintroduction of human representations at the Bronze Age/Iron Age transition occurs at multiple spatial scales, and may be an expression of a collective worldview. Unlike the *Kreisgrabenanlagen*, however, which may have served to bring people together at the local and regional scales, the way human representations were employed appears to separate people into different castes at the local scale while forging a common identity of elites at the regional or macro-regional scale. Similarly, changes in male burial assemblages during the early medieval period appear to represent a *Zeitgeist* of exclusivity. In both cases, however, similarities at the macro-scale suggest networks with shared ideologies.

Our case studies are all situated in periods of transition and high social instability; it seems likely that the identity-generating aspect of *Zeitgeist* was (and perhaps still is) of particular importance during times of great change and social fragmentation. *Zeitgeist*, as a widely shared materialised worldview, provides people with a temporal identity and a rootedness in their time, just at the point when times are changing.

References

Anati, E. (1994) *Valcamonica Rock Art*. Camunian Studies 13. Capo di Ponte, Edizioni del Centro.

Andersen, N.H. (1993) Causewayed enclosures of the Funnel Beaker culture. In S. Hvass and B. Storgaard (eds) *Digging into the Past: 25 years of archaeology in Denmark*, 100–3. Copenhagen and Aarhus, Royal Society of Northern Antiquaries-Jutland Archaeological Society.

Arrhenius, B. (1986) Enige christliche Paraphrasen aus dem 6. Jahrhundert. In H. Roth (ed.) *Zum Problem der Deutung frühmittelalterlicher Bildinhalte*, 129–51. Sigmaringen, Jan Thorbecke Verlag.

Bailey, D.W. (2000) *Balkan Prehistory: exclusion, incorporation, and identity*. London, Routledge.

Barbiera, I. (2005) *Changing Lands in Changing Memories*. Florence, All' Insegna del Gigllio.

Barr, D.P. (2006) *Unconquered: the Iroquois League at war in colonial America*. Westport, CT, Praeger.

Behr, C. (2012) The working of gold and its symbolic significance. In A. Pesch and R. Blankenfeldt (eds) *Goldsmith Mysteries: archaeological, pictorial and documentary evidence from the 1st millennium AD in northern Europe*, 51–8. Neumünster, Wachholtz Verlag.

Bertók, G. and Gáti, C. (2011) Neue Angaben zur spätneolithischen Siedlungsstruktur in Südosttransdanubien. *Acta Archaeologica Academiae Scientiarum Hungaricae* 62, 1–28.

Biel, J. (1985) *Der Keltenfürst von Hochdorf*. Stuttgart, Theiss.

Bierbrauer, V. (1994) Archeologia degli Ostrogoti in Italia. In V. Bierbrauer (ed.) *I Goti*, 170–213. Milano, Electa Lombardia.

Bierbrauer, V. (2003) The cross goes north: from late antiquity to Merovingian times south and north of the Alps. In M.O.H. Carver (ed.) *The Cross goes North: processes of conversion in northern Europe, AD 300-1300*, 429–42. York, York Medieval Press.

Binford, L.R. (1983) *In Pursuit of the Past: decoding the archaeological record*. London, Thames and Hudson.

Bintliff, J. (1991) The contribution of an annaliste/structural history approach to archaeology. In J. Bintliff (ed.) *The Annales School and Archaeology*, 1–33. Leicester, Leicester University Press.

Birch, T. (2011) Living on the edge: making and moving iron from the 'outside' in Anglo-Saxon England. *Landscape History* 32, 5–25.

Boardman, J. (1998) *Early Greek Vase Painting (11th-6th centuries BC): a handbook*. London, Thames and Hudson.

Böhme, H.W. (1993) Adelsgräber im Frankenreich. *Jahrbuch des Römisch-Germanischen Zentralmuseums* 40, 397–534.

Böhme, H.W. (1996) Adel und Kirche bei den Alamannen der Merowingerzeit. *Germania* 74, 477–507.

Böhme, H.W. (1998a) Franken und Romanen im Spiegel spätrömischer Grabfunde im nördlichen Gallien. In D. Geuenich (ed.) *Die Franken und die Alemannen bis zur „Schlacht bei Zülpich" (496/97)*, 31–58. Reallexikon der Germanischen Altertumskunde/Ergänzungsband 19. Berlin, Walter de Gryuter.

Böhme, H.W. (1998b) Goldblattkreuze. In R. Müller (ed.) *Reallexikon der Germanischen Altertumskunde* 12, 312–18. Berlin, Walter de Gruyter.

Bollenbeck, G. (2007) *Eine Geschichte der Kulturkritik*. München, C.H. Beck.

Bradley, R. (2006) Danish razors and Swedish rocks: cosmology and the Bronze Age landscape. *Antiquity* 80, 372–89.

Brather, S. (2000) Ethnische Identitäten als Konstrukte der frühgeschichtlichen Archäologie. *Germania* 78, 139–77.

Buchanan, M. (2002) *Nexus: small worlds and the groundbreaking science of networks*. New York, Norton.

Bujna, J. and Romsauer, P. (1986) Siedlung und Kreisanlage der Lengyel-Kultur in Bučany. In B. Chropovský and H. Friesinger (eds) *Internationales Symposium über die Lengyel-Kultur*, 27–35. Nitra, Archäologisches Institut der Slowakischen Akademie der Wissenschaften.

Chapman, J. (1981) *The Vinča Culture of South-East Europe: studies in chronology, economy and society*. 2 vols. BAR International Series 119. Oxford, British Archaeological Reports.

Childe, V.G. (1925) *The Dawn of European Civilization*. London, Kegan Paul.

Childe, V.G. (1950) *Prehistoric Migrations in Archaeology*. Instituttet for Sammenlignende Kulturforskning. Serie A: Forlesninger. Oslo, H. Aschehoug & Co.

Clark, G. (1952) *Prehistoric Europe: the economic basis*. London, Methuen.

Clark, S. (1999) *The Annales School: critical assessments*. London and New York, Routledge.

Coles, J. (2005) *Shadows of a Northern Past. Rock carvings of Bohuslän and Østfold*. Oxford, Oxbow Books.

Conway, S. and Steward, F. (2009) *Managing and Shaping Innovation*. Oxford, Oxford University Press.

Coyne, J.H. (1903) Galinée's narrative and nap (1669–70). In *Ontario Historical Society, Papers and Records* 4, 2–75. Toronto, ON, Ontario Historical Society.

Daim, F. and Neubauer, W. (eds) (2005) *Zeitreise Heldenberg, geheimnisvolle Kreisgräben: Niederösterreichische Landesausstellung 2005. Katalog des Niederösterreichischen Landesmuseums, Neue Folge 459*. St Pölten, Berger.

Daniel, G. (1963) *The Megalith Builders of Western Europe*. 2nd edn. London, Hutchinson.

Darvill, T.C. and Thomas, J. (eds) (2001) *Neolithic Enclosures in Atlantic Northwest Europe*. Neolithic Studies Group Seminar Papers 6. Oxford, Oxbow Books.

Diaz-Del-Rio, P. (2004) Copper Age ditched enclosures in central Iberia. *Oxford Journal of Archaeology* 23, 107–21.

Dobiat, C. (1982) Menschendarstellungen auf ostalpiner Hallstattkeramik. Eine Bestandsaufnahme. *Acta Archaeologica Academiae Scientiarum Hungaricae* 34, 279–322.

Fehr, H. (2002) *Volkstum* as paradigm: Germanic people and Gallo-Romans in early medieval archaeology since the 1930s. In A. Gillett (ed.) *On Barbarian Identity. Critical approaches to ethnicity in the Early Middle Ages*, 177–200. Studies in the Early Middle Ages 4. Turnhout, Brepols.

Foucault, M. (ed.) (1969 [2005]) *Archaeology of Knowledge*. London and New York, Routledge.

Geake, H. (1997) *The Use of Grave-goods in Conversion-period England, c.600–c.850*. BAR British Series 261. Oxford, John and Erica Hedges.

Gell, A. (1998) *Art and Agency: an anthropological theory*. Oxford, Clarendon Press.

Gervautz, M. and Neubauer, W. (2005) Sonne, Mond und Sterne. In Daim and Neubauer 2005, 73–4.

Ginsberg, J., Mohebbi, M.H., Patel, R.S., Brammer, L., Smolinski, M.S. and Brilliant, L. (2009) Detecting influenza epidemics using search engine query data. *Nature* 457, 1012–14.

Goffart, W. (1989) The theme of 'the Barbarian Invasions' in late Antique and modern historiography. In E.K. Chrysos and A. Schwarcz (eds) *Das Reich und die Barbaren*, 87–107. Wien, Böhlau.

Goldman, G. (1977) A tiszapolgári kultúra települése Bélmegyeren. Die Siedlung der Tiszapolgár Kultur in Bélmegyer. *Archaeologiai Értesítő* 104, 221–33.

Gramsch, A. (2006) Eine kurze Geschichte des archäologischen Denkens in Deutschland. *Leipziger online-Beiträge zur Ur- und Frühgeschichtlichen Archäologie* 19, 1–18.

Granovetter, M.S. (1973) The strength of weak ties. *American Journal of Sociology* 76, 1360–80.

Granovetter, M.S. (1983) The strength of weak ties. a network theory revisited. *Sociological Theory* 1, 201–33.

Haaland, R. (2004) Technology, transformation and symbolism: ethnographic perspectives on European iron working. *Norwegian Archaeological Review* 37, 1–19.

Haarnagel, W. (1962) Die Grabung Feddersen-Wierde und ihre Bedeutung für die Erkenntnis der bäuerlichen Besiedlung im Küstengebiet in dem Zeitraum vom 1. vor bis 5. Jahrhundert nach Chr. *Zeitschrift für Agrargeschichte und Agrarsoziologie* 10, 145–57.

Hakelberg, D. (2001) Deutsche Vorgeschichte als Geschichtswissenschaft – Der Heidelberger Extraordinarius Ernst Wahle im Kontext seiner Zeit. In H. Steuer (ed.) *Eine hervorragend nationale Wissenschaft,* 199–310. Ergänzungsbände zum Reallexikon der Germanischen Altertumskunde 29. Berlin and New York, Walter de Gruyter.

Hakenbeck, S. (2009) 'Hunnic' modified skulls: physical appearance, identity and the transformative nature of migrations. In H. Williams and D. Sayer (eds) *Mortuary Practices and Social Identities in the Middle Ages,* 64–80. Exeter, Exeter University Press.

Hakenbeck, S. (2011) *Local, Regional and Ethnic Identities in Early Medieval Cemeteries in Bavaria.* Contributi di Archaeologia Medievale/Premio Ottone d'Assia e Riccardo Frankovich 5. Firenze, All'Insegna del Giglio.

Hakenbeck, S., McManus, E., Geisler, H., Grupe, G. and O'Connell, T.C. (2010) Diet and mobility in Early Medieval Bavaria: a study of carbon and nitrogen stable isotopes. *American Journal of Physical Anthropology* 143, 235–49.

Härke, H. (1991) All quiet on the western front? Paradigms, methods and approaches in West German archaeology. In I. Hodder (ed.) *Archaeological Theory in Europe,* 187–222. London and New York, Routledge.

Härke, H. (1995) The Hun is a methodical chap. In P. Ucko (ed.) *Theory in Archaeology,* 46–60. London and New York, Routledge.

Harris, A. (2003) *Byzantium, Britain and the West.* Stroud and Charleston, Tempus.

Harrison, R.J. (2004) *Symbols and Warriors: images of the European Bronze Age.* Bristol, Western Academic.

Hase, F.-W.v. (2005) Die Verbindungen zwischen Etrurien/Altitalien und der Hallstattwelt im 8.–6. Jahrhundert v. Chr. In S. Celestino Pérez and J. Jiménez Ávila (eds) *El Periodo Orientalizante. Actas des III Simposio Internacional de Arqueología de Mérida: Protohistoria del Mediterráneo Occidental,* 107–14. Anejos de Archivo Español de Arqueología 35. Mérida, Archivo Español de Arqueología.

Haseloff, G. (1984) Stand der Forschung: Stilgeschichte Völkerwanderungs- und Merowingerzeit. In M. Høgestøl, J.H. Larsen, E. Straume and B. Weber (eds) *Festskrift til Thorleif Sjøvold på 70-årsdagen,* 109–124. Universitetets oldsaksamlings skrifter. Ny rekke 5. Oslo, Universitetets oldsaksamling.

Hedeager, L. (2000) Migration Period Europe: the formation of a political mentality. In F. Theuws and J.L. Nelson (eds) *Rituals and Power,* 15–57. Transformations of the Roman World 8. Leiden, Brill.

Hegedűs, K. (1981) Újkőkori Lakótelep Csanytelek Határából (Excavations at the Neolithic Settlement of Csanytelek-Újhalastó). *Archaeologiai Értesítő* 108, 1–12.

Hegel, G.W.F. (1821 [2001]) *Philosophy of Right.* Tr. S.W. Dyde. Kitchener, Batoche Books.

Heinrich-Tamaska, O. (2005) Deutung und Bedeutung von Salins Tierstil II zwischen *Langobardia* und *Avaria.* In W. Pohl and P. Erhart (eds) *Die Langobarden. Herrschaft und Identität,* 281–99. Forschungen zur Geschichte des Mittelalters 9. Vienna, Verlag der Österreichischen Akademie der Wissenschaften.

Helms, M.W. (2006) Joseph the Smith and the salvational transformation of matter in early medieval Europe. *Anthropos* 101, 451–71.

Henning, J. (1991) Schmiedegräber nördlich der Alpen. Germanisches Handwerkszeug zwischen keltischer Tradition und römischem Einfluß. *Saalburg-Jahrbuch* 46, 65–82.

Hiery, H.J. (2001) Zur Einleitung: Der Historiker und der Zeitgeist. In H.J. Hiery (ed.) *Der Zeitgeist und die Historie,* 1–6. Bayreuther Historische Kolloquien 15. Dettelbach, J.H. Röll.

Hills, C. and Lucy, S. (2013) *Spong Hill. Part IX, chronology and synthesis.* McDonald Institute Monographs. Cambridge, McDonald Institute for Archaeological Research.

Hodder, I. (ed.) (1987) *The Archaeology of Contextual Meanings.* Cambridge, Cambridge University Press.

Horváth, F. (1987) Hódmezővásárhely-Gorzsa: a settlement of the Tisza culture. In P. Raczky (ed.) *The Late Neolithic of the Tisza Region,* 31–46. Budapest-Szolnok, Kossuth Kiadó.

Huth, C. (2003) *Menschenbilder und Menschenbild. Anthropomorphe Bildwerke der frühen Eisenzeit.* Berlin, Reimer.

Kalicz, N. and Raczky, P. (1984) Preliminary report on the 1977–1982 excavations at the Neolithic and Bronze Age tell settlement of Berrettyóújfalu-Herpály, Part 1. *Acta Archaeologica Hungaricae* 36, 85–136.

Kalicz, N. and Raczky, P. (1987) The Late Neolithic of the Tisza region: a survey of recent archaeological research. In L. Tálas and P. Raczky (eds) *The Late Neolithic of the Tisza Region*, 11–29. Budapest-Szolnok, Kossuth Kiadó.

Kaul, F. (2004) *Bronzealderens religion. Religion of the Bronze Age: studies of the iconography of the Nordic Bronze Age.* Copenhagen, Det Kongelige Nordiske Oldskriftselskab.

Klotz, C.A. (ed.) (1767) *Beytrag zur Geschichte des Geschmacks und der Kunst aus Münzen.* Altenburg, Richterische Buchhandlung.

Knüsel, C. (2002) More Circe than Cassandra: the Princess of Vix in ritualised social context. *European Journal of Archaeology* 5, 275–308.

Koch, U. (1984) Handwerker in der alamannischen Höhensiedlung auf dem Runden Berg bei Urach. *Archäologisches Korrespondenzblatt* 14, 99–109.

Koch, U. (1996) Die Menschen und der Tod. In A. Wieczorek (ed.) *Die Franken*, 723–37. Wegbereiter Europas 2. Mainz, Philipp von Zabern.

Kohring, S. (2007) *Pottery Technologies and the Materialization of Society: Late Copper Age community practices in western Spain.* PhD Thesis. University of Cambridge.

Konersmann, R. (2004) Zeitgeist. In J. Ritter, K. Gründer and G. Gabriel (eds) *Historisches Wörterbuch der Philosophie* 12, 1266–70. Darmstadt, Wissenschaftliche Buchgesellschaft.

Konersmann, R. (2006) Der Hüter des Konsenses. Zeitgeist-Begriff und Zeitgeist-Paradox. In M. Gamper and P. Schnyder (eds) *Kollektive Gespenster. Die Masse, der Zeitgeist und andere unfassbare Körper*, 247–63. Freiburg im Breisgau, Rombach.

Kossack, G. (1954) *Studien zum Symbolgut der Urnenfelder- und Hallstattzeit Mitteleuropas.* Römisch-Germanische Forschungen 20. Berlin, Walter de Gruyter.

Kossack, G. (ed.) (1969) *Hallstatt und Italien. Gesammelte Aufsätze zur frühen Eisenzeit in Italien und Mitteleuropa.* Mainz, Römisch-Germanisches Zentralmuseum.

Kossinna, G. (1896) Die vorgeschichtliche Ausbreitung der Germanen in Deutschland. *Zeitschrift des Vereins für Volkskunde* 6, 1–14.

Kossinna, G. (1911) *Die Herkunft der Germanen.* Leipzig, Kabitzsch.

Kromer, K. (1986) Das östliche Mitteleuropa in der frühen Eisenzeit (7.–5. Jh. v. Chr.). Seine Beziehungen zu Steppenvölkern und antiken Hochkulturen. *Jahrbuch des Römisch-Germanischen Zentralmuseums* 33, 1–97.

Latour, B. (2005) *Reassembling the Social: an introduction to Actor-Network Theory.* Oxford and New York, Oxford University Press.

Louis, M. and Isetti, G. (1964) *Les gravures préhistoriques du Mont-Bego.* Itinéraires Ligures 9. Bordighera, Institut international d'Études Ligures.

Lucas, G. (2005) *The Archaeology of Time. Themes in archaeology.* London, Routledge.

Lucy, S. (1998) *The Early Anglo-Saxon Cemeteries of East Yorkshire.* BAR British Series 272. Oxford, British Archaeological Reports.

Lucy, S. (2000) *The Anglo-Saxon Way of Death: burial rites in early England.* Stroud, Sutton.

Lucy, S. (2002) Burial practice in early medieval eastern Britain: constructing local identities, deconstructing ethnicity. In S. Lucy and A. Reynolds (eds) *Burial in Early Medieval England and Wales*, 72–87. London, Society for Medieval Archaeology.

Makkay, J. (1983) Eine Kultstätte der Bodrogkeresztúr-Kultur in Szarvas und Fragen der sakralen Hügel. *Mitteilungen des Archäologischen Instituts der Ungarischen Akademie der Wissenschaften* 10–11, 45–57.

Martin, M. (1995) Schmuck und Tracht des frühen Mittelalters. In M. Martin and J. Prammer (eds) *Frühe Baiern im Straubinger Land*, 40–71. Straubing, Gäubodenmuseum Straubing.

Martin, T.F. (2020) Casting the net wider: network approaches to artefact variation in post-Roman Europe. *Journal of Archaeological Method and Theory* 27, 861–86.

Meller, H. (ed.) (2004) *Der geschmiedete Himmel. Die weite Welt im Herzen Europas vor 3600 Jahren.* Stuttgart, Theiss.

Nebelsick, L.D. (1992) Figürliche Kunst der Hallstattzeit am Nordostalpenrand im Spannungsfeld zwischen alteuropäischer Tradition und italischem Lebensstil. In A. Lippert and K. Spindler (eds) *Festschrift zum 50jährigen Bestehen des Institutes für Ur- und Frühgeschichte der Leopold-Franzens-Universität Innsbruck*, 401–32. Universitätsforschungen zur prähistorischen Archäologie 8. Bonn, Habelt.

Orschiedt, J. and Haidle, M.N. (2006) The LBK enclosure at Herxheim: theatre of war or ritual centre? References from osteoarchaeological investigations. *Journal of Conflict Archaeology* 2, 153–67.

Oswald, A., Dyer, C. and Barber, M. (2001) *The Creation of Monuments: Neolithic causewayed enclosures in the British Isles.* London, English Heritage Publications.

Otto, R. (1769 [1990]) *Johann Gottfried Herder, Kritische Wälder*, vol. 1. Berlin and Weimar, Aufbau-Verlag.

Owoc, M.A. (2004) A phenomenology of the buried landscape: soil as material culture in the Bronze Age of south-west Britain. In N. Boivin and M.A. Owoc (eds) *Soils, Stones and Symbols: cultural perceptions of the mineral world*, 107–22. London, UCL Press.

Palincaş, N. (2010) Reconfiguring anatomy: ceramics, cremation and cosmology in the Late Bronze Age in the Lower Danube. In K. Rebay-Salisbury, M.L.S. Sørensen and J. Hughes (eds) *Body Parts and Bodies Whole: changing relations and meanings*, 72–88. Oxford, Oxbow Books.

Parkinson, W.A. and Duffy, P.R. (2007) Fortifications and enclosures in European prehistory: a cross-cultural perspective. *Journal of Archaeological Research* 15, 97–141.

Parkinson, W.A. and Gyucha, A. (2012) Long-term social dynamics and the emergence of hereditary inequality: a prehistoric example from the Carpathian Basin. In T.K. Kienlin and A. Zimmermann (eds) *Beyond Elites: alternatives to hierarchical systems in modelling social formations*, 243–49. Universitätsforschungen zur prähistorischen Archäologie 215. Bonn, Rudolf Habelt.

Parkinson, W.A., Gyucha, A., Yerkes, R.W., Morris, M.R., Sarris, A. and Salisbury, R.B. (2010) Early Copper Age settlements in the Körös Region of the Great Hungarian Plain. *Journal of Field Archaeology* 35, 164–83.

Parkinson, W.A., Yerkes, R.W. and Gyucha, A. (2004) The transition to the Early Copper Age on the Great Hungarian Plain: the Körös Regional Archaeological Project excavations at Vésztő-Bikeri and Körösladány-Bikeri, Hungary, 2000–2002. *Journal of Field Archaeology* 29, 101–21.

Pásztor, E., Barna, J.P. and Roslund, C. (2008) The orientation of rondels of the Neolithic Lengyel culture in Central Europe. *Antiquity* 82, 910–24.

Pavúk, J. (1991) Lengyel-culture fortified settlements in Slovakia. *Antiquity* 65, 348–57.

Pearce, J., Millett, M. and Struck, M. (eds) (2000) *Burial, Society and Context in the Roman World.* Oxford, Oxbow Books.

Pesch, A. (2012a) Fallstricke und Glatteis: Die germanische Tierornamentik. In H. Beck, D. Geuenich and H. Steuer (eds) *Altertumskunde – Altertumswissenschaft – Kulturwissenschaft*, 633–87. Berlin and Boston, Walter de Gruyter.

Pesch, A. (2012b) The goldsmith, his apprentice and the gods. A fairy tale. In A. Pesch and R. Blankenfeldt (eds) *Goldsmith Mysteries*, 37–48. Neumünster, Wachholtz Verlag.

Petrasch, J. (1990) Mittelneolithische Kreisgrabenanlagen in Mitteleuropa. *Bericht der Römisch-Germanischen Kommission* 71, 407–564.

Quast, D. (1998) Vom Einzelgrab zum Friedhof. In K. Fuchs, M. Kempa, R. Redies, B. Theune-Großkopf and A. Wais (eds) *Die Alamannen*, 171–201. Stuttgart, Theiss.

Raczky, P., Domboróczki, L. and Hajdú, Z. (2007) The site of Polgár-Csőszhalom and its cultural and chronological connections with the Lengyel culture. In J.K. Kozłowski and P. Raczky (eds) *The*

Lengyel, Polgár and Related Cultures in the Middle/Late Neolithic in Central Europe, 49–70. Kraków, The Polish Academy of Arts and Sciences.

Rebay-Salisbury, K. (2016) *The Human Body in Early Iron Age Central Europe. Burial Practices and Images of the Hallstatt World.* London, Routledge.

Rebay-Salisbury, K. and Hakenbeck, S. (2009) Zeitgeist (session report). *The European Archaeologist* 32, 34.

Rebay, K.C. (2006) *Das hallstattzeitliche Gräberfeld von Statzendorf, Niederösterreich.* Universitätsforschungen zur Prähistorischen Archäologie 135. Bonn, Rudolf Habelt.

Riemer, E. (1999) Zu Vorkommen und Herkunft italischer Folienkreuze. *Germania* 77, 609–36.

Robb, J. (2008) Introduction. *Cambridge Archaeological Journal* 18, 57–9.

Robb, J. and Harris, O.J.T. (eds) (2013) *The Body in History. Europe from the Palaeolithic to the Future.* Cambridge, Cambridge University Press.

Robb, J. and Pauketat, T. (eds) (2008) Special section: time and change in archaeological interpretation. *Cambridge Archaeological Journal* 18.1, 57–99.

Salin, B. (1904) *Die altgermanische Thierornamentik: typologische Studie über germanische Metallgegenstände aus dem IV. bis IX. Jahrhundert, nebst einer Studie über irische Ornamentik.* Stockholm, K.L. Beckmans Buchdruckerei.

Salisbury, R.B. (2012) Engaging with soil, past and present. *Journal of Material Culture* 17, 23–41.

Salisbury, R.B., Bertók, G. and Bácsmegi, G. (2013) Integrated prospection methods to define small-site settlement structure: a case study from Neolithic Hungary. *Archaeological Prospection* 20, 1–10.

Sarris, A., Papadopoulos, N., Agapiou, A., Salvi, M.C., Hadjimitsis, D.G., Parkinson, W.A., Yerkes, R.W., Gyucha, A. and Duffy, P.R. (2013) Integration of geophysical surveys, ground hyperspectral measurements, aerial and satellite imagery for archaeological prospection of prehistoric sites: the case study of Vésztő-Mágor Tell, Hungary. *Journal of Archaeological Science* 40, 1454–70.

Sassaman, K.E. (2005) Poverty point as structure, event, process. *Journal of Archaeological Method and Theory* 12, 335–64.

Sassaman, K.E. and Rudolphi, W. (2001) Communities of practice in the early pottery traditions of the American Southeast. *Journal of Anthropological Research* 57, 407–25.

Shennan, S. (2013) Demographic continuities and discontinuities in Neolithic Europe: evidence, methods and implications. *Journal of Archaeological Method and Theory* 20, 300–11.

Siegfried-Weiss, A. (1979) *Der Ostalpenraum in der Hallstattzeit und seine Beziehungen zum Mittelmeergebiet.* Hamburger Beiträge zur Archäologie 6. Hamburg, Buske.

Siegmund, F. (1996) Kleidung und Bewaffnung der Männer im östlichen Frankenreich. In A. Wieczorek (ed.) *Die Franken*, 691–706. Wegbereiter Europas 2. Mainz, Philipp von Zabern.

Skeates, R. (2002) The Neolithic ditched enclosures of the Tavoliere, south-east Italy. In G. Varndell and P. Topping (eds) *Enclosures in Neolithic Europe: essays on causewayed and non-causewayed sites*, 51–8. Oxford, Oxbow Books.

Smolla, G. (1979/1980) Das Kossinna-Syndrom. *Fundberichte aus Hessen* 19/20, 1–9.

Sørensen, M.L.S. and Rebay, K.C. (2008) From substantial bodies to the substance of bodies: analysis of the transition from inhumation to cremation during the Middle Bronze Age in Central Europe. In D. Borić and J. Robb (eds) *Past Bodies. Body-centred research in archaeology*, 59–68. Oxford, Oxbow Books.

Steuer, H. (1982) *Frühgeschichtliche Sozialstrukturen in Mitteleuropa.* Göttingen, Vandenhoeck and Ruprecht.

Suphan, B. (1877) Briefe zur Beförderung der Humanität. In *Herders sämmtliche Werke* 17, 72–414. Berlin, Weidmann.

Taylor, T. (2012) Concentric ambiguities: a theoretical approach to Neolithic Kreisgrabenanlagen and the social implications of polythetic variance. In F. Bertemes and H. Meller (eds) *Neolithische*

Kreisgrabenanlagen in Europa. Internationale Arbeitstagung vom 7. Bis 9. Mai 2004 in Goseck, 349–61. Tagungen des Landesmuseums für Vorgeschichte Halle Band 8. Halle (Saale), Beier and Beran.

Theune, C. (2004) *Germanen und Romanen in der Alamannia: Strukturveränderungen aufgrund der archäologischen Quellen vom 3. bis zum 7. Jahrhundert*. Ergänzungsbände zum Reallexikon der germanischen Altertumskunde 45. Berlin, Walter de Gruyter.

Theuws, F. and Alkemade, M. (2000) A kind of mirror for men: sword deposition in late antique northern Gaul. In F. Theuws and J.L. Nelson (eds) *Rituals of Power*, 401–76. Transformations of the Roman World 8. Leiden, Brill.

Tringham, R.E. (1971) *Hunters, Fishers and Farmers of Eastern Europe 6000–3000 BC*. London, Hutchinson.

Trnka, G. (1991) *Studien zu mittelneolithischen Kreisgrabenanlagen*. Vienna, Österreichische Akademie der Wissenschaften.

von Carnap-Bornheim, C. (2001) The social position of the Germanic goldsmith AD 0–500. In B. Magnus (ed.) *Roman Gold and the Development of the Early Germanic Kingdoms*, 263–28. Kungl. Vitterhets Historie och Antikvitets Akademien Konferenser 51. Stockholm, Almqvist and Wiksell.

Von Rummel, P. (2010) Gotisch, barbarisch oder römisch? Methodologische Überlegungen zur ethnischen Interpretation von Kleidung. In W. Pohl and M. Mehofer (eds) *Archaeology of Identity – Archäologie der Identität*, 51–77. Forschungen zur Geschichte des Mittelalters 17. Vienna, Verlag der Österreichischen Akademie der Wissenschaften.

Voß, H.-U. (2008) Fremd – nützlich – machbar. Römische Einflüsse im germanischen Feinschmiedehandwerk. In S. Brather (ed.) *Zwischen Spätantike und Frühmittelalter*, 343–65. Ergänzungsbände zum Reallexikon der Germanischen Altertumskunde 57. Berlin and New York, Walter de Gryuter.

Watts, D.J. (1999) *Small Worlds: the dynamics of networks between order and randomness*. Princeton, NJ, Princeton University Press.

Welch, M.G. (2011) The mid-Saxon 'final phase'. In H. Hamerow, D.A. Hinton and S. Crawford (eds) *The Oxford Handbook of Anglo-Saxon Archaeology*, 266–87. Oxford, Oxford University Press.

Wenger, E. (1998) *Communities of Practice: learning, meaning, and identity*. Cambridge, Cambridge University Press.

Werner, J. (1961) Fernhandel und Naturalwirtschaft im östlichen Merowingerreich nach archäologischen und numismatische Zeugnissen. *Bericht der Römisch-Germanischen Kommission* 42, 307–46.

Werner, J. (1970) Zur Verbreitung frühgeschichtlicher Metallarbeiten (Werkstatt – Wanderhandwerk – Handel – Familienverbindung). *Antikvarisk Arkiv (Early Medieval Studies I)* 38, 65–81.

Werner, J. (1973 [1950]) Zur Entstehung der Reihengräberzivilisation. In F. Petri (ed.) *Siedlung, Sprache und Bevölkerungsstruktur im Frankenreich*, 285–325. Darmstadt, Wissenschaftliche Buchgesellschaft.

Whittle, A. (1996) *Europe in the Neolithic: the creation of new worlds*. Cambridge World Archaeology. Cambridge, Cambridge University Press.

Wirth, S. (2006) Vogel – Sonnen – Barke. In H. Beck, D. Geuenich and H. Steuer (eds) *Reallexikon der Germanischen Altertumskunde 32*, 552–63. Berlin and New York, Walter de Gruyter.

Woolf, A. (2011) *Barbarians and Pseudo-Barbarians in Late Antiquity*. Cambridge Late Antiquity Network Seminar. Seminar paper given at the Centre for Research in the Arts, Social Sciences and Humanities, University of Cambridge.

Zeitgeist: The Movie (2007) Directed by Peter Joseph, Gentle Machine Productions. World Wide, Peter Joseph.

Zipf, G.E. (2006) *Studien zu den Anfängen figürlicher Darstellungen im endbronze- und früheisenzeitlichen Frankreich und Italien. Motive, Dekorträger und Kontexte*. Thesis, Freie Universität Berlin.

Zotti, G. and Neubauer, W. (2011) Astronomical aspects of Kreisgrabenanlagen (Neolithic circular ditch systems) – an interdisciplinary approach. *Proceedings of the International Astronomical Union* 7, 349–56.

Chapter 3

From systems of power to networks of knowledge: the nature of El Argar culture (southeastern Iberia, c. 2200–1500 BC)

Borja Legarra Herrero

El Argar culture has been depicted traditionally as a series of highly hierarchical geo-political systems that were mainly interested in the internal control and organisation of their territory. This article reinterprets new archaeological evidence to suggest an alternative vision of Argaric societies that emphasises interconnectivity between a mosaic of differing regions and a more fluid socio-political organisation. Network approaches emerge as a useful theoretical and methodological referent to make sense of the complexity of the archaeological data and help to place El Argar within the typical Mediterranean themes of connectivity, volatility and fragmentation that so well suit the study of the landscapes of southeastern Iberia.

Key words: network analyses, Argar culture, prehistory, Iberia, Mediterranean, social complexity

1. Introduction: networks, the Mediterranean and El Argar

El Argar culture characterises the archaeology of southeastern Spain during the end of the third to the middle of the second millennium BC. Once a 'classic' culture in the handbooks of European prehistory (Childe 1957), it commanded less attention from the academic world outside Spain in the second half of the twentieth century. This marginalisation is being addressed by a new wave of publications that reconnects the study of the region with wider archaeological interests (Cámara Serrano and Molina González 2006; Lull *et al.* 2010b; 2014; Gilman 2013; Scarre 2013; Aranda Jiménez *et al.* 2015). Much of this renewed impetus relies on the lively debate around the concept of state and its applicability to the understanding of Argaric culture (Chapman 2003; Contreras Cortés *et al.* 2004; Lull and Micó 2011; Bartelheim 2012; Gilman 2013; Legarra Herrero 2014; Aranda Jiménez *et al.* 2015).

The recent studies have brought a new growing acknowledgement of regional differences in the Argaric world with the identification of temporal and spatial variations in the way typical Argaric traits were deployed (Chapman 2008; Ramos Millán 2013) and how these interacted with other local traditions (Aranda Jiménez 2013). The studies are breaking down cultural history assumptions that El Argar culture was a homogeneous phenomenon that covered the entirety of southeastern Iberia. Therefore, authors have started to move away from the label 'culture' and start to refer to the Argaric 'norm' (Aranda Jiménez *et al.* 2015, 8) to try to convey more accurately the diversity in the way Argaric traits appear in the record of Bronze Age southeastern Iberia.

Mediterranean paradigms of fragmentation, uncertainty and connectivity (Horden and Purcell 2000; Broodbank 2013) are also starting to influence novel approaches to El Argar. At the geographical level, southeastern Spain can be defined as a typically fragmented Mediterranean landscape (Horden and Purcell 2000), with an arid and unstable climate (Castro *et al.* 1998; Carrión *et al.* 2010). The river valleys (Vinalopó, Almanzora, Segura) contrast with the arid badlands typical of the region and against the high-altitude landscapes of the interior. At the same time, those valleys create routes that connect the mountains with the Mediterranean coast, bringing together the various landscapes and the unique resources in each of them such as metals (Murillo-Barroso *et al.* 2015).

It could be argued that Argaric societies may not fit well in the Mediterranean paradigm of interconnectivity (Horden and Purcell 2000) as long trade connections do not seem to be part of the essence of the Iberian Bronze Age. The presence of ivory, amber and ostrich eggs in several sites proves that exchange routes connecting Argaric sites with Africa existed (López Padilla 2009; Lillios 2014; Murillo Barroso *et al.* 2018) but it is true that the number of such items is relatively low (but see Nocete *et al.* 2013; Lull *et al.* 2014) and may reflect tenuous links between southeastern Spain and the rest of the Mediterranean.

But the Mediterranean paradigm does not just rely on long distance networks, and the evidence for significant exchange links at the short and medium scale in south Iberia is much stronger than normally recognised. The presence of distinct Argaric materials and cultural traits across southeastern Spain constitutes in itself strong evidence of the significance of movement and trade in the Bronze Age (Fig. 3.1). The above-mentioned variability in the Argaric record indicates a wealth of different types of links between regions. Further support is presented by new studies that have identified how raw materials moved in fluid networks across a large geographical area (Montero Ruiz and Murillo-Barroso 2010) and the importance of placing sites near main routes of communication (Andrés Rodriguez 2017).

The time has come to consider how this new information impacts the understanding of Argaric societies, moving the focus of investigation away from their internal organisation that the discussion of the 'Argaric state' has favoured towards the interactions between communities. As part of this effort, network approaches

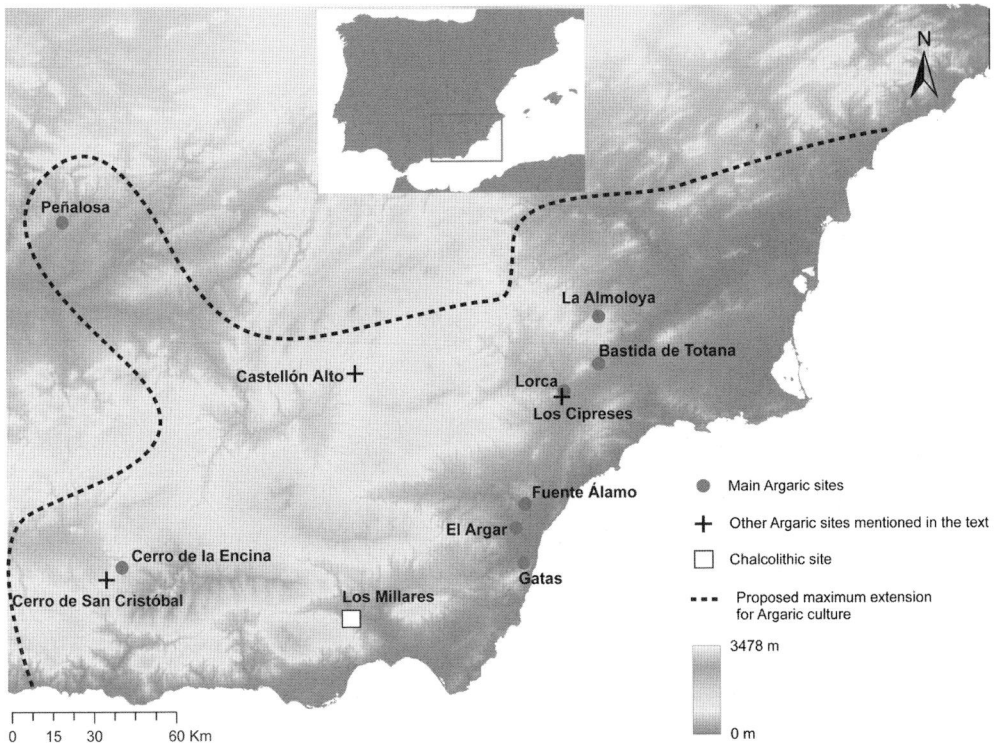

Figure 3.1 Sites mentioned in the text and proposed maximum extension of the Argaric culture.

(Brughmans 2010; 2013; Knappett 2011; Collar *et al.* 2015) may offer particular advantages to study the challenges that the Argaric record presents. In particular, many of the questions regarding socio-political complexity may be better understood by including the fluid nature of social and economic relationships amongst Argaric communities (Schortman 2014) rather than paying attention solely to the internal organisation of each community or region.

2. El Argar: a 500-word introduction

Third-millennium BC southern Spain is starting to be recognised as an extremely dynamic period, with an increasing number of large settlements and imported materials identified in the archaeological record (Nocete *et al.* 2008; García Sanjuán and Murillo-Barroso 2013). It is about 2200 BC when the last of the large Chalcolithic sites, Los Millares (Fig. 3.1 for sites mentioned in the text), goes out of use, coinciding with the appearance of a distinctive group of sites in southeastern Spain, centred first in the areas of modern north Almeria and south Murcia (Lull *et al.* 2010a).

Argaric sites were first investigated in the nineteenth century by the Siret brothers, two Belgian engineers who defined this culture archaeologically (Siret and Siret

Figure 3.2 View of the site of Fuente Álamo (top of hill) from below.

1890) using the name of the most important site discovered, El Argar (Fig. 3.1; modern Almeria, Spain). Argaric culture was defined through two main features: highly defensible sites found on hilltops (Fig. 3.2), and individual burials in cists, pits and jars normally found nearby or underneath houses (Fig. 3.3; Lull 1983; 2000; Aranda *et al.* 2009; Aranda Jiménez *et al.* 2015). Argaric communities also have a distinct material culture, particularly with the use of highly burnished black ceramics replacing the incised and impressed vessels of the Chalcolithic period (Fig. 3.4; Siret and Siret 1890; Lull 1983) and with new shapes added to the repertoire such as pedestalled cups, and the carinated and biconical jars normally found in burials. Metal items occur more regularly in the archaeological record, normally in the form of ornaments and tools (Montero Ruiz 1991) with a small number of specialised weapons (Aranda Jiménez *et al.* 2009; Lull *et al.* 2010b).

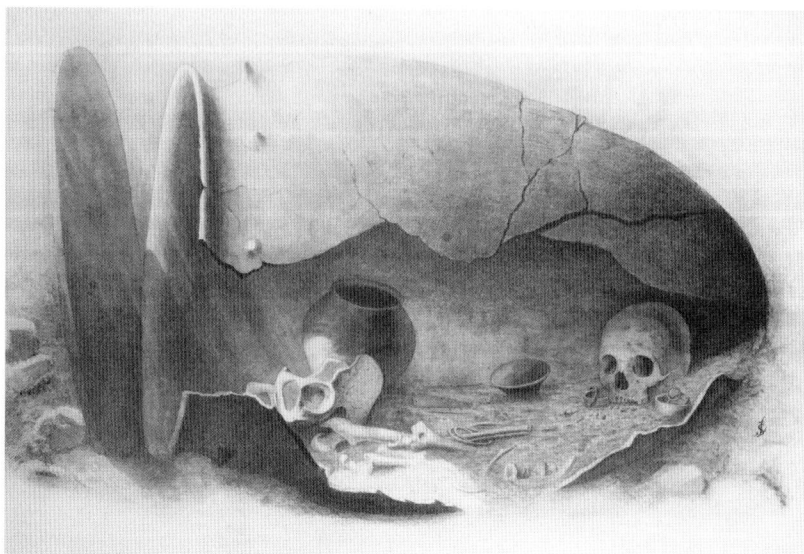

Figure 3.3 Tomb 9 in El Argar (Siret and Siret 1890, plate 35).

Figure 3.4 Ceramic vases from El Argar site tombs (1/4 actual size) (Siret and Siret 1890, plate 55).

Traditionally, it was thought that Argaric society reached its zenith around 1750–1550 BC (Lull 1983; Aranda Jiménez *et al.* 2015), a moment in which Argaric sites appear across most of southeastern Spain (Fig. 3.1). Recent discoveries, however, are rapidly reshaping the chronological and geographical framework. The formative period of Argaric societies at the end of the third millennium BC is being redrawn by new discoveries at the site of La Bastida, where large fortifications have been dated to 2200 BC (Lull *et al.* 2014). The early date of such formidable construction does not fit well with the evolutionary understanding of Argaric societies (Lull 1983) and it raises questions about the early development of Argaric communities and their relation to earlier Chalcolithic sites such as Los Millares. Similarly, the regional configuration of Argaric communities is undergoing major reinterpretation. The first area in which Argaric culture appeared is being expanded to include the region of modern south-central Murcia (Lull *et al.* 2014). This is part of an attempt to define more precisely the varying character of Argaric culture across different regions of southeastern Spain (Chapman 2008; Jover Maestre and López Padilla 2009). It is increasingly evident that each region underwent different trajectories in the Argaric period with distinctive regional settlement patterns (Legarra Herrero 2014; López Padilla *et al.* 2015), resource exploitation strategies (Moreno Onorato and Contreras Cortés 2010), and relationships between Argaric cultural traits and contemporaneous local traditions (Aranda Jiménez 2013).

3. The inward view: El Argar as a system

Despite new advances in the understanding of the spatio-temporal framework, the prevalent view of Argaric societies still relies heavily on a study of the organisation of each community and regional system in isolation. Traditional approaches in the nineteenth and twentieth centuries that depended heavily on diffusionist paradigms (Siret and Siret 1890; Aranda *et al.* 2015, 8–10) were replaced in the 1980s and 1990s by a wave of new approaches interested in the internal development of Argaric societies (Lull 1983; Gilman and Thornes 1985; Chapman *et al.* 1987; Chapman 1990). The most discussed view proposed that Argaric society was organised in at least three distinct classes: a small elite, a group of free men and a class of dependants and/or slaves (Lull and Estévez 1986). The elite would have exercised control over the production and transformation of basic resources, such as cereal and metals, using violence as a practical but also ideological means to secure authority over the population (Chapman 1990; 2003; Lull 2000; Lull *et al.* 2009; 2010b). Other voices, such as Gilman's (Gilman 1981; Gilman and Thornes 1985) and Mathers' (1994) proposed that Argaric societies were more akin to 'chiefdoms' in which central figures had a looser political and economic control. Despite the significant differences amongst approaches, all these studies were mostly concerned with internal socio-economic factors.

This focus on the internal structure continues to be popular (Lull *et al.* 2009; Molina González and Cámara Serrano 2009), such as statistical approaches that aim to identify wealth levels in burials that support the idea of three distinct social classes (Lull and Estévez 1986; Lull 2000; Lull Santiago *et al.* 2005). Locational studies have also tried to find a link between wealthy tombs and their privileged spatial position at the centre of the sites that would reinforce the idea of a separate elite class living at the core of the major sites (Cámara Serrano and Molina González 2004; 2010).

This strict socio-political order is projected into the geo-political organisation of Argaric landscapes (Jover Maestre and López Padilla 1999; Arteaga Matute 2000; Chapman 2003; Eiroa García 2004; Molina González and Cámara Serrano 2004; Cámara Serrano and Molina González 2010; Lull *et al.* 2010b; López Padilla *et al.* 2014). The more distinguished social elites occupied the largest hilltop settlements from which they controlled a significant territory. Fortified areas at the centre of the large settlements are argued to be elite residences, and large storage areas such as cisterns in many of the larger settlements have been seen as evidence of the close control of subsistence resources (Castro *et al.* 2001). At the second level, smaller hilltop settlements helped to control those areas further away from the central site. At the third level, most of the lower classes lived in small sites normally in lowlands with easy access to agricultural land. In this view, Argaric culture was formed by a specialised territorial organisation in which each part of the society had a well-defined role, implying that Argaric culture could be divided in distinct regions with well-defined political boundaries, each of them headed by a 'capital' (Arteaga Matute 2000).

The study of trade and interaction between each Argaric group has been largely limited to the movement of metals (Molina González and Cámara Serrano 2009; Lull *et al.* 2010b). The scarcity of metal, and its unique properties (hardness, appearance) would have made copper and silver ideal materials for elites to construct and maintain a hierarchical socio-political order. Elites would have secured exclusive access to metals giving them a militaristic advantage and exclusive access to the prestigious identities attached to weaponry and silver adornments. Leaders would also have regulated the circulation of metals to other social groups as a mechanism of securing socio-political control (Lull *et al.* 2010b). Specialised metallurgical centres in the highlands, such as Peñalosa would have been controlled by central Argaric sites and the movement of metals would have been done through highly restricted and directional channels under the supervision of the elites (Lull *et al.* 2010b; Moreno Onorato and Contreras Cortés 2010) leaving most of the population out of the exchange activities. Distribution and interaction within each Argaric group would also have been organised in highly hierarchical re-distribution systems in which metals would move downwards and basic staples upwards.

4. Elements of critique: El Argar as a fluid phenomenon

A new impetus in fieldwork in recent years has produced more fine-grained understanding of the archaeological record and one of the immediate outcomes of these new patterns of data is the need for more fluid interpretations of Argaric societies.

4.1. Territorial configuration and basic resource access

Major emphasis has been placed on the study of the relationship of Argaric settlements with surrounding resources (Gilman and Thornes 1985; Risch 1998; 2002; Carrión Marco 2004; Delgado Raack 2008) including some large projects around the area of Gatas (Chapman *et al.* 1987; Castro Martínez *et al.* 1999), Aguas (Mederos Martín 1994; Castro *et al.* 1998) and Antas (Cámalich Massieu and Martín Socas 1998). This legacy data has been recently reviewed for a new investigation of the relationship between communities, demography, territoriality and regional organisation (Serrano Ariza 2012; Ramos Millán 2013; Legarra Herrero 2014).

Recent research has questioned the view of a strictly organised territory, presenting a more fragmented and chaotic picture (Legarra Herrero 2014). The Vera region has in the past been presented as a geo-political unit in which the site of El Argar acted as the capital to a number of subordinate settlements that exploited different areas of the region (Arteaga Matute 2000; Schubart and Arteaga 1986). The data provided by intensive surface survey (Cámalich Massieu and Martín Socas 1998; see detailed discussion in Legarra Herrero 2014) has shown, however, that El Argar (c. 2.2 ha) is not significantly larger than several other sites in the region (Fig. 3.5) that appear to have comparable populations (Legarra Herrero 2014). It is difficult to envision such compact communities being able to control territories beyond their immediate hinterland (Feinman 2011). Under these sites, there seems to be only a second tier of smaller settlements (c. 0.1–0.2 ha) normally located at the edge of the catchment areas of the central sites, and probably somehow related to the latter.

Investigation of the resources available in the one-hour catchment area for each potential central site (Fig. 3.6) indicated that each of the possible settlements had direct access to the necessary agricultural resources for its subsistence (Legarra Herrero 2014). The fact that the catchment areas did not overlap, and the evidence that most abiotic resources were procured mainly from the immediate landscape surrounding each site (Risch 2002; Haro Navarro *et al.* 2006), adds to the picture of a region divided mainly into autonomous communities with a handful of hamlets in their hinterland.

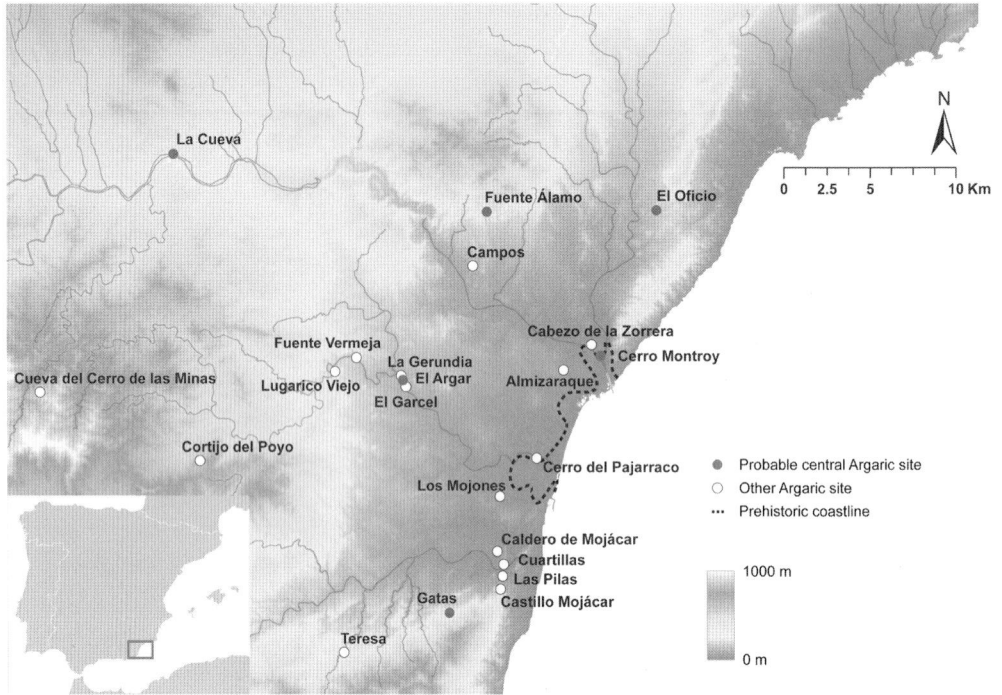

Figure 3.5 Known Argaric sites in the Vera region.

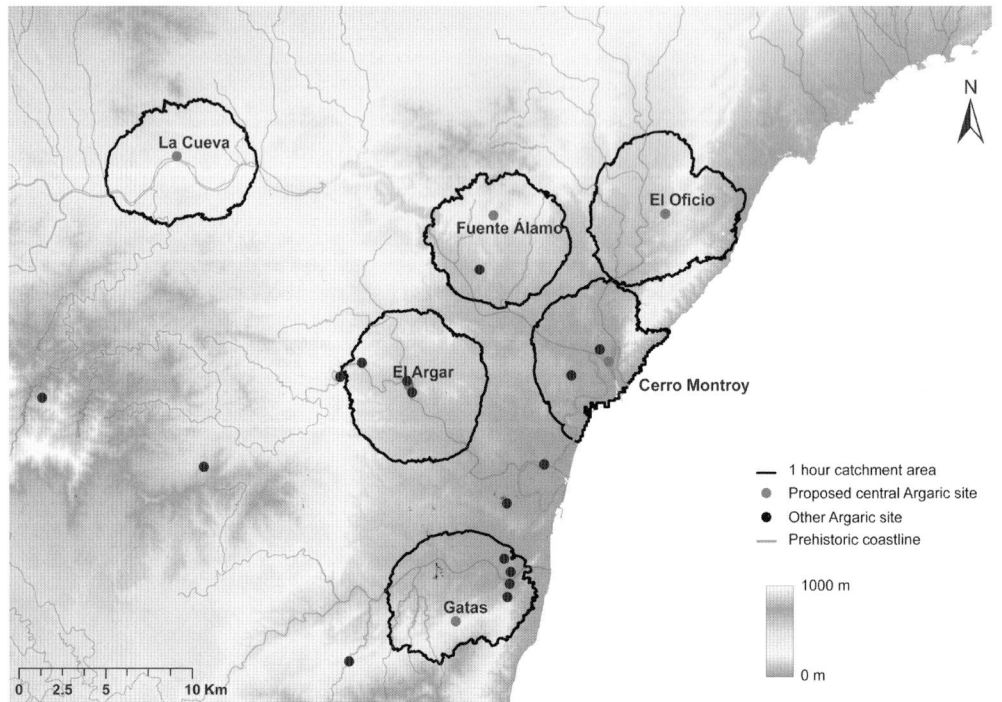

Figure 3.6 One-hour catchment areas of the main Argaric sites in the Vera region.

An alternative view presents the region as a mosaic of small independent communities perched on top of hilltops that controlled the immediate territory around them, enough to secure their subsistence. Small sites may have helped to expand these territories slightly or just survived in the spaces between larger sites. The two-tier settlement hierarchy and the constrained geographical imprint of each site encourages the interpretation of the Vera Basin as a region constructed over a flexible configuration of several comparable socio-political units. While these units may rely heavily in their own resources, their small size does not allow them to remain autarchic. Exogamy would be a major issue in such small communities, but also the creation of social and economic links with other communities as mechanisms for risk aversion (Halstead 1989) and in order to secure basic resources such as metals. The malleable regional structure would mean that the history of the Vera region was ever changing socially, economically and politically as the balance between sites varied depending on short-term contingencies (Legarra Herrero 2014).

Settlement size and frequency of settlements in several Argaric regions are similar to that identified in Vera, perhaps indicating comparable organisations (Chapman 2008; Serrano Ariza 2012; Ramos Millán 2013). In some other cases, larger sites such as Lorca (12 ha; Fontella Ballesta *et al.* 2004) and La Bastida de Totana (4–6 ha; Lull *et al.* 2014) may suggest a different territorial organisation. In Granada, the location of el Cerro de la Encina (Aranda Jiménez *et al.* 2008; Legarra Herrero 2014) in an area with very little direct access to agricultural resources but only a few kilometres away from of El Cerro de San Cristobal, which is located in the middle of the rich agricultural plain (Aranda Jiménez *et al.* 2012), may indicate a specific dynamic for this region.

Considering Argaric settlement patterns as small highly independent units that adapted differently to specific regional situations helps explain the variability encountered in the record. The interaction of the different settlements in specific geographical settings would produce different histories and regional organisations. There may be cases in which these evolved in larger territorial organisations but the fluidity at the basis of the system may have kept these instances rare and short-lived. The main point here is that the conceptualisation of Argaric communities as independent or semi-independent units makes the study of the relationships between settlements more relevant than ever and intrinsically linked to the investigation of their internal organisation.

4.2. Metallurgy and long-distance resource access

Recent archaeometallurgical analyses are providing a wealth of new information, shifting considerably the understanding of the processes of extraction, production and consumption of silver and copper by Argaric communities (Montero Ruiz and Murillo-Barroso 2010; Moreno Onorato and Contreras Cortés 2010; Hunt Ortiz *et al.* 2011; Bartelheim *et al.* 2012; Murillo-Barroso *et al.* 2014; 2015).

In particular, a new wave of lead isotope analyses is helping to build a much more complex picture of the movement of metals around the Argaric landscapes (Bartelheim *et al.* 2012; Murillo-Barroso *et al.* 2015). Analyses of Argaric silver items have only identified the use of native silver (Bartelheim *et al.* 2012), available in just a few areas in southeastern Iberia. It also suggests that the production of silver items would have involved relatively simple procedures that may not have required full-time specialists. The analysis has also revealed that silver seems to have moved across Argaric landscapes through quite fluid channels, with metals of diverse origin appearing in different settlements (Bartelheim *et al.* 2012).

This complex picture has been corroborated by lead isotope analyses of copper items (Murillo-Barroso *et al.* 2015). They provide a similar picture as copper of different origins was found across the different Argaric landscapes in complex distribution patterns. The more focused analysis of material at Cerro de San Cristobal and Cerro de la Encina has shown not only that the copper in these closely located sites comes from different origins, but also that the metal within each site had several origins (Murillo-Barroso *et al.* 2015). Evidence for manufacturing metal items is found in most excavated Argaric sites, normally at a domestic level, without real indication of specialised workshops, and therefore denoting a local, decentralised activity (Montero Ruiz and Murillo-Barroso 2010). Production, exchange and consumption of metals may therefore be explained as locally determined activities with metals from different regions moving through several types of exchange involving different parts of a society and with products being produced mainly locally (Bartelheim 2007; Montero Ruiz and Murillo-Barroso 2010; Murillo-Barroso *et al.* 2015).

4.3. *Burial customs, heterogeneity and interaction*

Burial analysis in recent decades has mainly concerned the study of tombs in relation to socio-economic differentiation (Cámara Serrano *et al.* 1996; Lull 2000; Contreras Cortés and Cámara Serrano 2002; Lull *et al.* 2004; 2009; Aranda Jiménez 2008) which has led to other aspects of funerary ritual remaining understudied (Montón-Subías 2010). This focus on socio-economic factors has normally assumed that the comparable nature of most burials indicates a similar relation between funerary rituals and social, economic and ideological aspects across the Argaric landscapes. Such an assumption is based on the striking similarities in burials that are hundreds of kilometres apart, with very similar burial rites, material assemblages and tomb types appearing in distant regions.

But these facts should not obscure the actual variability encountered in burials across Argaric landscapes (Aranda Jiménez *et al.* 2015, 130–7). Tombs appear in Argaric sites in many ways. Some houses included burials, while others did not, as in the case of Fuente Álamo (Pingel *et al.* 2003) and Castellón Alto (Molina González *et al.* 2003). Single inhumations tended to be the norm but double ones were not rare, and a few cases of tombs with multiple individuals have been recorded (Aranda Jiménez *et al.* 2015, 130–7). The proportion of single and multiple burials was not regular amongst settlements, and in some of them such as Cerro de la Encina, there was a much higher proportion of double and triple burials than in most other sites (Aranda and Molina 2006).

There may have been also differences in the number of burials per settlement, although this is more difficult to document due to different levels of preservation and excavation. In the El Argar settlement more than 1000 burials were reported (Siret and Siret 1890; Kunter 1990). At the neighbouring site of Fuente Alamo 120 were excavated, but the site may have housed more than 1000 tombs (Bartelheim 2012, 347). What seems clear is that only a small part of the population was buried in each site (Bartelheim 2012), and it may be possible that the choices about whom to bury varied for each settlement. Such a possibility is further supported by differences in the demography of the burials; for example, in the well excavated settlements of Gatas and Fuente Álamo adult males were underrepresented (Aranda Jiménez *et al.* 2015). Therefore, it becomes extremely difficult to understand the rules that governed interment. Why were some people buried while others were not? Why were some buried inside houses and others not? How do these differences relate to other types of variability in the tombs, such as wealth (Aranda Jiménez *et al.* 2015, 127–30)? The tendency to locate wealthy burials at the central areas of sites suggested in the cases of Castellón Alto and Peñalosa (Cámara Serrano 2001; Molina González and Cámara Serrano 2009), does not seem to be corroborated by data from Cerro de la Encina or Fuente Álamo (Aranda Jiménez *et al.* 2015). While wealth differences in burials can be recognised as elements of hierarchisation, it is difficult to match the funerary evidence with a society rigidly organised in classes (Bartelheim 2012; Gilman 2013; Montón Subías 2007) and aspects of gender (Montón-Subías 2010), and identity (Aranda Jiménez 2013) may explain much of the variability of tombs. This quick overview aims to raise the possibility that the presence of burials with Argaric traits may have obeyed different customs across southeastern Spain, or at least that the canons that regulated burial customs in Argaric societies were open enough to allow communities to make their own interpretations.

In order to understand better this tension between similarities and differences in the burial record, it may be worth considering the Argaric funeral as a charged cultural context that helped to articulate interaction between Argaric communities. Similar burials would express similar ideological and social conventions that could be played out in shared practices. In particular, the strong homogeneity of Argaric burnished wares found in tombs (Fig. 3.3; Aranda 2001), defying patterns of regional material variation, may provide evidence of ideologically significant practices that were very similar in every Argaric community. The association with drinking of certain ceramic shapes (cups, small jars) common in Argaric burials (Aranda Jiménez 2010; Aranda Jiménez and Montón Subías 2011) may indicate that there was much impor-tance bestowed on certain liquid consumption practices across the Argaric territory.

Prescribed consumption rituals organised under a set of similar rules across Argaric populations would have been important cultural arenas for interaction, familiar to all. One of the roles of such practices may have been to provide a sort of culturally agreed context in which people that otherwise had very little knowledge of each other could meet under a familiar set of rules. The shared knowledge of what to expect and how to behave would have tempered many of the uncertainties of meeting a stranger and would have offered a common ground on which they develop an understanding of each other.

The most highly burnished cups and lenticular vases, closely imitating metal counterparts, are rare items and they were probably largely made specifically for the wealthiest burials. The recent discovery in La Almoloya of a ceramic jar decorated with silver bands further prove that drinking practices in which burnished wares were used constituted significant social arenas of communication where wealth and prestige differences could be stated.

Argaric funerary evidence presents a complex relationship between material culture, burial customs and identity that results in a seemingly contradictory set of homogeneous traits and heterogeneous behaviours. Argaric mortuary customs not only refer to local choices in the way death was related to the living, but they also offer evidence of the significance of a common set of practices, a shared cultural language, that enabled interaction between Argaric societies.

5. The Argaric network: potential and limitations

The patchy nature of the archaeological data precludes the implementation of formal network analyses in Argaric Iberia (*e.g.* Brughmans 2013). Nevertheless, network-based approaches can contribute significantly to the interpretation of the variability and fluidity found in the record, providing new information that otherwise would be difficult to obtain (Collar *et al.* 2015). It also opens new avenues in the study of social complexity in Argaric groups by emphasising the significance of interaction in such processes (Mizoguchi 2009; Schortman 2014).

The potential of network analysis is evident when considering settlement patterns and the interrelation between sites in Argaric landscapes. In the Vera basin, the fluid nature of the regional configuration (Legarra Herrero 2014) suits a network approach well. The settlement probably provided a distinct social identity to its residents that regulated major parts of their lives such as access to land, political and social rights, and so forth. The densely packed habitation of most of the major sites further suggests closely knit relationships between its inhabitants, and their location on visible hill tops visually underlined the common identity of its dwellers to the outsider. The use of Argaric settlements in a network analysis would tie the analysis of social interactions with the realities of Argaric geography (Brughmans 2013), providing new insights into the nature of Argaric territorial configuraton. For example, in the case of the Vera Basin, thinking about central sites as connected nodes exploiting a densely habited region poses questions about the gaps in the archaeological record of the region and the possible presence of other major sites in the area (Fig. 3.7). Such evidence not only can help in future territorial analyses but it can also inform efforts in the preservation of the archaeology of the region.

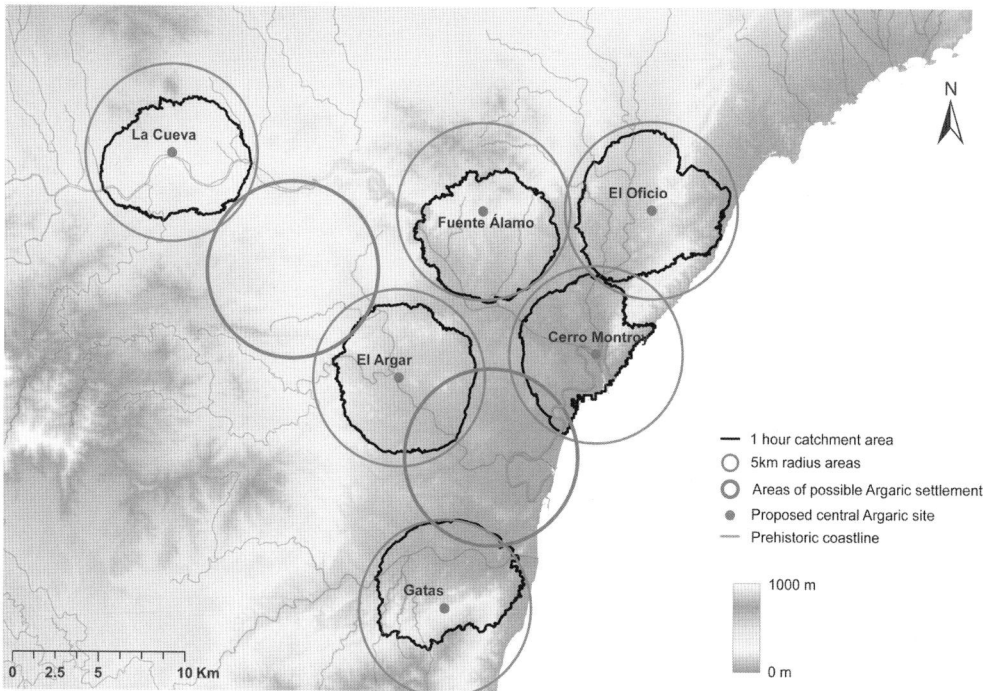

Figure 3.7 Proposed missing Argaric sites in the Vera region.

The use of network approaches can also provide fresh insights in the understanding of socio-political complexity in Argaric societies. In particular, the application of a small-world network model (Brughmans 2010, 278–80; Knappett 2011, 126–7) could offer a way to explain variability and homogeneity in the record in relation to processes of social differentiation. Under this model, each Argaric region would present a densely connected network, while the links between the regions would rely on more sporadic connections. Argaric societies lived by combining a variety of types of interaction at several scales with different types of relationships, information and materials moving in the intra-regional and inter-regional levels (Robb 2007).

Most resources present in Argaric sites were obtained from areas immediate to the site (Legarra Herrero 2014) suggesting communities that were organised primarily around small geographical scales. It seems reasonable to propose that many of the necessary relationships beyond the settlement (exogamy, networks of social and economic support, Halstead 1989; Robb 2007) would be established with nearby populations creating a dense network of closely located sites. The relationships that would fuel these small networks would have been varied in their nature, including economic, social and ideological transactions and would have included a wide spectrum of the population. Traditionally defined Argaric regions, such as Vera, Orce (Schüle 1986), the Granada plain (Molina González and Cámara Serrano 2009) or the area of Villena (Jover Maestre *et al.* 2015; López Padilla *et al.* 2015) are good candidates for such densely connected regions. The configuration of each region would vary depending on local geography and resources ending in different contingent histories.

Interaction occurring beyond the scale of each region is well attested by metal trade, by the expansion of Argaric sites and by shared customs and practices as indicated in the burials. These longer distance connections involve a more restricted, although highly important, set of materials and ideas. This is well exemplified by the consumption practices marked by burnished wares in burials. They indicate a set of practices with a strong cultural value that would probably have helped to override the challenges of establishing social and economic relationships beyond the regional scale. Such practices could have funnelled the distribution of key materials and ideas across large areas of southeastern Iberia. Such a ritualised type of interaction does not preclude other types of connections, and the fluid picture coming from metal analyses opens the possibility of other types of more commercially oriented trading activities.

Small-world network approaches therefore would allow for the explanation of independent regional paths as adaptations to the specific situation of a geographical region while at the same time acknowledging the importance of long-distance connections. Such a framework provides a basis for explaining complexity in the heterogeneous Argaric world.

It has been argued that the mapping and understanding of the relationships of distinct social groups in a landscape may help to explain the appearance of hierarchies and complexity (Schortman 2014). Privileged location of certain communities may provide them with the necessary advantages to gain wealth and regional dominance in highly connected landscapes. Certain sites would arise as political and economic powerhouses by controlling the movement of materials in exchange networks (*e.g.* Broodbank 1993). Such sites are not necessarily the producers, nor the final consumers, but those in key positions at the middle of the exchange networks. Those communities able to articulate local advantageous characteristics (resources, agricultural potential, demographic density) and large-scale ones (location with respect to main transportation routes, metal resources) would have been in particularly strong positions.

In terms of network-based approaches, the exceptionality of certain Argaric sites could be studied through the measurement of concepts such as degree centrality (rank based on number of edges or connections for each node), betweenness (rank based on the location of a node in the connection joining two other sites) and closeness (rank based on the calculation of how many steps are necessary to reach a node from another node; Mizoguchi 2009; Schortman 2014; Collar *et al.* 2015). While these may be difficult to implement until a more extensive knowledge of Argaric settlement patterns is achieved, it provides a hypothesis for thinking about power differences and political and economic inequalities within the heterogeneous character of the Argaric record. Recent studies have established that the location of certain Argaric sites responds to the interest in controlling communication routes (Andrés Rodríguez 2017), and support the relevance of network studies for the Bronze Age of southeastern Iberia.

6. Conclusions

There is obvious work ahead to fulfil the potential of network approaches in southeastern Spain, starting from intensive archaeological surveys that provide a better understanding of settlement patterns in several Argaric regions. More extensive petrographic analysis of ceramics from Argaric tombs and settlements could provide a picture of how material moved (Knappett 2011) that would complement the data provided by archaeometallurgical studies. Ceramic analyses have proved to be particularly useful in understanding interaction both at the large (Day *et al.* 2011) and at the local levels (Whitelaw *et al.* 1997) in the Mediterranean.

Still, this study has tried to prove the potential of network analysis and 'Mediterranean' approaches in order to move beyond static conceptions of culture and to explain better the mix of diversity and similarity that characterise the Argaric archaeological record. It enables us to understand the importance of interaction and mobility for the Argaric communities and to relate these aspects to more local processes of resource exploitation and internal social organisation. This mixture of local, regional and large-scale patterns opens new ways to understand socio-political complexity in the Bronze Age of southeastern Iberia.

References

Andrés Rodríguez, L. (2017) El poblamiento Argárico en la costa de la Depresión de Vera (Almería, España) en el II milenio BC. Un acercamiento mediante el análisis espacial de base SIG. *Arqueología y Territorio* 14, 35–45.

Aranda, G. (2001) *El análisis de la relación forma-contenido de los conjuntos cerámicos del yacimiento arqueológico del Cerro de la Encina (Granada, España)*. Oxford, Archaeopress.

Aranda, G., Montón-Subías, S., Sánchez-Romero, M. and Alarcón, E. (2009) Death and everyday life. The Argaric societies from Southeast Iberia. *Journal of Social Archaeology* 9, 139–62.

Aranda Jiménez, G. (2008) Cohesión y distancia social. El consumo comensal de bóvidos en el ritual funerario de las sociedades argáricas. *Cuadernos de Prehistoria y Arqueología de la Universidad de Granada* 18, 107–23.

Aranda Jiménez, G. (2013) Against uniformity cultural diversity: the 'others' in Argaric societies. In M.C. Berrocal, L. García Sanjuán and A. Gilman (eds) *The Prehistory of Iberia. Debating early social stratification and the state*, 99–118. New York, Routledge.

Aranda Jiménez, G., Alarcón García, E., Murillo-Barroso, M., Montero Ruiz, I., Jiménez Brobeil, S.A., Sánchez Romero, M. and Rodríguez Ariza, M.O. (2012) El yacimiento argárico del cerro de San Cristóbal (Ogíjares, Granada). *Menga. Revista de Prehistoria de Andalucía* 3, 141–66.

Aranda, G. and Molina, F. (2006) Wealth and power in the Bronze Age of the south-east of the Iberian Peninsula: the funerary record of Cerro de la Encina. *Oxford Journal of Archaeology* 25, 47–59.

Aranda Jiménez, G., Molina González, F., Fernández Martín, S., Sánchez Romero, M., Al Oumaoui, I., Jiménez Brobeil, S.A. and Roca, M.G. (2008) El poblado y necrópolis argáricos del Cerro de la Encina (Monachil, Granada): Las campañas de excavación de 2003–05. *Cuadernos de Prehistoria y Arqueología de la Universidad de Granada* 18, 219–64.

Aranda Jiménez, G. and Montón Subías, S. (2011) Feasting death: funerary rituals in the Bronze Age societies of south-eastern Iberia. In G. Aranda Jiménez, S. Montón Subías and M. Sánchez Romero (eds) *Guess Who's Coming to Dinner: feasting rituals in the prehistoric societies of Europe and the Near East*, 130–57. Oxford, Oxbow Books.

Aranda Jiménez, G., Montón Subías, S. and Jiménez Brobeil, S.A. (2009) Conflicting evidence? Weapons and skeletons in the Bronze Age of south-east Iberia. *Antiquity* 83, 1038–51.

Aranda Jiménez, G., Montón Subías, S. and Sánchez Romero, M. (2015) *The Archaeology of Bronze Age Iberia. Argaric societies.* London, Routledge.

Arteaga Matute, O. (2000) La sociedad clasista inicial y el origen del Estado en el territorio de El Argar. *Revista Atlántico Mediterránea de Prehistoria y Arqueología Social* 3, 121–219.

Bartelheim, M. (2007) *Die Rolle der Metallurgie in vorgeschichtlichen Gesellschaften. Sozioökonomische und kulturhistorische Aspekte der Ressourcennutzung; ein Vergleich zwsichen Andalusien, Zypern un dem Nordalpenraum.* Rahden/Westf., Verlag Marie Leidorf.

Bartelheim, M. (2012) Detecting social structures in the Bronze Age of southeastern Spain. In T. Kienlin and A. Zimmermann (eds) *Beyond Elites. Alternatives to hierarchical systems in modelling social formations. International conference at the Ruhr-Universität Bochum, Germany, October 22–24, 2009. Teil 1*, 339–54. Bonn, Habelt.

Bartelheim, M., Cortés, F.C., Onorato, A.M., Murillo-Barroso, M. and Pernicka, E. (2012) The silver of the south Iberian El Argar culture: a first look at production and distribution. *Trabajos de Prehistoria* 69, 293–309.

Blake, E. (2013) Social networks, path dependence, and the rise of ethnic groups in pre-Roman Italy. In C. Knappett (ed.) *Network Analysis in Archaeology: new approaches to regional interaction*, 203–22. Oxford, Oxford University Press.

Broodbank, C. (1993) Ulysses without sails: trade, distance, knowledge and power in the early Cyclades. *World Archaeology* 24, 315–31.

Broodbank, C. (2013) *The Making of the Middle Sea. A history of the Mediterranean from the beginning to the emergence of the Classical world.* London, Thames and Hudson.

Brughmans, T.O.M. (2010) Connecting the dots: towards archaeological network analysis. *Oxford Journal of Archaeology* 29, 277–303.

Brughmans, T.O.M. (2013) Thinking through networks: a review of formal network methods in archaeology. *Journal of Archaeological Method and Theory* 20, 623–62.

Cámalich Massieu, M.D. and Martín Socas, D. (1998) *El territorio almeriense desde los inicios de la producción hasta fines de la antigüedad: un modelo, la depresión de Vera y cuenca del Río Almanzora.* Sevilla, Consejería de Cultura, Servicio de Investigación y Difusión del Patrimonio Histórico. Junta de Andalucía.

Cámara Serrano, J.A. (2001) *El ritual funerario en la Prehistoria Reciente en el Sur de la Península Ibérica.* Oxford, John and Erica Hedges Ltd.

Cámara Serrano, J.A., Contreras Cortés, F., Pérez Bareas, C. and Lizcano Prestel, R. (1996) Enterramientos y diferenciación social II. La problemática de la Edad del Bronce en el Alto Guadalquivir. *Trabajos de Prehistoria* 53, 91–108.

Cámara Serrano, J.A. and Molina González, F. (2004) El megalitismo en el sureste de la Península Ibérica. Ideología y control territorial. *Mainake* 26, 139–63.

Cámara Serrano, J.A. and Molina González, F. (2006) Selection of data, determinism and scientific relevance in interpretations of social development in the late prehistory of the Iberian Southeast. In P. Díaz-del-Río and L. García Sanjuán (eds) *Social Inequality in Iberian Late Prehistory*, 21–36. Oxford, Archaeopress.

Cámara Serrano, J.A. and Molina González, F. (2010) Relaciones de clase e identidad en El Argar: Evolución social y segregación espacial en los Altiplanos granadinos (c. 2000–1300 cal. A.C.). *Arqueología espacial* 28, 21–40.

Cámara Serrano, J.A. and Molina González, F. (2011) Jerarquización social en el mundo argárico (2000–1300 aC). *Quaderns de Prehistòria i Arqueologia de Castelló* 29, 77–100.

Carrión, J.S., Fernández, S., Jiménez-Moreno, G., Fauquette, S., Gil-Romera, G., González-Sampériz, P. and Finlayson, C. (2010) The historical origins of aridity and vegetation degradation in south-eastern Spain. *Journal of Arid Environments* 74, 731–36.

Carrión Marco, Y. (2004) Análisis antracológico del yacimiento de Fuente Álamo (Cuevas de Almanzora, Almería): uso de la madera y paleovegetación. In L. Hernández Alcaráz and M.S. Hernández Pérez (eds) *La Edad del Bronce en tierras valencianas y zonas limítrofes*, 477–86. Alicante, Ayuntamiento de Villena, Instituto Alicantino de Cultura Juan Gil-Albert.

Castro Martínez, P.V., Chapman, R.W., Gili I Suriñach, S., Lull, V., Micó, R., Rihuete Herrada, C., Risch, R. and Sanahuja Yll, M.E. (1999) *Proyecto Gatas 2. La dinámica arqueoecológica de la ocupación prehistórica*. Sevilla, Junta de Andalucía.

Castro, P., Chapman, R., Gili, S., Lull, V., Micó, R. and Rihuete, C. (eds) (1998) *Aguas Project. Palaeoclimatic reconstruction and the dynamics of human settlement and land use in the area of the middle Aguas (Almería) in the south-east of the Iberian Peninsula*. Luxemburg, European Comission.

Castro, P.V., Chapman, R.W., Gili Suriñach, S., Lull, V., Micó Pérez, R., Rihuete Herrada, C., Risch, R. and Sanahuja Yll, M.E. (2001) La sociedad argárica. In M. Ruiz-Gálvez Priego (ed.) *La Edad del Bronce, ¿Primera Edad de Oro de España? Sociedad, economía e ideología*, 181–217. Barcelona, Crítica Arqueología.

Chapman, R. (2008) Producing inequalities: regional sequences in later prehistoric southern Spain. *Journal of World Prehistory* 21, 195–260.

Chapman, R. (2014) Scales, interaction, and movement in later Mediterranean prehistory. In S. Souvatzi and A. Hadji (eds) *Space and Time in Mediterranean Prehistory*, 32–48. New York, Routledge.

Chapman, R., Lull, V., Picazo, M. and Sanahuja, M.E. (1987) *Proyecto Gatas. Sociedad y Economía en el Sudeste de España c. 2500–800 a.n.e. 1. La prospección arqueoecológica*. Oxford, British Archaeological Reports.

Chapman, R.W. (1990) *Emerging Complexity: the later prehistory of south-east Spain, Iberia and the west Mediterranean*. Cambridge, Cambridge University Press.

Chapman, R.W. (2003) *Archaeologies of Complexity*. London, Routledge.

Childe, V.G. (1957) *The Dawn of European Civilization*. London, Routledge and Paul.

Collar, A., Coward, F., Brughmans, T.O.M. and Mills, B.J. (2015) Networks in archaeology: phenomena, abstraction, representation. *Journal of Archaeological Method and Theory* 22, 1–32.

Contreras Cortés, F. and Cámara Serrano, J.A. (2002) *La jerarquización en la Edad del Bronce del Alto Guadalquivir (España). El poblado de Peñalosa (Baños de la Encina, Jaén)*. Oxford, Archaeopress.

Contreras Cortés, F., Cámara Serrano, J.A., Moreno Onorato, M.A. and Aranda Jiménez, G. (2004) Las sociedades estatales de la Edad del Bronce en el Alto Guadalquivir (proyecto Peñalosa 2ª fase). Quinta campaña de excavaciones (2001). *Anuario Arqueológico de Andalucía* 2001, 24–38.

Day, P.M., Rutter, J.B., Quinn, P.S. and Kilikoglou, V. (2011) A world of goods: transport jars and commodity exchange at the Late Bronze Age harbor of Kommos, Crete. *Hesperia*, 80.4, 511–58.

Delgado Raack, S. (2008) *Prácticas económicas y gestión social de recursos (macro)líticos en la prehistoria reciente (III-I milenios aC) del Mediterráneo occidental*. PhD Thesis. Universitat Autónoma de Barcelona.

Delgado Raack, S. and Risch, R. (2006) La tumba nº 3 de Los Cipreses y la metalurgia Argárica. *Alberca: Revista de la Asociación de Amigos del Museo Arqueológico de Lorca* 4, 21–50.

Feinman, G.M. (2011) Size, complexity, and organizational variation: a comparative approach. *Cross-Cultural Research* 45, 37–58.

Eiroa García, J.J. (2004) *La Edad del Bronce en Murcia*. Murcia, Real Academia Alfonso X El Sabio.

Fontella Ballesta, S., Gómez Martínez, J.A. and Miras García, M. (2004) Lorca, poblado más extenso y primigenio de la cultura del Argar. *Alberca: Revista de la Asociación de Amigos del Museo Arqueológico de Lorca* 2, 39–52.

García Sanjuán, L. and Murillo-Barroso, M. (2013) Social complexity in Copper Age southern Iberia (ca. 3200–2200 Cal BC): reviewing the state hypothesis at Valencina de la Concepción (Seville, Spain). In M.C. Berrocal, L. García Sanjuán and A. Gilman (eds) *The Prehistory of Iberia. Debating early social stratification and the state*, 119–40. New York, Routledge.

Gilman, A. (1981) The development of social stratification in Bronze Age Europe. *Current Anthropology* 22, 1–23.

Gilman, A. (2013) Were there states during the later prehistory of southern Iberia? In M.C. Berrocal, L. García Sanjuán and A. Gilman (eds) *The Prehistory of Iberia. Debating early social stratification and the state*, 10–28. New York, Routledge.

Gilman, A. and Thornes, J.B. (1985) *Land-use and Prehistory in South-east Spain*. London, George Allen & Unwin.

Halstead, P. (1989) The economy has a normal surplus: economic stability and social change among early farming communities of Thessaly, Greece. In P. Halstead and J. O'Shea (eds) *Bad Year Economics: cultural responses to risk and uncertainty*, 68–80. Cambridge, Cambridge University Press.

Haro Navarro, M., Carrión Méndez, F. and García González, D. (2006) Territorio y georrecursos en el Cabo de Gata (Níjar, Almería) durante la edad del cobre. In G. Martínez Fernández, A. Morgado Rodríguez and J A. Afonso Marrero (eds) *Sociedades prehistóricas, recursos abióticos y territorio*, 315–26. Granada, Fundación Ibn al-Jatib de Estudios de Cooperación Cultural.

Hernández Pérez, M.S. (2009) Tiempos de cambio. El final del Argar en Alicante. In M.S. Hernández Pérez, J.A. Soler Díaz and J.A. López Padilla (eds) *En los confines del Argar: una cultura de la Edad del Bronce en Alicante en el centenario de Julio Furgús*, 292–305. Alicante, Fundación Marq.

Hérnandez Pérez, M.S., Soler Díaz, J.A. and López Padilla, J. (eds) (2009) *En los confines del Argar: una cultura de la Edad del Bronce en Alicante en el centenario de Julio Furgús*. Alicante, Fundación MARQ.

Horden, P. and Purcell, N. (2000) *The Corrupting Sea. A study of Mediterranean history*. Oxford, Blackwell.

Hunt Ortiz, M., Contreras Cortés, F. and Arboledas Martínez, L. (2011) La procedencia de los recursos minerales metálicos en el poblado de la Edad de Bronce de Peñalosa (Baños de la Encina, Jaén). In J.M. Mata Perelló, L. Torrí I Abat, M.N. Fuentes Prieto, A. Niera Campo and O. Puche Riart (eds) *Actas del Quinto Congreso Internacional sobre Minería y Metalurgia Históricas en el Suroeste Europeo, León, 19-21 de Junio de 2008. Libro en Homenaje a Claude Domergue*, 195–206. La Poble de Segur, Sociedad Española para la Defensa del Patrimonio Geológico y Minero.

Jover Maestre, F.J. and López Padilla, J.A. (1999) Caracterización del patrón de asentamiento en la cuenca del Río Vinalopó (Alicante) durante el II milenio ANE. *XXIV Congreso Nacional de Arqueología: Cartagena 1997*, 241–9. Cartagena, Gobierno de la Región de Murcia, Instituto de Patrimonio Histórico.

Jover Maestre, F.J. and López Padilla, J.A. (2004) 2.100–1.200 BC. Aportaciones al proceso histórico en la cuenca del río Vinalopó. In L. Hernández Alcaráz and M.S. Hernández Pérez (eds) *La Edad del Bronce en tierras valencianas y zonas limítrofes*, 285–302. Alicante, Ayuntamiento de Villena, Instituto Alicantino de Cultura Juan Gil-Albert.

Jover Maestre, F.J. and López Padilla, J.A. (2009) Más allá de los confines del Argar. Los inicios de la Edad del Bronce y la delimitación de las áreas culturales en el cuadrante suroriental de la Península Ibérica, 60 años después. In M.S. Hernández Pérez, J.A. Soler Díaz and J.A. López Padilla (eds) *En los confines del Argar: una cultura de la Edad del Bronce en Alicante en el centenario de Julio Furgús*, 268–91. Alicante, Fundación Marq.

Jover Maestre, F.J., López Padilla, J.A. and Martínez Monleón, S. (2015) Espacios sociales en la Edad del Bronce: La Cubeta de Villena como caso de estudio. In M.J. De Pedro Micho and B. Soler Mayor (eds) *Vivir junto al Turia hace 4.000 años. La Lloma del Betxí*, 118–23. Valencia, Museu de Prehistòria de València. Àrea de Cultura. Diputació de València.

Knappett, C. (2011) *An Archaeology of Interaction: network perspectives on material culture and society*. Oxford, Oxford University Press.

Kunter, M. (1990) *Menschliche Skelettreste aus Siedlungen der El Argar-Kultur. Ein Beitrag der prähistorischen Anthropologie zur Kenntnis bronzezeitlicher Bevölkerungen Südostspaniens*. Mainz am Rhein, P Von Zabern.

Legarra Herrero, B. (2014) Estructura territorial y estado en la cultura Argárica. *Menga. Revista de Prehistoria de Andalucía* 4, 21–43.

Lillios, K.T. (2014) Crossing borders: death and life in second millennium BC southern Iberia and North Africa. In A.B. Knapp and P. Van Dommelen (eds) *The Cambridge Prehistory of the Bronze and Iron Age Mediterranean*, 554–70. Cambridge, Cambridge University Press.

López Padilla, J.A. (2009) El irresistible poder de la ostentación: la artesanía del marfil en la época del Argar. *Alberca: Revista de la Asociación de Amigos del Museo Arqueológico de Lorca* 7, 7–23.

López Padilla, J.A., Jover Maestre, F.J. and Martínez Monleón, S. (2014) San Antón y los orígenes de la Edad del Bronce en el sur de Alicante. *Orihuela. Arqueología y Museo*, 80–103. Alicante, MARQ. Museo Arqueológico de Alicante. Diputación de Alicante.

López Padilla, J.A., Martínez Monleón, S. and Jover Maestre, F.J. (2015) Estudio y caracterización del territorio argárico alicantino. In M.J. De Pedro Micho and B. Soler Mayor (eds) *Vivir junto al Turia hace 4.000 años. La Lloma del Betxí*, 124–31. Valencia, Museu de Prehistòria de València. Àrea de Cultura. Diputació de València.

Lull, V., Micó Pérez, R., Rihuete Herrada, C. and Risch, R. (2004) Las relaciones de propiedad en la sociedad argárica. Una aproximación a través del análisis de las tumbas de individuos infantiles. *Mainake* 2004, 233–72.

Lull Santiago, V., Micó Pérez, R., Rihuete Herrada, C. and Risch, R. (2005) Property relations in the Bronze Age of south-western Europe: an archaeological analysis of infant burials from El Argar (Almeria, Spain). *Proceedings of the Prehistoric Society* 71, 247–68.

Lull Santiago, V., Micó Pérez, R., Rihuete Herrada, C. and Risch, R. (2010) Las relaciones políticas y económicas de El Argar. *Menga. Revista de Prehistoria de Andalucía* 1, 11–35.

Lull, V. (1983) *La 'cultura' de El Argar: Un modelo para el estudio de las formaciones económico-sociales prehistóricas*. Madrid, Akal.

Lull, V. (2000) Argaric society: death at home. *Antiquity* 74, 581–90.

Lull, V. and Estévez, J. (1986) Propuesta metodológica para el estudio de las necrópolis argáricas. *Homenaje a Luis Siret (1934-1984)*, 441–52. Sevilla, Junta de Andalucía.

Lull, V. and Micó, R. (2011) *Archaeology of the Origin of the State: the theories*. Oxford, Oxford University Press.

Lull, V., Micó, R., Rihuete-Herrada, C. and Risch, R. (2014) The La Bastida fortification: new light and new questions on Early Bronze Age societies in the western Mediterranean. *Antiquity* 88, 395–410.

Lull, V., Micó, R., Rihuete Herrada, C. and Risch, R. (2010a) Límites históricos y limitaciones del conocimiento arqueológico: la transición entre los grupos arqueológicos de Los Millares y El Argar. In P. Bueno, A. Gilman, C. Martín Morales and F.J. Sánchez-Palencia (eds) *Arqueología, sociedad, territorio y paisaje. Estudios sobre prehistoria reciente, protohistoria y transición al mundo romano en homenaje a Ma. Dolores Fernández Posse*, 75–94. Madrid, Consejo Superior de Investigaciones Científicas.

Lull, V., Micó, R., Rihuete Herrada, C. and Risch, R. (2010b) Metal and social relations of production in the 3rd and 2nd millennia BCE in the southeast of the Iberian peninsula. *Trabajos de Prehistoria* 67, 323–47.

Lull, V., Micó, R., Risch, R. and Rihuete Herrada, C. (2009) El Argar: la formación de una sociedad de clases. In M.S. Hernández Pérez, J.A. Soler Díaz and J.A. López Padilla (eds) *En los confines del Argar: una cultura de la Edad del Bronce en Alicante en el centenario de Julio Furgús*, 224–45. Alicante, Fundación Marq.

Mathers, C. (1994) Goodbye to all that? Contrasting patterns of change in the south-east Iberian Bronze Age c. 24/2200–600 BC. In C. Mathers and S. Stoddart (eds) *Development and Decline in the Mediterranean Bronze Age*, 21–72. Sheffield Archaeological Monographs 8. Sheffield, J.R. Collis.

Mederos Martín, A. (1994) *Los estados incipientes del sureste de la Península Ibérica. Repercusiones en las cuencas de los ríos Aguas, Antas y Almanzora. Almería (4500-1300 a.C./5300-1600 a.C.)*. PhD Thesis. Universidad de La Laguna.

Mizoguchi, K. (2009) Nodes and edges: a network approach to hierarchisation and state formation in Japan. *Journal of Anthropological Archaeology* 28, 14–26.

Molina González, F. and Cámara Serrano, J.A. (2004) Urbanismo y fortificaciones en la cultura de El Argar: homogeneidad y patrones regionales. In M.R. García Huerta and J. Morales Hervás (eds) *La Península Ibérica en el II milenio A.C.: poblados y fortificaciones*, 9–56. Cuenca, Universidad de Castilla-La Mancha.

Molina González, F. and Cámara Serrano, J.A. (2009) La cultura argárica en Granada y Jaén. In M.S. Hernández Pérez, J.A. Soler Díaz and J.A. López Padilla (eds) *En los confines del Argar: una cultura de la Edad del Bronce en Alicante en el centenario de Julio Furgús*, 196–223. Alicante, Fundación Marq.

Molina González, F., Rodríguez Ariza, M.O., Jiménez, S.A. and Botella López, M. (2003) La sepultura 121 del yacimiento argárico de El Castellón Alto (Galera, Granada). *Trabajos de Prehistoria* 60, 153–8.

Montero Ruiz, I. (1991) *Estudio arqueometalúrgico en el sudeste de la Península Ibérica*. PhD Thesis. Universidad Complutense de Madrid.

Montero Ruiz, I. and Murillo-Barroso, M. (2010) La producción metalúrgica en las sociedades argáricas y sus implicaciones sociales: una propuesta de investigación. *Menga. Revista de Prehistoria de Andalucía* 1, 37–52.

Montón-Subías, S. (2010) Muerte e identidad femenina en el mundo argárico. *Trabajos de Prehistoria* 67, 119–37.

Montón Subías, S. (2007) Interpreting archaeological continuities: an approach to transversal equality in the Argaric Bronze Age of south-east Iberia. *World Archaeology* 39, 246–62.

Moreno Onorato, A. and Contreras Cortés, F. (2010) La organización social de la producción metalúrgica en las sociedades argáricas: el poblado de Peñalosa. *Menga. Revista de Prehistoria de Andalucía* 1, 53–76.

Murillo-Barroso, M., Montero Ruiz, I. and Aranda Jiménez, G. (2015) An insight into the organisation of metal production in the Argaric society. *Journal of Archaeological Science: Reports* 2, 141–55.

Murillo-Barroso, M., Aranda Jiménez, G. and Montero Ruiz, I. (2014) Aspectos sociales del cambio tecnológico: nuevos datos para valorar la introducción de la aleación del bronce en las sociedades argárica. In E. García Afonso and B. Ruíz González (eds) *Movilidad, Contacto y Cambio. II Congreso de Prehistoria de Andalucía. Antequera 15-17 de febrero de 2012*, 417–27. Sevilla, Consejería de Educación, Cultura y Deporte de la Junta de Andalucía.

Nocete, F., Queipo, G., Sáez, R., Nieto, J.M., Inácio, N., Bayona, M.R., Peramo, A., Vargas, J.M., Cruz-Auñón, R., Gil-Ibarguchi, J.I. and Santos, J.F. (2008) The smelting quarter of Valencina de la Concepción (Seville, Spain): the specialised copper industry in a political centre of the Guadalquivir Valley during the third millennium BC (2750–2500 BC). *Journal of Archaeological Science* 35, 717–32.

Murillo-Barroso, M., Peñalver, E., Bueno, P., Barroso, R., de Balbín, R., Martinón-Torres, M. (2018) Amber in prehistoric Iberia: New data and a review. *PLoS ONE* 13.8 e0202235. https://doi.org/10.1371/journal.pone.0202235.

Nocete, F., Vargas, J.M., Schuhmacher, T.X., Banerjee, A. and Dindorf, W. (2013) The ivory workshop of Valencina de la Concepción (Seville, Spain) and the identification of ivory from Asian elephant on the Iberian Peninsula in the first half of the 3rd millennium BC. *Journal of Archaeological Science* 40, 1579–92.

Pingel, V., Schubart, H., Arteaga, O., Roos, A.M. and Kunst, M. (2003) Excavaciones arqueológicas en la ladera sur de Fuente Álamo: campaña de 1999. *Spal* 12, 179–230.

Ramos Millán, A. (2013) Villages of wealth and resistance in paradise: Millaran and Argaric chiefdoms in the Iberian southeast. In M.C. Berrocal, L. García Sanjuán and A. Gilman (eds) *The Prehistory of Iberia. Debating early social stratification and the state*, 74–98. New York, Routledge.

Risch, R. (1998) Análisis paleoeconómico y medios de producción líticos: el caso de Fuente Alamo. In G. Delibes (ed.) *Minerales y metales en la prehistoria reciente: algunos testimonios de su explotación y laboreo en la Península Ibérica*, 105–54. Valladolid, Universidad de Valladolid.

Risch, R. (2002) *Recursos naturales, medios de producción y explotación social: un análisis económico de la industria lítica de Fuente Alamo (Almeria), 2250-1400 antes de nuestra era.* Mainz am Rhein, P. von Zabern.

Robb, John. (2007) *The Early Mediterranean Village: agency, material culture, and social change in Neolithic Italy.* Cambridge, Cambridge University Press.

Scarre, C. (2013) Social stratification and the state in prehistoric Europe: the wider perspective. In M.C. Berrocal, L. García Sanjuán and A. Gilman (eds) *The Prehistory of Iberia. Debating early social stratification and the state,* 381–406. New York, Routledge.

Schortman, E.M. (2014) Networks of power in archaeology. *Annual Review of Anthropology* 43, 167–82.

Schubart, H. and Arteaga, O. (1986) Fundamentos arqueológicos para el estudio socio-económico y cultural del area de El Argar. *Homenaje a Luis Siret (1934-1984). Actas del Congreso, Cuevas del Almanzora,* 289–307. Sevilla, Junta de Andalucía.

Schüle, A. (1986) El Cerro de la Virgen, Orce (Granada): consideraciones sobre su marco ecológico y cultural. *Homenaje a Luis Siret (1934-1984). Actas del Congreso, Cuevas del Almanzora,* 208–20. Sevilla, Junta de Andalucía.

Serrano Ariza, R. (2012) Fotificaciones y estado en la cultura argárica. *Arqueología y Territorio* 9, 49–72.

Siret, E. and Siret, L. (1890) *Las primeras edades del metal en el sudeste de España.* Barcelona, Henrich & Co.

Whitelaw, T.M., Day, P.M., Kiriatzi, E., Kilikoglou, V. and Wilson, D.E. (1997) Ceramic traditions at EM IIB Myrtos, Fournou Korifi. In R. Laffineur and P.P. Betancourt (eds) *TEXNH: Craftsmen, craftswomen and craftsmanship in the Aegean Bronze Age. Proceedings of the 6th International Aegean Conference/6e Rencontre égéenne internationale, Philadelphia, Temple University, 18-21 April 1996,* 265–74. Liège, Université de Liège.

Chapter 4

The breakdown of knowledge: people and pottery at the Bronze Age tell at Százhalombatta-Földvár, Hungary

Joanna Sofaer

The site of Százhalombatta-Földvár, situated on the west bank of the Danube 30 km south of Budapest, is one of the most important fortified Bronze Age temperate tell settlements in the region. Occupied from the Early Bronze Age to the beginning of the Late Bronze Age, this site offers an opportunity to trace the construction and breakdown of networks in which craft knowledge was accumulated through investigation of changes in ceramic production. While a sophisticated ceramic tradition flourished in earlier periods, it appears to have disintegrated with social breakdown in the later phases. The identification of social networks through changes in both the manufacture of ceramics and the transmission of knowledge of how to make them enables us to trace this process of social collapse.

Key words: networks, ceramics, knowledge transmission, Hungary, Bronze Age

1. Introduction

Networks provide a means for the learning of craft knowledge (Sofaer 2006; Rebay-Salisbury *et al.* 2014). Disruption to networks may consequently have substantial implications for material change. Craft knowledge is participative. It is actively generated through complex responsive processes and situated in relationships between people (Lave and Wenger 1991; Wenger 2000; Stacey 2001; Gamble 2002; Stark *et al.* 2008). Thus, when these relationships are severed leading to disruption of the networks in which they are positioned, knowledge may be lost, resulting in the disappearance of elements of a material repertoire. In other cases, where the break in the network is only partial, or links in the network are discontinuous (Borgatti *et al.* 2009), people may attempt to fill in 'knowledge gaps' (Tichenor *et al.* 1970) resulting in more subtle changes to material expression. In this chapter I want to use a network perspective as a lens through which to understand rapid changes in ceramic vessels at the end of the Middle Bronze Age at the tell settlement at Százhalombatta-Földvár, Hungary. My aim is to explore the circumstances under which learning networks may have broken down, how people responded to the challenges this presented, and the potential implications for larger scale changes at the end of the Middle Bronze Age in the Carpathian Basin.

2. The Bronze Age tell at Százhalombatta-Földvár and the end of the Middle Bronze Age

The site of Százhalombatta-Földvár is situated on the west bank of the Danube, 30 km south of Budapest. It is one of the most important fortified Bronze Age temperate tell settlements in the region with occupation layers up to 6 m deep. The site today is 200 m × 100 m in area although up to one third of the original settlement may have been destroyed during clay extraction by a local brick factory and erosion by the River Danube (Poroszlai 2000). The site was first occupied at the end of the Early Bronze Age (c. 2000 BC) and was continuously inhabited through the Vatya and Koszider phases of the Middle Bronze Age until the start of the Late Bronze Age (c. 1400 BC). The site was subsequently abandoned until relatively small-scale occupation in the Urnfield phase of the Late Bronze Age during which the site was in use into the Iron Age, when it again expanded. The most recent excavations, ongoing since 1998, focus on domestic contexts and are producing detailed new data, revealing a picture of settlement structure, architecture and life inside Bronze Age houses (Vicze 2005; Sofaer 2010; 2011; Sørensen 2010; Vicze *et al.* 2017). Although a fraction of the original surface, the present 20 m × 20 m trench is the largest ever Bronze Age tell excavation in Hungary.

The tell at Százhalombatta-Földvár offers an opportunity to trace the construction and breakdown of networks in which craft knowledge was accumulated through investigation of changes in ceramic production. An extraordinarily sophisticated pottery-making tradition flourished here, reaching its zenith at the end of the Middle Bronze Age in the Koszider phase (c. 1600–1400 BC). The upper levels of the site have yielded large quantities of distinctive, elaborate Koszider ceramics including tripartite table ware vessels with *ansa lunata* handles decorated with impressed dots and incised inverted triangles, table ware bowls and domestic cooking pots with distinctive bossed rims, and storage vessels with lentil shaped impressions and groove decoration around applied bosses (Bóna 1975; Vicze 2011) (Fig. 4.1).

Although Koszider pottery is increasingly known from other sites including settlements, cemeteries and hoards (Vicze *et al.* 2013), at Százhalombatta-Földvár the depth of cultural layers provides a unique opportunity to follow the development of these ceramic types. The genesis, duration and dating of the Koszider phase has been a subject of long-standing debate (see Vicze 2013; Vicze and Sümegi 2013) but the finds from Százhalombatta-Földvár indicate that Koszider pottery was an unbroken development of earlier Classical Vatya forms with gradual exaggeration of decorative embellishments (Poroszlai 2013). Furthermore, in contrast to views of the Koszider

Figure 4.1 Koszider vessels from Százhalombatta-Földvár (Photograph: Matrica Museum Százhalombatta).

phase as one of a short period of radical change, destruction and subsequent aban-donment of settlements due to incomers – an interpretation based primarily on identification of a Koszider bronze hoard horizon (Mozsolics 1967; David 2002) – there is no break in the settlement sequence that might speak to such disruption. Instead, the abandonment of the settlement took place at the end of an extended Koszider phase lasting 150–200 years (Uhnér 2010; Jaeger-Kulcsár 2013).

These findings augment those from elsewhere in the Carpathian Basin that have demonstrated that the Koszider phase is of greater duration and more widely distrib-uted than was previously understood (Bóna and Nováki 1982; Bóna 1992; Vicze 2013). Recent analysis of the large, well-preserved ceramic assemblage from the cemetery at Dunaújváros-Duna-dűlő has resulted in the development of an internal chronol-ogy for the Koszider phase that divides it into early and late sub-phases (Vicze 2011; 2013). The early Koszider pottery sees the introduction of new decorative motifs to previously plain Vatya vessel types, as well as minor increases in rim thickness and in the size of inverted rims. In addition, there are some new vessel types, in particular bowls, and modifications to the shape of some urns (Vicze 2013, 19). Late Koszider ceramics are much more baroque and readily identifiable although the 'flamboyant' decoration was still applied to traditional ceramic forms, thereby indicating continuity (Vicze 2013, 20). Decorative motifs include zigzags, incised or grooved garlands, and pointed bosses of increasing size, which were placed in designated positions (body or rim) depending on vessel type. Specific aspects of vessels are further exaggerated, including the development of *ansa lunata* handles or the shape of rims on urns or bowls. The latter also show the further development of new forms (Vicze 2011; 2013). Despite these developments, however, techniques of vessel manufacture and fabrics remained unchanged and continued to follow long-established practices (Vicze 2013).

The end of the Koszider phase is little understood. The abandonment of tell settlements, including at Százhalombatta-Földvár, has been attributed to the socio-economic collapse of Middle Bronze Age societies (Reményi 2013). It has been proposed that 'unstable social organization was built on unstable elite control over resources' (Reményi 2013, 39) that was brought to the brink by climatic deterioration in the mid-second millennium; consequent economic crisis in the region is deemed to have resulted in a sudden collapse (Reményi 2013; Sümegi 2013). The environmental evidence certainly speaks to a wetter and colder climate throughout the continent contemporary with the Koszider phase. This may have had an important effect on tell communities situated along the river systems in the central Carpathian Basin where an increase in the size of floodplains would have reduced the extent of pasture, pushing herds into more elevated arable land and thereby reducing the area available for cultivation (Sümegi 2013, 171). However, to date the evidence for social collapse has been less clear. In order to explore this, it is to social networks and their identification through the ceramics at Százhalombatta-Földvár that I now wish to turn.

3. Networks for the acquisition of potting knowledge at Százhalombatta-Földvár in the Koszider phase

The Koszider assemblage at Százhalombatta-Földvár comprises a range of domestic vessels for cooking, storage vessels and table wares, including cups, bowls, jugs, sieves, fish dishes, deep domestic (cooking) bowls, cooking pots and storage vessels. There are also miniature forms that replicate the assemblage as a whole. The range of Koszider vessel forms is smaller than in the preceding Vatya phase of the Middle Bronze Age, but as at Dunaújváros-Duna-dűlő there is noticeable elaboration and exaggeration of existing forms (Sofaer 2006; Budden 2007; Vicze 2011). Some of the more elaborate vessels may have been highly valued; research on Vatya cemeteries suggests that ceramics replaced metalwork as prestige objects in mortuary contexts (Vicze 2011). Elsewhere I have suggested that some vessels, such as Swedish helmet bowls, may have been used to tell cosmological stories (Sofaer 2013).

A number of vessel types were made in specific size ranges with typologically identical shapes used for different functions. For example, there are small cups and bowls used for individual portions, and large vessels of the same types likely used as jugs and serving dishes. The Koszider assemblage is extremely rule-bound. Each vessel type has specific forms of decoration, fabric types, wall thickness and size ranges, although they do not fall easily into traditional categorisations of coarse and fine wares (Budden 2007; Budden and Sofaer 2009; Vicze 2011). In particular, the late Koszider pottery from Százhalombatta-Földvár has a distinct quality and style, notably in the high-quality table wares (Budden 2007). Petrological and geochemical work has demonstrated that the overwhelming majority of the pottery at the site is locally made (Kreiter *et al.* 2007).

The Koszider assemblage from Százhalombatta-Földvár can be divided into four groups of vessels along a spectrum of technical difficulty relating to vessel size and morphological characteristics (Budden and Sofaer 2009); smaller, simpler forms require less skill to produce than large complex ones (Rye 1981; Caiger-Smith 1995; Michelaki 2008). Thus, small simple cups represent the easiest vessels made at the site. Domestic vessels of moderate size with comparatively neutral shapes are of intermediate difficulty. Large urns with complex morphologies, additions and embellishments are very technically demanding. Table wares with complex tripartite forms, highly exaggerated morphology, complex handles, embellishments and very thin walls are the most technically demanding of all (Budden and Sofaer 2009). The late Koszider vessels include some exceptionally technically complex forms that demand substantial skill and experience to produce. In all cases, however, the making of ceramics is a very physical process that requires the potter to engage bodily with his or her clay and tools (Budden and Sofaer 2009). The acquisition of potting skill is a matter of practice. In other words, it is a gradual process requiring the repeated performance of specific vessel-appropriate potting actions. Thus, it has been noted that there is a tendency for older potters to produce more complex items because of an incremental increase in skill with age and experience (Kramer 1985; Stark and Longacre 1993). Potting constitutes the development of embodied knowledge.

Existing embodied knowledge can be overlain, or added to, with new or more advanced knowledge. Under usual circumstances it is impossible to 'unlearn' embodied knowledge, since it becomes cumulatively and more competently incorporated into practices of manufacture through time (Sofaer and Budden 2012). Thus, for example, one cannot normally imagine unlearning to drive a car or write with a pencil. Although it is possible to lose the facility to craft objects, through for example degenerative changes associated with old age, this does not necessarily constitute a lack of knowledge but is rather the inability to execute body knowledge appropriately. Crown (2001) notes that once potters can no longer satisfy the necessary criteria for production they simply stop potting. Since clay is a plastic additive medium, embodied knowledge can be traced in the ceramic record. The level of acquisition of embodied knowledge can be assessed by recording the degree of skill exercised by a potter for different elements of vessel manufacture against the expected outcome for a given vessel type (Budden 2007; 2008; Budden and Sofaer 2009).

Recent studies of ceramic production at Százhalombatta-Földvár have revealed that simple vessel forms such as cups used less well-prepared clays and display relatively less skill and greater numbers of errors than more technically demanding fine wares with highly levigated clays, thin walls, complex shapes and embellishments (Budden 2008; Budden and Sofaer 2009). This pattern runs contrary to what one might expect in as much as it could be anticipated that where potters of similar ability make a range of different vessels, then pots that are more technically challenging ought to display more errors than vessels that are technically easier. Given that the prevalence of error decreases from easier to more complex vessel forms, the data from Százhalombatta-Földvár suggests a gradient of potting experience and embodied knowledge. It is therefore likely that that a structured system of potting apprenticeship operated at the site (Budden 2007; 2008; Budden and Sofaer 2009). Less skilled potters for whom there was a greater risk of making mistakes learnt their craft on easier vessel forms made from less valuable resources. More experienced or master potters who were more technically accomplished made complex fine wares using better prepared clays (Budden 2007; Budden and Sofaer 2009; Sofaer and Budden 2012). An apprenticeship system constitutes a network in which structure and function are closely related. Knowledge was transmitted and acquired through participation in the network (Wendrich 2013) but it is important to note that power and access to resources was also invested within it; at Százhalombatta-Földvár this was expressed in relation to individuals and their degree of potting skill.

Although simpler vessels were clearly more suited to learners, the use of cups as 'practice pieces' was also made possible because they did not fulfill the same social role as table wares. It is likely that cups, although implicated in ritual events linked to family and kinship (including hoarding and burial) (Budden 2007; Poroszlai 2013), did not have the same prestige role as more complex vessels. Hence, they would be considered acceptable as long as they fitted into general cultural conventions regarding shape and decoration. It was not therefore crucial for the same consistently high standards of manufacture to be applied to cups, allowing their production to be part of a learning process and a higher social tolerance of error. By contrast, at the other end of the spectrum of technical difficulty, complex table wares were high status objects strongly implicated in social display and subject to close visual scrutiny (Sofaer 2006; 2010; Budden and Sofaer 2009; Vicze 2011). High-quality clay, manufacture and decoration were therefore critical to their social function, resulting in a reduced social tolerance of error. Nonetheless, both cups and table wares, including those indicating less developed embodied potting knowledge, are overwhelmingly well-fired with full reduction to a rich black. This uniformity in firing is not, therefore, consistent with the number and range of errors found for other technological variables. It strongly suggests that there were skilled practitioners who took on the firing of different vessel types, perhaps in a centrally organised manner.

With the exception of firing, it is likely that most vessels were made by a single potter who was responsible for all aspects of the vessel; for any given vessel the overall level of skill in execution is generally consistent for a range of technological variables (Sofaer and Budden 2012). Nonetheless, a few vessels seem to send 'mixed messages', displaying contradictory skill levels for different elements of the potting process. In particular, the technically easiest vessels tend to show more 'mixed messages' in terms of skill than other categories of vessels (Budden and Sofaer 2012). It may be that such pots reveal a relationship between novice and experienced potters, both contributing to the making of individual vessels (cf. Crown 2007). Such collaborations seem to have been *ad hoc* since there does not appear to be any clear direction in the data regarding which processes were more frequently carried out by novices or experienced potters.

Novice potters thus worked on their own but acted within a wider environment where they were able to draw on the help and support of others. The nature of the wider social and economic setting in which potters learnt was, however, highly structured. Potters of all skill levels from novice to master worked within a system of progression where skill was not only required, but also rewarded by moving on to the making of more complex vessels and access to better quality resources once relevant skills had been acquired. The expression of ceramic rules seen within the assemblage may therefore be traced to a well-regulated and hierarchical scaffolded system of learning (Budden and Sofaer 2009) that affirms and reiterates the 'right' way to do things and the social 'place' of both people and particular object forms within the network.

Traditions arise from continuity and stability in the transfer of knowledge (Costin 1998; Wendrich 2013). The gradual development of ceramic forms from the Vatya through to the late Koszider speaks to the strength and solidity of this network throughout most of the Middle Bronze Age, contradicting suggestions that social organisation was intrinsically unstable (Reményi 2013). Based on evidence for cross-craft relationships and ethnographic data, I have elsewhere suggested that at Százhalombatta-Földvár links between craftspeople may have been based around relations between kin (Sofaer 2006). Such networks provide strong support for individuals, thereby reducing potential strains, as well as providing opportunities for guided learning. However, at the very end of the Koszider phase they seem to have unraveled dramatically.

4. Breaking potting networks at the end of the Koszider phase

The final Koszider table wares at Százhalombatta-Földvár show a distinct and rapid overall decline in technical competence. Although typologically they are clearly late Koszider vessel types, the overall quality of the clays decreases as less attention was paid to clay preparation; clays were not as finely levigated and include large quartz inclusions. Previously tight and consistent fabrics are replaced by looser, more coarsely tempered and variable ones. Vessel wall thickness, previously highly standardised for vessel types, becomes erratic with some individual vessels showing a dramatic increase.

Figure 4.2 Changes over time in inverted rim table ware bowls at the end of the Koszider phase; left (earliest) to right (latest). The vessel on the right is from the last Koszider level at Százhalombatta-Földvár (Photograph: J. Sofaer).

Furthermore, firing is not as consistent with fewer successful attempts at full reduction and more fire clouding on pots (Fig. 4.2). This decline in 'finesse' does not represent a deliberate change in aesthetic as, with the exception of firing, it is not noticeable in complete vessels. Nor is it likely to have been a positive choice on the part of potters given the longstanding technical excellence of vessels in the rest of the Middle Bronze Age; Koszider potters were highly sophisticated and mindful craftspeople who had a clear awareness of differences in clay qualities and ascribed them value. In addition, Vatya and Koszider innovation had previously taken place in vessel form rather than in other aspects of vessel manufacture. At the end of the Koszider there therefore seems to have been an attempt to maintain previous complex vessel forms at the top of the hierarchy of skill but without full implementation of a number of other aspects of the potting process. In other words, vessels conformed visually to the Koszider tradition but were made using different resources and in different ways; there seems to have been a sudden decline in embodied knowledge.

The ability to pot is related to the social and physical environment, opportunities for learning through doing, access to visual stimuli, access to materials and the social status of craft within society (Crown 1999, 26; Sofaer and Budden 2012). Research on continuity and change in textile production has demonstrated that rapid changes (within the space of a generation) can take place in a previously long-standing craft tradition if the degree of scaffolding or supervision of novices is reduced (Greenfield 2000); less scaffolded learning situations lead to innovation and difference as novices are creative in solving problems and devising new ways of doing things. Similarly, weaker ties within networks have been identified as being beneficial for creativity (Perry-Smith and Shalley 2003). Given the combination of changes seen in the ceramics at Százhalombatta-Földvár, this may indicate that the last generation of Koszider potters was unable to develop fully their embodied knowledge and access the high-quality resources required to make such pots. Social networks that had nourished the Koszider pottery tradition were breaking down with more fragile ties within apprenticeship networks. In addition, while simple knowledge is easily diffused between actors that are socially close or distant to the source of knowledge, complex knowledge resists diffusion and is accessible only to those close to its source (Sorenson *et al.* 2006). A breakdown in the network would therefore create difficulties in accessing knowledge from elsewhere. Thus, in order for potters to continue to produce socially acceptable vessels they needed to find ways to fill their knowledge gaps, then responded by creative problem solving or 'making do'. They improvised within the remit of what knowledge they had but were unable to execute vessels with the same degree of skill as their predecessors. The reduction in quality of clays also suggests a lack of pre-planning and disregard for an earlier practice of laying down clays for the future; finely levigated clays take time to produce, indeed historical examples frequently point to potters laying down clays for the following generation (de Waal 2015). At Százhalombatta-Földvár the inability to access high-quality resources led to improvisation and creative substitution, a human response seen in other contrasting contexts where people face similar issues (see Sofaer 2005; 2015).

To understand the conditions under which networks of knowledge may break down it is useful to turn to the ethnographic record. In his study of craftspeople on the island of Crete, Herzfeld reveals a hegemonic system where masters have almost unlimited power over their apprentices (Herzfeld 2004). Master craftspeople are reluctant to show their apprentices all the skills of their trade, partly because it is expensive in time and materials, but also because passing on all their knowledge would create new masters who would then constitute a threat to existing ones. Apprentices in their turn resort to all kinds of devious methods to uncover their master's secrets (Herzfeld 2004). Similarly, in Japan potters' apprentices are forced to 'steal' their master's secrets if they wish to progress (Singleton 1989); such circumstances reveal the original meaning of the word 'crafty'. Since table wares at Százhalombatta-Földvár were prestige objects used in display (Sofaer 2006; 2013), knowledge regarding how to make them would be highly valuable and worth protecting. If 'knowledge is power', then it may be that at the end of the Middle Bronze Age existing power structures embedded within the apprenticeship system become almost too effective.

Apprentices were therefore unable to fully acquire the embodied knowledge to make a pot because the access to knowledge channels was curtailed. The impact of such a removal of access to knowledge would be particularly swift in a pre-literate society with a strongly hierarchical learning system where the acquisition of knowledge took place under supervised conditions.

5. Networks, knowledge and the collapse of Koszider society

The interpretation presented above implies a change in motivation in order for the protection of knowledge to outweigh a pre-existing, long-standing tradition of passing it on. It may be that the value of highly skilled objects peaked, creating an incentive for the protection of knowledge and disinvestment in the wider community of practice; a prioritisation of individual interests over those of the group. Alternatively (or in addition), concern with the protection of knowledge may indicate internal power struggles and a change in kin networks. Thus, the pots at Százhalombatta-Földvár may describe the fault lines of a wider social fracture in which the collapse of a hierarchical craft production network was part of a reconfiguration of the wider social system at the end of the Middle Bronze Age.

It is worth noting that the density of houses in the settlement at Százhalombatta-Földvár, and therefore the closeness of living on the tell, was necessarily one in which an awareness of social and behavioural rules must have been of importance. There seems to have been a consistency in the size of house plots suggesting a kind of community orderliness, control and agreement regarding the equitable division of space on the tell overall, the notion of the household and how much space individual households required (Vicze 1992; Sørensen 2010; Sofaer 2011; Sofaer *et al.* 2015). This kind of social living was another kind of network – a network of neighbours that was also a network of shared social understandings where the actions of individuals would have impacted on people living close by. It is easy to imagine that the close knit lifestyle of living on a tell may have become impossible to sustain in the wake of a collapse in mutual understanding and breakdown in communication by people in the social network, whether linked specifically to craft production or part of a wider disintegration of social and knowledge structures. The current excavations at Százhalombatta-Földvár have revealed that the tell was a dynamic community (Sørensen and Vicze 2013; Vicze *et al.* 2014; Sofaer 2015). In this sense the breakdown in social networks may have contributed to creation of the conditions for the abandonment of tells and the eventual severing of the deep-seated connection to place that was previously integral to tell-dwelling.

6. Conclusion

At Százhalombatta-Földvár, continuity in the production of technically complex ceramic vessels was closely linked to the sustainability of social networks in which novices were taught how to produce objects by more experienced and knowledgeable master potters. The embodied nature of potting means that systems of apprenticeship work well when social relations are stable, however, once they come into question then continuity in craft production may become vulnerable to disruption. Networks are dynamic entities that work through sustained and negotiated social relationships between people (Emirbayer and Goodwin 1994). The breakdown of networks of potting knowledge at the site does not initially seem to have been complete as at the end of the Koszider phase only specific aspects of pottery making were affected; complete severing of the network is indicated by the total absence of any Koszider forms in the following Late Bronze Age.

It is useful to explore the implications of the observation that the first signs of a breakdown are visible in ceramic forms requiring the highest skill levels. While these vessels are the most technically challenging to make, in terms of the complexity of the network in which they are embedded they are simultaneously the most straight-forward as they were made wholly by single individuals; in other words by master potters. By contrast, the technically easiest vessels, in particular the 'mixed message' vessels used as practice pieces, involved more social interaction since they were the focus of learning and teaching communities. Thus, while such vessels are simple to make, they were, in fact, socially complex; the greater the number of people involved, the more social engagement and negotiation is required.

Although it is likely that these different social networks would have been inter-related, given their contrasting nature it may be that the production of different types of vessels was subject to different kinds of strain. Complex networks may be put under strain when one of the supporting links falls down, or when the output of craftspeople presents increased demands for labour either directly or indirectly related to pottery production (for example, a need for increased manpower to extract and sort clays) (Crown 2007). However, such networks also provide strong support for individuals, and the greater the number of people involved the greater the possibility that individuals may step in to cover the roles of others, thereby reducing potential strains. This is particularly so in kin-based networks where responsibility is shared and mutual interests are recognised. Less complex networks may be more vulnerable and less resilient because while they represent a smaller set of relationships and a smaller number of potential breaking points, these same features mean that they are unable to adapt their structure (Allenby and Fink 2005; Schiller 2014). Their failure may therefore be more catastrophic; there are fewer people available to step in to subsidise knowledge and consequently vested interests are greater. When vested interests start to erode then this may provide opportunities for a closing down of access to channels of knowledge.

The master-apprentice relationship is an asymmetrical relationship in which the master exercises a form of positional control (Gamble 2003) and which can be used to create cross-generational alliances (Gosselain 2008). My interpretation of changes to ceramics at the end of the Koszider period – in terms of the breakdown of knowledge and lack of access to resources for the production of complex vessels – therefore locates the disruption to networks of potting knowledge as 'top down' within the crafting community of practice and as related to power dynamics. Such an observation recognises the agency of people within the network (Emirbayer and Goodwin 1994). It places the actions of individuals at the heart of changes to material culture rather than attributing the end of the Koszider phase to an unspecified general failure of the social and economic system. There remain many questions regarding the end of the Middle Bronze Age in the Carpathian Basin and how observations in the ceramic record were related to wider material, environmental and social changes. It is, for example, currently unclear whether the small-scale changes at Százhalombatta-Földvár are echoed at other contemporary settlements. Nonetheless, the data from Százhalombatta-Földvár open a window onto the unravelling of networks at a larger scale.

Acknowledgements

I would like to thank Magdolna Vicze for her helpful comments on a draft of this paper and Marie Louise Stig Sørensen for many stimulating conversations on related issues. Colleagues in the Matrica Museum, Százhalombatta kindly provided me with the photograph of Koszider vessels.

References

Allenby, B. and Fink, J. (2005) Toward inherently secure and resilient societies. *Science* 309 (5737), 1034–6.
Bóna, I. (1975) Die Mittlere Bronzezeit Ungarns Und Ihre Südöstlichen Beziehungen. Budapest, Akadémiai Kiadó.
Bóna, I. (1992) Bronzezeitliche Tell-Kulturen in Ungran. In W. Meier-Arendt (ed.) *Bronzezeit in Ungarn. Forschungen in Tell Siedlungen an Donau und Theiss*, 9–41. Frankfurt am Main, Stadt Frankfurt Dez. Kultur u. Wissenschaft.
Bóna, I. and Nováki, Gy. (1982) Alpár bronzkori és Árpád-kori vára. *Cumania* 7, 17–268.
Borgatti, S., Mehra, A., Brass, D. and Labianca, G. (2009) Network analysis in the social sciences. *Science* 323 (5916), 892–5.
Budden, S. (2007) Renewal and Reinvention: The role of learning strategies in the Early to Late Middle Bronze Age of the Carpathian Basin. PhD Thesis. Southampton University.
Budden, S. (2008) Skill amongst the sherds: understanding the role of skill in the Early to Late Middle Bronze Age in Hungary. In I. Berg (ed.) *Breaking the Mould: challenging the past through pottery*, 1–17. Oxford, Archaeopress.
Budden, S. and Sofaer, J. (2009) Non-discursive knowledge and the construction of identity. Potters, potting and performance at the Bronze Age tell of Százhalombatta, Hungary. *Cambridge Archaeological Journal* 19.2, 203–20.
Caiger-Smith, A. (1995) *Pottery, People and Time*. Somerset, Richard Dennis.
Costin, C. (1998) Introduction: craft and social identity. *Archaeological Papers of the American Anthropological Association* 8, 3–16.
Crown, P. (1999) Socialisation in American southwest pottery decoration. In J.M. Skibo and G.M. Feinman (eds) *Pottery and People*, 25–43. Salt Lake City, University of Utah Press.
Crown, P. (2001) Learning to make pottery in the prehispanic American southwest. *Journal of Anthropological Research* 57, 451–69.

Crown, P. (2007) Life histories of pots and potters: situating the individual in archaeology. *American Antiquity* 72, 677–90.

David, W. (2002) Studien zu Ornamentik und Datierung der bronzezeitlichen Depotfundgruppe Hajdúsámson-Apa-Ighiel-Zajta. Bibliotheca Musei Apulensis XVIII. Alba Iulia, Verlag Altip S.A.

De Waal, E. (2015) *The White Road: a pilgrimage of sorts*. London, Chatto & Windus.

Emirbayer, M. and Goodwin, J. (1994) Network analysis, culture and the problem of agency. *American Journal of Sociology* 99.6, 1411–54.

Gamble, J. (2002) Teaching without words: tacit knowledge in apprenticeship. *Journal of Education* 28, 63–82.

Gamble, J. (2003) Tacit Knowledge in Craft Pedagogy: a sociological analysis. PhD Thesis. University of Cape Town.

Gosselain, O. (2008) Mother Bella was not a bella: inherited and transformed traditions in southwestern Niger. In M. Stark, B. Bowser, and L. Horne (eds) *Cultural Transmission and Material Culture: breaking down boundaries*, 150–77. Tucson, AZ, University of Arizona Press.

Greenfield, P. (2000) Children, material culture and weaving: historical change and developmental change. In J. Sofaer Derevenski (ed.) *Children and Material Culture*, 72–86. London, Routledge.

Herzfeld, M. (2004) The Body Impolitic. Artisans and artifice in the global hierarchy of value. Chicago, University of Chicago Press.

Jaeger, M. and Kulcsár, G. (2013) Kakucs–Balla-Domb a case study in the absolute and relative chronology of the Vatya culture. *Acta Archaeologica Academiae Scientiarum Hungaricae* 64, 289–320.

Kramer, C. (1985) Ceramic ethnoarchaeology. *Annual Review of Anthropology* 14, 77–102.

Kreiter, A.B., Bajnóczi, P., Sipos, G., Szakmány, G. and Tóth, M. (2007) Archaeometric examination of Early and Middle Bronze Age ceramics from Százhalombatta-Földvár, Hungary. *Archeometriai Műhely* 2, 33–46.

Lave, J. and Wenger, E. (1991) *Situated Learning: legitimate peripheral participation*. Cambridge, Cambridge University Press.

Michelaki, K. (2008) Making pots and potters in the Bronze Age Maros villages of Kiszombor-Új-Élet and Kláraflava-Hajdova. *Cambridge Archaeological Journal* 18.3, 355–80.

Mozsolics, A. (1967) *Bronzefunde des Karpatenbeckens, Depotfundhorizonte von Hajdúsámson und Kosziderpadlás*. Budapest, Akadémiai Kiadó.

Perry-Smith, J. and Shalley, C. (2003) The social side of creativity: a static and dynamic social network perspective. *Academy of Management Review* 28.1, 89–106.

Poroszlai, I. (2000) Excavation campaigns at the Bronze Age tell site at Százhalombatta-Földvár. In I. Poroszlai, and M. Vicze (eds) *Százhalombatta Archaeological Expedition Annual Report 1*, 13–73. Százhalombatta, Archaeolingua.

Poroszlai, I. (2013) The Koszider phase at Százhalombatta-Földvár. In M. Vicze, I. Poroszlai and P. Sümegi (eds) *Koszider: Hoard, Phase, Period? Round table conference on the Koszider problem*, 9–11. Százhalombatta, Matrica Museum.

Rebay-Salisbury, K., Brysbaert, A. and Foxhall, L. (2014) (eds) *Material Crossovers: knowledge networks and the movement of technological knowledge between craft traditions*. London, Routledge.

Reményi, L. (2013) Remains of the Koszider period from the area of Budapest. In M. Vicze, I. Poroszlai and P. Sümegi (eds) *Koszider: Hoard, Phase, Period? Round table conference on the Koszider problem*, 31–54. Százhalombatta, Matrica Museum.

Rye, O. (1981) *Pottery Technology: principles and reconstruction*. Washington, DC, Taraxum.

Schiller, F., Penn, A. and Basson, L. (2014) Analyzing networks in industrial ecology – a review of social-material network analyses. *Journal of Cleaner Production* 76.1, 1–11.

Singleton, J. (1998) Craft and art education in Mashiko pottery workshops. In J. Singleton (ed.) *Learning in Likely Places. Varieties of apprenticeship in Japan*, 122–33. Cambridge, Cambridge University Press.

Sofaer, J. (2006) Pots, houses and metal. Technological relations at the Bronze Age tell at Százhalombatta, Hungary. *Oxford Journal of Archaeology* 25.2, 127–47.

Sofaer, J. (2011) Human ontogeny and material change at the Bronze Age tell of Százhalombatta, Hungary. *Cambridge Archaeological Journal* 21.2, 217–27.

Sofaer, J. (2013) Cosmologies in clay: Swedish helmet bowls in the Middle Bronze Age of the Carpathian Basin. In S. Bergerbrant and S. Sabatin (eds) *Counterpoint: essays in archaeology and heritage studies in honour of Professor Kristian Kristiansen*, 361–65. Oxford, Archaeopress.

Sofaer, J. (2015) *Clay in the Age of Bronze. Essays in the archaeology of prehistoric creativity*. Cambridge, Cambridge University Press.

Sofaer, J. and Budden, S. (2012) Many hands make light work: embodied knowledge at the Bronze Age Tell at Százhalombatta, Hungary. In M.L.S. Sørensen, L. Bender Jørgensen and K. Rebay-Salisbury (eds) *Embodied Knowledge*, 117–27. Oxford, Oxbow Books.

Sofaer, J., Sørensen, M.L.S. and Vicze, M. (2015) Hierarchical or not? How can we interpret Bronze Age tells? *Bronze Age Forum*. University of Exeter.

Sofaer, J., with contributions by Bech, J.-H., Budden, S., Choyke, A., Eriksen, B.V., Horváth, T., Kovács, G., Kreiter, A., Muhlenbock, C. and Sticka, H.-P. (2010) Chapter 7. Technology and craft. In T. Earle and K. Kristiansen (eds) *Organising Bronze Age Societies. European society in late prehistory: a comparative approach*, 185–217. Cambridge, Cambridge University Press.

Sofaer, J. with Sofaer, R. (2005) Yellow potatoes. *Postcolonial Studies* 8.1, 97–103.

Sorenson, O., Rivkin, J. and Fleming, L. (2006) Complexity, networks and knowledge flow. *Research Policy* 35.7, 994–1017.

Sørensen, M.L.S. (2010) Households. In T. Earle and K. Kristiansen (eds) *Organising Bronze Age Societies. European society in late prehistory: a comparative approach*, 122–54. Cambridge, Cambridge University Press.

Sørensen, M.L.S. and Vicze, M. (2013) Locating household activities on a Bronze Age tell. In M. Madella, G. Kovács, B. Kulcsárné-Berzsényi and I. Brizi Godino (eds) *The Archaeology of Household*, 159–78. Oxford, Oxbow Books.

Stacey, R. (2001) *Complex Responsive Processes in Organisations. Learning and knowledge creation*. London, Routledge.

Stark, M.T. and Longacre, W.A. (1993) Kalinga ceramics and new technologies: social and cultural contexts of ceramic change. In W.D. Kingery (ed.) *The Social and Cultural Contexts of New Ceramic Technologies*, 1–32. Westerville, OH American Ceramic Society.

Stark, M., Bowser, B. and Horne, L. (eds) (2008) *Cultural Transmission and Material Culture. Breaking down boundaries*. Tucson, AZ, University of Arizona Press.

Sümegi, P. (2013) A comparative geoarchaeological report and environmental history of the Bronze Age tell of Polgár-Kenderföld. In M. Vicze, I. Poroszlai and P. Sümegi (eds) *Koszider: Hoard, Phase, Period? Round table conference on the Koszider problem*, 153–91. Százhalombatta, Matrica Museum.

Tichenor, P.A., Donohue, G.A. and Olien, C.N. (1970) Mass media flow and differential growth in knowledge. *Public Opinion Quarterly*, 34.2, 159–70.

Uhnér, C. (2010) *Makt och samhälle. Politisk ekonomi under bronsåldern i Karpaterbäckenet*. Gotarc Series B, Gothenburg Archaeological Theses, No. 54. Gothenburg, Göteborg Universitet.

Vicze, M. (1992) Baracs-Földvár. In W. Meier-Arendt (ed.) *Bronzezeit in Ungarn. Forschungen in Tell Siedlungen an Donau und Theiss*, 146–48. Frankfurt am Main, Stadt Frankfurt Dez. Kultur u. Wissenschaft.

Vicze, M. (2005) Excavation methods and some preliminary results of the SAX Project. In I. Poroszlai and M. Vicze (eds) *Százhalombatta Archaeological Expedition. Report 2*, 65–77. Százhalombatta, Archaeolingua.

Vicze, M. (2011) *Bronze Age Cemetery at Dunaújváros-Duna-dűlő*. Dissertationes Pannonicae series IV, vol.1. Budapest, Eötvös Loránd University, Institute of Archaeological Sciences.

Vicze, M. (2013) Koszider: break or continuity? In M. Vicze, I. Poroszlai and P. Sümegi (eds) *Koszider: Hoard, Phase, Period? Round table conference on the Koszider problem*, 15–29. Százhalombatta, Matrica Museum.

Vicze, M., Sofaer, J. and Sørensen, M.L.S. (2014) Glimpsing social organisation – evidence from the Bronze Age tell at Százhalombatta-Földvár. *Hungarian Archaeology E-Journal* Summer 2014, 1–4.

Vicze, M. and Sümegi, P. (2013) Foreword. In M. Vicze, I. Poroszlai and P. Sümegi (eds) *Koszider: Hoard, Phase, Period? Round table conference on the Koszider problem*, 7–8 (Százhalombatta Matrica Museum).

Vicze, M., Poroszlai, I. and Sümegi, P. (eds) (2013) *Koszider: Hoard, Phase, Period? Round table conference on the Koszider problem*. Százhalombatta, Matrica Museum.

Vicze, M., Sørensen, M.L.S. and Sofaer, J. (2017) Advances in tell research. Methodological reflections on the SAX Project. In G. Kulcsár and G.V. Szabó (with V. Kiss and G. Váczi) (eds) *Advances in Hungarian Bronze Age Studies*, 487–95. Ősrégészeti Tanulmányok/Prehistoric Studies II, State of the Hungarian Bronze Age Research. Budapest, Institute of Archaeology, Research Centre for the Humanities, Hungarian Academy of Sciences; Institute of Archaeological Sciences, Faculty of Humanities, Eötvös Loránd University; Ősrégészeti Társaság/Prehistoric Society.

Wendrich, W. (2013) Recognizing knowledge transfer in the archaeological record. In W. Wendrich (ed.) *Archaeology and Apprenticeship. Body knowledge, identity and communities of practice*, 255–62. Tucson, AZ, University of Arizona Press.

Wenger, E. (2000) *Communities of Practice. Learning, meaning and identity*. Cambridge, Cambridge University Press.

Chapter 5

Connecting the world of the Bronze Age

Anthony Harding

This chapter considers the utility of network theory and network thinking for understanding the complexity of Bronze Age Europe, including but moving well beyond, the Mediterranean. Scholars now generally agree that this was a highly interconnected world, but precisely how those connections worked is less easy to understand. Core-periphery (World Systems Theory) models are generally imposed on the data from above, while the possibility of operating at the micro-scale offered by network approaches is likely to be truer to the data. The potential of network analysis for understanding the interconnections involved in the production and movement of metals and amber is highlighted.

Key words: Bronze Age, interaction, networks

1. The world of Bronze Age Europe

The world of Bronze Age Europe was a complex one. A series of studies in recent years have shown that it was far from the undeveloped, 'primitive' one that might have seemed the case fifty years ago. While the cultures of Bronze Age Greece have always been thought to have been highly developed, a version of the palace societies of the Near East, the cultural manifestations of the main continent have often seemed shrouded in darkness, with little available with which to understand the nature of economy and society.

A series of recent finds, as well as renewed discussion in the literature, have brought about a radical rethink of former views. Among the new finds it is worth mentioning just a few. The most spectacular and informative is undoubtedly the Uluburun shipwreck (Yalçın *et al.* 2005), since it provides unrivalled archaeological (as opposed to textual) evidence for contact between different parts of the east Mediterranean. The many extraordinary objects recovered from its cargo include items from many parts of the Mediterranean, as well as a few that probably emanated from the north or from the Black Sea area, for instance amber beads, the stone sceptre with curled end, with its best parallels in Bulgaria, Romania and Moldova (Buchholz 1999; Yalçın *et al.* 2005, 149–53), or double axes (Harding 2007, 51 with references). The movement of copper and tin, which was the main trade commodity of the vessel, is reflected in other cargo finds: the hoard from Langdon Bay near Dover, southeast England, and the series of finds made near Salcombe in Devon, southwest England. The former, coupled with the find of a boat by the shore at Dover (Clark 2004), is very suggestive of cross-channel trading voyages, involving – at least in part – bronzes; the latter, of which only a part is published (Needham *et al.* 2013; Wang *et al.* 2016; 2018) seems especially significant in view of the proximity of this part of the southern English coast to the tin resources of Dartmoor, to which river valleys give easy access. Tin was seemingly a commodity with limited sources in the ancient world; those in southwest England have always been thought to have been of particular importance, and the Salcombe finds provide welcome corroboration of this. It is considered likely by modern analysts that many finds across Europe and the Mediterranean made use of Cornish tin, for instance the Nebra disc (Brügmann *et al.* 2015) or ingots from Haifa (Berger *et al.* 2018; 2019); the latter especially interesting in view of the distance involved. It is striking, however, that the tin ingots on the Uluburun ship came from a different source.

Shipwrecks and ships' cargoes represent movement *par excellence*, which is why they have attracted especial attention from scholars. But individual objects can often be shown to have been made in a place far from their archaeological find-place; this is the case for many important recent Bronze Age finds. Amber has long been a material of special interest, since the vast majority of archaeological amber in Europe has been shown to come from the 'Baltic' sources (which may not always be very close to Baltic shores). The considerable quantities of amber in Mycenaean Greece reflect movement very directly; the form of certain beads, notably spacer-plates, provides a much more specific connection, between Greece, southern England and Central Europe (mainly southern Germany). This debate has been under way for many years, but has recently acquired renewed significance in view of the highly detailed work carried out by Dr Katharine Verkooijen, which is set to change views about the place of origin of the plates, and their possible connections, given the fairly wide range of dates that separates them (Verkooijen 2014). Interestingly a series of new finds has been made in recent years, which changes the distribution pattern as previously known, especially in England. The other extraordinary amber finds, rather later in date, come from the kurgans at Hordiivka in Ukraine, where numerous beads of Tiryns and Allumiere type are present (Berezenskaja and Kločko 1998) (Fig. 5.1). These bead forms are distinctively central Mediterranean and Adriatic, as studied by several authors (Harding 1984, 82–5; Negroni Catacchio 1999; 2014), so their appearance in Ukraine, a distance from the presumed manufacture area of some 1600 km as the crow flies, and much further by way of sea, is truly remarkable (Fig. 5.2). On the other hand, the amber beads from Bernstorf, Lkr. Freising, Bavaria (Gebhard and Rieder 2002; Gebhard and Krause 2016), among which is one engraved with what is purported to be Linear B signs and another with a bearded face, are highly unlikely to be genuine; the same is true for the gold

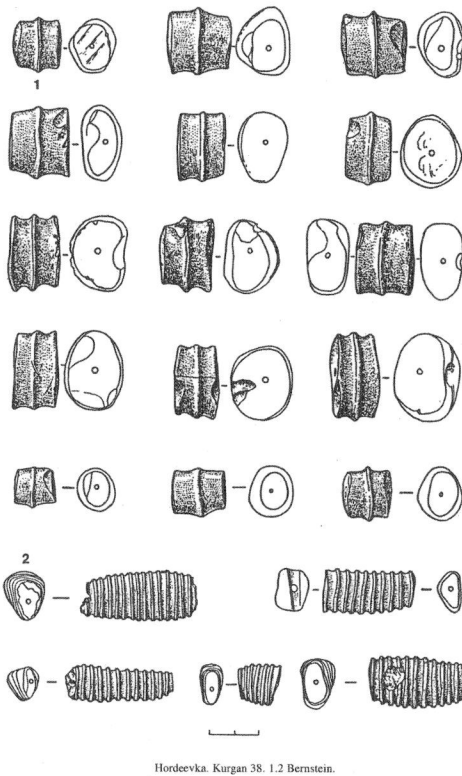

Hordeevka. Kurgan 38. 1.2 Bernstein.

Figure 5.1 Amber beads from Kurgan 38 at Hordiivka, Ukraine (source: Berezanskaja and Kločko 1998).

that was found on the same site, in spite of protestations to the contrary. (Strong arguments against the authenticity of the gold have appeared (Pernicka 2014) and a detailed examination of the amber confirmed the commonly held view that it is modern (Verkooijen 2017). Unfortunately, some unwise commentators have rushed into print with fantasy accounts, apparently without a proper appreciation of the difficulties with the find context (Janko 2015). Reviews of Gebhard and Krause 2016 have been uniformly negative.)

Other individual objects that demonstrate far-reaching connections, or claims of such, might be thought less significant. One cannot deny the importance of, for instance, the Nebra disc (Meller 2010), showing as it does an apparently sophisticated appreciation of the heavenly bodies; but its wider context is more controversial, not just the meaning of the depictions on the disc, but also its possible connections with advanced civilisations to the southeast. (I refrain from discussing a recent attempt to date it to the Iron Age on the basis that it was not really associated with the other objects believed to come from the same findspot (Gebhard and Krause 2020). This redating has to be seen in the wider context of the dispute over the authenticity of the Bernstorf amber and gold.)

On the other hand, finds of oxhide ingots have multiplied in recent years (Lo Schiavo *et al.* 2009) (Fig. 5.3): although not a new find, the identification of an ingot fragment in a south German hoard by Margarita Primas was a notable step (Primas and Pernicka 1998), and another piece comes from the hoard at Şarköy on the north side of the Sea of Marmara (Harmankaya 1995). Further north, in Bulgaria and Romania, several ingots are present (Rotea 2002–2003 (2004); Leshtakov 2007; Doncheva 2012), so the metal network spread far and wide around southern seas, and penetrated inland as well: not only into Bulgaria, but also into Anatolia, since one example comes from Boğazköy (Müller-Karpe 1980). A miniature example comes from the Makarska hoard on the Dalmatian coast in Croatia (Vagnetti 1971; Sherratt 2012), arguably part of a group of Cypriot objects that were part of the movement of Cypriot goods westwards in the Bronze Age; and the so-called 'cushion ingots' found in the hoards along the Sava have sometimes been called miniature oxhide ingots (Vinski-Gasparini 1973,

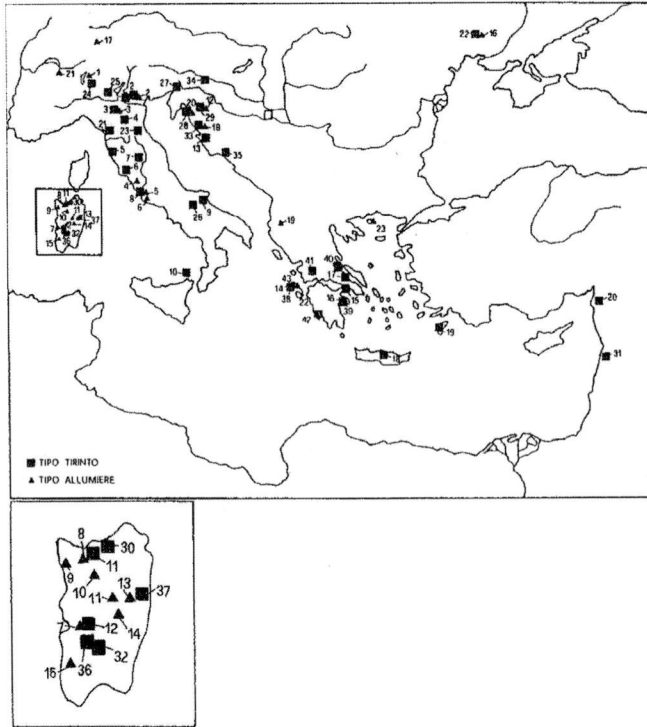

Figure 5.2 Distribution of amber beads of Tiryns and Allumiere types (source: Negroni Catacchio 2014).

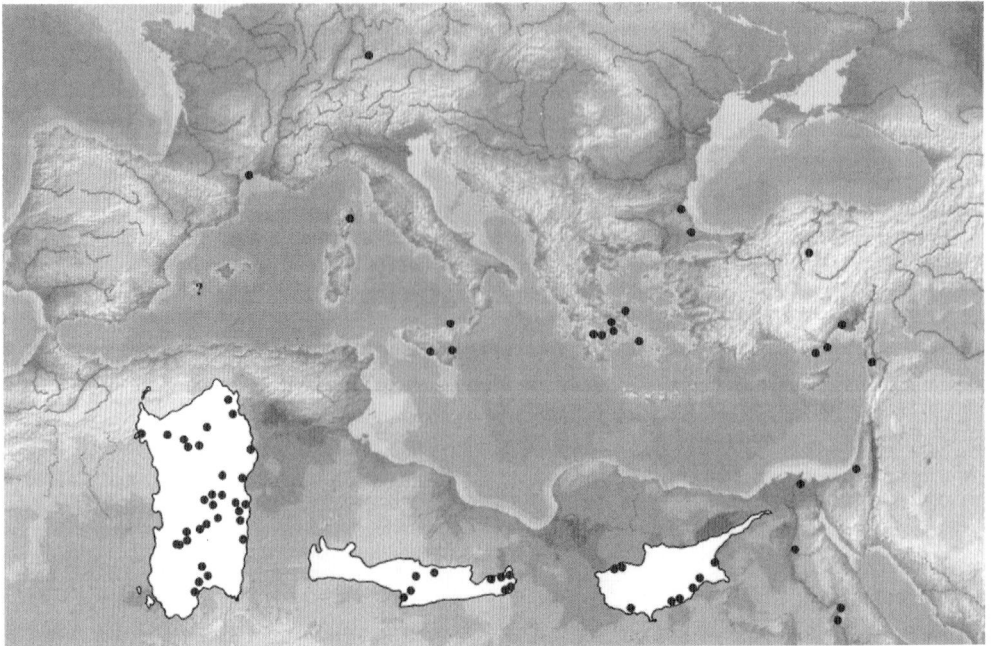

Figure 5.3 Distribution of oxhide ingots (source: R. Maddin in Lo Schiavo et al. 2009).

139–40, 181 pl. 96 (Kloštar Ivanić), referred to as a 'Keftiu-ingot' and measuring 6.8 × 5.7 cm). One does not need to go as far as some scholars have in viewing certain enigmatic designs on Scandinavian rock as oxhide ingots (Ling and Stos-Gale 2015) to believe that the movement of copper metal in ingot form was widespread not only in the Mediterranean but also had outliers in the Black Sea area and further north.

Individual objects such as the Mycenaean bronze cup from Dohnsen, Kr. Celle (Sprockhoff 1961; Matthäus 1977–78) or spearheads of Cypriot type (Gerloff 1975, 149–52, 255–7; Watkins 1976; Brandherm 2000; 2017), while undoubtedly genuine objects of Mediterranean manufacture, provide limited help for the discussion in view of their lack of context. They may, however, be used to help build up the wider picture of contact and connection in the Bronze Age world.

The Cypriot spearheads or daggers (properly called hook-tang weapons) are a particularly interesting case in point (Fig. 5.4). Opinions have varied over the years as to whether they are genuine ancient imports into Central and Western Europe, or stray finds emanating from the antiquities trade. For many years I was sceptical about

Figure 5.4 Distribution of 'Cypriot daggers' (hook-tang weapons).

their usefulness in offering information on Bronze Age trade (Harding 1984, 171), but in the light of a number of new finds since Gerloff and Watkins wrote, it becomes increasingly unlikely that all the objects could have chanced to arrive in northern Europe through anything other than ancient movement by people, whether in trade, gift exchange or something else. The largest number come from France, though none with a proper context. In Britain, an old find from Egton Moor in Yorkshire is now joined by one in western Scotland, one in Devon and a group of five also from Devon about which almost nothing is known (and which have now disappeared) (Fig. 5.5). This

Figure 5.5 'Cypriot daggers' from Britain. Left: Egton Moor, North Yorkshire (Whitby Museum, photo courtesy of Roger Pickles); Centre: Rubha a' Bhodaich, Bute, Argyll (Kelvingrove Art Gallery and Museum, Glasgow, photo courtesy of Dirk Brandherm); Right: Torrington, Devon (Royal Albert Memorial Museum, Exeter; photo RAMM, by permission).

situation is admittedly unsatisfactory, but the existence of so many pieces demands an explanation. In the absence of anything satisfactory, the objects are best treated as part of the wider pattern of inter-cultural exchange during the Bronze Age.

To this we can now add the evidence of glass beads from north Germany and Denmark, recently discussed by Jeanette Varberg and colleagues (2015; 2016). The analysis of glass beads from Scandinavia shows a composition that is so close to that of Egyptian and Mesopotamian examples that it is concluded they must have been imported.

The increasing volume of material clearly indicating Europe-wide contacts and movements therefore needs to be considered within a wider framework. This has been the rationale for a number of attempts at understanding such movement as part of a system or network.

2. World systems and networks

Understanding the nature of connections in the Bronze Age world has been the subject of many studies in recent years. Of particular importance has been the approach which sees these connections as part of a 'World System'; in the context of Bronze Age Europe the writings of Kristian Kristiansen have been especially influential (Kristiansen 1987; 1998; Kristiansen and Larsson 2005). This is not the place to embark on a critique of the approach, which I have undertaken previously (Harding 2000, 418–22; 2013); but it is worth reiterating that World Systems Theory (also known as core-periphery theory) has the disadvantage that it imposes a model from the top down, ignoring the role of actors on the ground, and removes independence of action from those in the periphery, who become little more than pawns in the power play of the dominant centres. Nevertheless, World Systems Theory does bring into focus the nature of the interplay, apparently intense at certain times in certain areas, between different parts of the Bronze Age world.

Recent years have seen the development of a quite different approach to connections in the ancient world: network analysis (Network Theory). Most archaeological applications have been to different periods of the past; some are general in nature (Brughmans 2010; 2012; Knappett 2011; 2013; Collar *et al.* 2015), and some specific (Coward 2013; Mills *et al.* 2013). For the European Bronze Age, Knappett's work with Evans and Rivers set the scene (Knappett *et al.* 2008), and his later works have built on this foundation; but for continental Europe the only application known to me is that on metalwork conducted by Gábor Váczi (Váczi 2013; 2014). Another was attempted for Italy by Emma Blake (Blake 2014). The potential for using network analysis has continued as a favoured topic in the ten years since it came to the attention of archaeologists more widely, with numerous publications appearing every year (*e.g.* Brughmans *et al.* 2016; Knappett 2017; Leidwanger and Knappett 2018; Peeples 2018).

Knappett *et al.* built on earlier work by Broodbank (2000) to build a gravity model of the Aegean area in the Middle Bronze Age, based on the principle that 'large sites choose preferentially to interact among themselves', on the basis that both population size and distance are important to a trading network, along with the available resources that a large site would necessarily imply. Knappett subsequently developed these ideas with particular reference to the situation within Crete, based on Minoan pottery production (Knappett 2011, chapters 4–6). More recently Knappett has developed these ideas in relation to connectivity and mobility, with particular reference to the process known as 'Minoanization' (Knappett 2018). The potential for different periods can be seen from the most successful applications, such as that by Per Östborn and Henrik Gerding on Hellenistic bricks from around the Mediterranean (Östborn and Gerding 2014; 2015).

Váczi started by conducting a seriation of 500 hoards of Urnfield date, giving seven phases of unequal composition and thus duration. This was followed by principal components analysis to determine the dominant artefact types in each phase, and correspondence analysis to determine the dominant associations between types. A 'connection analysis' followed, based on ornaments from each phase; though this part of the work is not described in detail, it appears that this was based on 'primary characterization and analyses of the functional groups of artefacts', leading to a series of network maps in which the importance of nodes is represented by the number of type elements present in each location, and the strength of the links by the number of connecting elements. The published maps do not include this information, other than that the size of the nodes (circles) is proportionate to the 'number of all dots', and the thickness of the connecting lines (links or edges) proportionate to the 'number of identical dots' (Váczi 2013, figs 9–13).

A new study by Paul Duffy combines Network Analysis with a detailed examination of Early and Middle Bronze Age cemeteries on the Great Hungarian Plain (Duffy 2020). In this he models:

> critical gateways in the Tisza river drainage and evaluates the concentration of metal on different topological nodes of the river network in an attempt to understand what parameters best explain the distribution of metals across this landscape … [finding] that proximity to important nodes in the river system is a good predictor of metal abundance in cemeteries. (Duffy 2020, 13)

In particular, the location of sites in relation to river catchments is discovered to find a reflection in the wealth in metal of the sites, though caution was found to be necessary in interpreting metal 'wealth' since metal weight is not necessarily correlated with absolute number of metal objects. This study shows the potential for using Network Analysis in fruitful ways to understand how inequality may relate to environmental factors. It is evident, however, that undertaking such a study is a complex and time-consuming process.

At this stage it is not possible to offer more than these pointers to what will surely become a much-used and helpful set of methods for understanding interconnections in archaeological situations, including those of the Bronze Age. Commodities such as amber, as well as metal goods, which were demonstrably moved about over long distances, may be susceptible to this approach, though such a study would have to be conducted within the framework of a wider frame of reference; for amber alone, a simple distribution map of types would probably tell one what one needed to know. This stricture applies to my earlier suggestion (2013) that the amber beads of Tiryns and Allumiere types could be subjected to such an approach; while in theory this might be possible, in practice not enough is known about the find contexts of many of the finds, including those at one of the most important sites, Frattesina in the Po plain.

In the archaeological use of network analysis, the nodes are usually considered to be sites or site contexts, with the finds from them forming the elements from which similarities are established and on the basis of which links ('edges') are created. Usually it is links between sites that are involved, but they can also be links between elements within single sites. The existence of a link, in the form of a similarity in artefact types, is one thing, but what is crucial is to establish the strength of such links. And that aspect is intimately bound up with the centrality question: how central to a network, in other words important, is an individual node? These are all matters that the current group of network scholars working in archaeology are trying to address. Archaeologists, of course, have to work with the fact that they can only deal with material culture, and specifically with the parts of material culture that survive from antiquity, unlike those who work with social networks at the present day, who can interrogate their subjects or experience networks themselves. Material culture is a reflection of behaviour in the past, though exactly how that behaviour reflects societal practices and beliefs is a matter of interpretation. Nevertheless, enough has been done for us to be able to have confidence that many of these issues will be resolved in the coming years.

That the world of the Bronze Age in Europe was strongly interconnected has never been in doubt. The strength and nature of that interconnection has been a matter of debate for several decades. Traditional methods of investigation, typically charting instances of phenomena (usually artefact types) and putting them on distribution maps, have their uses, and are often all that is possible given the nature of the evidence. Even the manifesto for an approach based on the 'structured transmission of a symbolic package' (Kristiansen and Larsson 2005, 14) is still based on the same procedures, the study of individual artefacts, singly and collectively. By contrast, a network approach offers the possibility of a method that seeks to set objects, and sites, within a robust framework that rests on an appreciation of material culture for what it really was, rather than what we, thousands of years after the events concerned, like to imagine it might have constituted. As the methodology develops, this will become more and more evident, to the great benefit of all those who study the ancient past.

References

Berezanskaja, S.S. and Kločko, V.I. (1998) *Das Gräberfeld von Hordeevka*. Archäologie in Eurasien, Band 5. Rahden/Westf., Verlag Marie Leidorf GmbH.

Berger, D., Brügmann, G. and Pernicka, E. (2019) Zum Stand der Zinnforschung: neue Erkenntnisse zu Zinnherkunft und -Handel anhand von Isotopen- und Spurenelement-Analysen spätbronzezeitlicher Zinnbarren. In C. Herm, S. Merkel, M. Schreiner and R. Wiesinger (eds) *Archäometrie und Denkmalpflege 2019 - Jahrestagung an der Akademie der Bildenden Künste Wien, Institut für Naturwissenschaften und Technologie in der Kunst, 11.-14. September 2019*, 192–5. METALLA Sonderheft 9. Bochum, Deutsches Bergbau-Museum.

Berger, D., Figueiredo, E., Brügmann, G. and Pernicka, E. (2018) Tin isotope fractionation during experimental cassiterite smelting and its implication for tracing the tin sources of prehistoric metal artefacts. *Journal of Archaeological Science* 92, 73–86.

Blake, E. (2014) *Social Networks and Regional Identity in Bronze Age Italy*. New York, Cambridge University Press.

Brandherm, D. (2000) Zyprische Griffangelklingen aus West- und Mitteleuropa? Zur Problematik einer Quellengruppe der frühen und mittleren Bronzezeit. *Kleine Schriftenreihe no. 4, Freiburger Institut für Palaeowissenschaftliche Studien* 1–22.

Brandherm, D. (2017) Zyprische Griffangelklingen & Co. aus West- und Mitteleuropa? Noch einmal zur Problematik einer Quellengruppe der frühen und mittleren Bronzezeit. In *Memento dierum antiquorum. Festschrift für Majolie Lenerz-de Wilde zum 70. Geburtstag*, 45–70. Hagen/Westfalen, Curach Bhán Publications.

Broodbank, C. (2000) *An Island Archaeology of the early Cyclades*. Cambridge, Cambridge University Press.

Brughmans, T. (2010) Connecting the dots: towards archaeological network analysis. *Oxford Journal of Archaeology* 29.3, 277–303.

Brughmans, T. (2012) Thinking through networks: a review of formal network methods in archaeology. *Journal of Archaeological Method and Theory* 20, 623–62.

Brughmans, T., Collar, A. and Coward, F. (eds) (2016) *The Connected Past: challenges to network studies in archaeology and history*. Oxford, Oxford University Press.

Brügmann, G., Berger, D., Pernicka, E. and Nessel, B. (2015) Zinn-Isotope und die Frage nach der Herkunft prähistorischen Zinns. In T. Gluhak, S. Greiff, K. Kraus and M. Prange (eds) *Archäometrie und Denkmalpflege - Jahrestagung an der Johannes Gutenberg-Universität Mainz 25.-28. März 2015*, 188–91. METALLA Sonderheft 7. Bochum, Deutsches Bergbau-Museum.

Buchholz, H.-G. (1999) Ein aussergewöhnliches Steinzepter im östlichen Mittelmeer. *Praehistorische Zeitschrift* 74, 68–78.

Clark, P. (ed.) (2004) *The Dover Bronze Age Boat*. Swindon, English Heritage.

Collar, A., Coward, F., Brughmans, T. and Mills, B.J. (2015) Networks in archaeology: phenomena, abstraction, representation. *Journal of Archaeological Method and Theory* 22.1, 1–32.

Coward, F. (2013) Grounding the net: social networks, material culture and geography in the Epipalaeolithic and Early Neolithic of the Near East (~21,000–6,000 cal BCE). In C. Knappett (ed.) *Network Analysis in Archaeology: new approaches to regional interaction*, 247–80. Oxford, Oxford University Press.

Doncheva, D. (2012) The northern 'journey' of Late Bronze Age copper ingots. In E. Paunov and S. Filipova (eds) *ΗΡΑΚΛΕΟΥΣ ΣΩΤΗΡΟΣ ΘΑΣΙΩΝ. Studia in honorem Iliae Prokopov sexagenario ab amicis et discipulis dedicata*, 671–714. Veliko Turnovo, Faber Publishers.

Duffy, P.R. (2020) River networks and funerary metal in the Bronze Age of the Carpathian Basin. *PLoSONE* 15.9. e0238526. doi: https://doi.org/10.1371/journal.pone.023852.

Gebhard, R. and Krause, R. (2016) *Bernstorf. Archäologisch-naturwissenschaftliche Analysen der Gold- und Bernsteinfunde vom Bernstorfer Berg bei Kranzberg, Oberbayern. Bernstorf-Forschungen, 1.* Abhandlungen und Bestandkataloge der Archäologischen Staatssammlung, Band 3. Frankfurter Archäologische Schriften, Band 31. München, Archäologische Staatssammlung.

Gebhard, R. and Krause, R. (2020) Critical comments on the find complex of the so-called Nebra Sky Disk. *Archäologische Informationen* 43, 1–22. [early view] http://journals.ub.uni-heidelberg.de/arch-inf.

Gebhard, R. and Rieder, K.H. (2002) Zwei bronzezeitliche Bernsteinobjekte mit Bild- und Schriftzeichen aus Bernstorf (Lkr. Freising). *Germania* 80, 115–133.

Gerloff, S. (1975) *The Early Bronze Age Daggers in Great Britain and a Reconsideration of the Wessex Culture.* Prähistorische Bronzefunde, Abt. VI, 2. Munich, Beck.

Harding, A. (1984) *The Mycenaeans and Europe.* London, Academic Press.

Harding, A. (2000) *European Societies in the Bronze Age.* Cambridge, Cambridge University Press.

Harding, A. (2007) Interconnections between the Aegean and continental Europe in the Bronze and Early Iron Ages: moving beyond scepticism. In I. Galanaki, H. Tomas, Y. Galanakis and R. Laffineur (eds) *Between the Aegean and Baltic Seas: prehistory across borders (Proceedings of the International Conference Bronze and Early Iron Age Interconnections and Contemporary Developments between the Aegean and the Regions of the Balkan Peninsula, Central and Northern Europe, Zagreb April 2005)*, 47–56. Aegaeum 27. Liège and Austin, TX, University de Liège and University of Austin at Texas.

Harding, A. (2013) World systems, cores and peripheries in prehistoric Europe. *European Journal of Archaeology* 16, 378–400.

Harmankaya, N.S. (1995) Kozman Deresi Mevkii (Şarköy, Tekirdağ) Maden Buluntulury. In Faculty of Letters University of Istanbul Section of Prehistory (ed.) *Readings in Prehistory: Studies Presented to Halet Çambel*, 217–54. Istanbul, Graphis.

Janko, R. (2015) Amber inscribed in Linear B from Bernstorf in Bavaria. New light on the Mycenaean kingdom of Pylos. *Bayerische Vorgeschichtsblätter* 80, 39–64.

Knappett, C. (2011) *An Archaeology of Interaction. Network perspectives on material culture and society.* Oxford, Oxford University Press.

Knappett, C. (2017) Globalization, connectivities and networks: an archaeological perspective. In T. Hodos (ed.) *Routledge Handbook of Archaeology and Globalization*, 29–41. London, Routledge.

Knappett, C. (2018) From network connectivity to human mobility: models for Minoanization. *Journal of Archaeological Method and Theory* 25.4, 974–95.

Knappett, C. (ed.) (2013) *Network Analysis in Archaeology. New approaches to regional interaction.* Oxford, Oxford University Press.

Knappett, C., Evans, T. and Rivers, R. (2008) Modelling maritime interaction in the Aegean Bronze Age. *Antiquity* 82, 1009–24.

Kristiansen, K. (1987) Center and periphery in Bronze Age Scandinavia. In M. Rowlands, M.T. Larsen and K. Kristiansen (eds) *Centre and Periphery in the Ancient World*, 74–85. Cambridge, Cambridge University Press.

Kristiansen, K. (1998) *Europe before History.* Cambridge, Cambridge University Press.

Kristiansen, K. and Larsson, T.B. (2005) *The Rise of Bronze Age Society. Travels, transmissions and transformations.* Cambridge, Cambridge University Press.

Leidwanger, J. and Knappett, C. (eds) (2018) *Maritime Networks in the Ancient Mediterranean World.* Cambridge, Cambridge University Press.

Leshtakov, K. (2007) Eastern Balkans in the system of Aegean economy in the LBA. Oxhide and bun-ingots in Bulgarian lands. In I. Galanaki, H. Tomas, Y. Galanakis and R. Laffineur (eds) *Between the Aegean and Baltic Seas. Proceedings of the International Conference Bronze and Early Iron Age Interconnections and Contemporary Developments between the Aegean and the Regions of the Balkan Peninsula, Central and Northern Europe, University of Zagreb, 11-14 April 2005*, 447–58, pls CIX–CX. Aegaeum 27. Liège and Austin, TX, University de Liège and University of Austin at Texas.

Ling, J. and Stos-Gale, Z. (2015) Representations of oxhide ingots in Scandinavian rock art: the sketchbook of a Bronze Age traveller? *Antiquity* 89, 191–209.

Lo Schiavo, F., Muhly, J.D., Maddin, R. and Giumlia-Mair, A. (eds) (2009) *Oxhide Ingots in the Central Mediterranean.* Biblioteca di Antichità Cipriote 8. Rome, A.G. Leventis Foundation; CNR – Istituto di Studi sulle Civiltà dell'Egeo e del Vicino Oriente.

Matthäus, H. (1977–78) Neues zur Bronzetasse aus Dohnsen, Kreis Celle. *Die Kunde* 28–29, 51–69.

Meller, H. (2010) Nebra: Vom Logos zum Mythos – Biographie eines Himmelsbildes. In H. Meller and F. Bertemes (eds) *Der Griff nach die Sternen. Wie Europas Eliten zu Macht und Reichtum kamen.*

Internationales Symposium in Halle (Saale) 16.-21. Februar 2005, 23–73. Tagungen des Landesmuseums für Vorgeschichte Halle (Saale) 5. Halle (Saale), Landesmuseum für Vorgeschichte.

Mills, B.J., Roberts, J.M.J., Clark, J.J., Haas, W.R., Huntley, D., Peeples, M.A., Borck, L., Ryan, S.C., Trowbridge, M. and Breiger, R.L. (2013) The dynamics of social networks in the Late Prehispanic US Southwest. In C. Knappett (ed.) *Network Analysis in Archaeology. New approaches to regional interaction*, 181–202. Oxford, Oxford University Press.

Müller-Karpe, A. (1980) Die Funde. In Peter Neve (ed.) Die Ausgrabungen in Boğazköy-Hattusa 1979. *Archäologische Anzeiger 1980*, 303–7.

Needham, S., Parham, D. and Frieman, C.J. (2013) *Claimed by the Sea: Salcombe, Langdon Bay, and other marine finds of the Bronze Age.* CBA Research Report 173. York, Council for British Archaeology.

Negroni Catacchio, N. (1999) Produzione e commercio dei vaghi d'ambra tipo Tirinto e tipo Allumiere alla luce delle recenti scoperte. In O. Paoletti (ed.) *Protostoria e Storia del 'Venetorum Angulus'. Atti del XX Convegno di studi etruschi ed italici, Portogruaro - Quarto d'Altini - Este - Adria, 16-19 ottobre 1996*, 241–65. Pisa and Rome, Instituti editoriali e poligrafici internazionali.

Negroni Catacchio, N. (2014) I vaghi tipo Tirinto e Allumiere come indicatori di status. Nuovi dati su cronologia e diffusione. In G. Baldelli and F.L. Schiavo (eds), *Amore per l'Antico, dal Tirreno all'Adriatico, dalla Preistoria al Medioevo e oltre. Studi di antichità in ricordo di Giuliano de Marinis, vol. 1*, 3–14. Rome, Scienze e Lettere.

Östborn, P. and Gerding, H. (2014) Network analysis of archaeological data: a systematic approach. *Journal of Archaeological Science* 46, 75–88.

Östborn, P. and Gerding, H. (2015) The diffusion of fired bricks in Hellenistic Europe: a similarity network analysis. *Journal of Archaeological Method and Theory* 22, 306–44.

Peeples, M.A. (2018) *Connected Communities: social networks, identity, and social change in the ancient Cibola world.* Tucson, AZ, University of Arizona Press.

Pernicka, E. (2014) On the authenticity of the gold finds from Bernstorf, community of Kranzberg, Freising district, Bavaria. *Jahresschrift für Mitteldeutsche Vorgeschichte* 94, 517–26.

Primas, M. and Pernicka, E. (1998) Der Depotfund von Oberwilflingen. Neue Ergebnisse zur Zirkulation von Metallbarren. *Germania* 76.1, 25–65.

Rotea, M. (2002–2003 [2004]) Non-ferrous metallurgy in Transylvania of Bronze Age. *Acta Musei Napocensis* 39–40, 7–17.

Sherratt, S. (2012) The intercultural transformative capacities of irregularly appropriated goods. In J. Maran and P.W. Stockhammer (eds) *Materiality and Social Practice: transformative capacities of intercultural encounters*, 152–72. Oxford, Oxbow Books.

Sprockhoff, E. (1961) Eine mykenische Bronzetasse von Dohnsen, Kr. Celle. *Germania* 39, 11–22.

Váczi, G. (2013) Cultural connections and interactions of Eastern Transdanubia during the Urnfield period. *Dissertationes Archaeologicae* Series 3 No. 1, 205–30.

Váczi, G. (2014) A hálózatelemzés régészeti alkalmazásának lehetőségei a késő bronzkori fémművesség tükrében (Potentials of the archaeological application of network analysis in the light of Late Bronze Age metallurgy). *Archaeologiai Értesítő* 139, 261–91.

Vagnetti, L. (1971) Osservazioni sul cosidetto ripostiglio di Makarska. *Studi Ciprioti e Rapporti di Scavo* 1, 203–16.

Varberg, J., Gratuze, B. and Kaul, F. (2015) Between Egypt, Mesopotamia and Scandinavia: Late Bronze Age glass beads found in Denmark. *Journal of Archaeological Science* 54, 168–81.

Varberg, J., Gratuze, B., Kaul, F., Hansen, A.H., Rotea, M. and Wittenberger, M. (2016) Mesopotamian glass from Late Bronze Age Egypt, Romania, Germany, and Denmark. *Journal of Archaeological Science* 74, 184–94.

Verkooijen, K. (2014) *Tears of the Sun: Bronze Age amber spacers from Britain and Europe.* PhD Thesis. University of Exeter.

Verkooijen, K. (2017) Report and catalogue of the amber found at Bernstorf, near Kranzberg, Freising district, Bavaria, Germany. *Jahresschrift fur Mitteldeutsche Vorgeschichte* 96, 139–230.

Vinski-Gasparini, K. (1973) *Kultura polja sa žarama u sjevernoj Hrvatskoj*. Zadar, Sveučilište u Zagrebu, Filozofski Fakultet – Zadar.

Wang, Q., Strekopytov, S. and Roberts, B.W. (2018) Copper ingots from a probable Bronze Age shipwreck off the coast of Salcombe, Devon: composition and microstructure. *Journal of Archaeological Science* 97, 102–17.

Wang, Q., Strekopytov, S., Roberts, B.W. and Wilkin, N. (2016) Tin ingots from a probable Bronze Age shipwreck off the coast of Salcombe, Devon: composition and microstructure. *Journal of Archaeological Science* 67, 80–92.

Watkins, T. (1976) Wessex without Cyprus. 'Cypriot daggers' in Europe. In J.V.S. Megaw (ed.) *To Illustrate the Monuments. Essays on archaeology presented to Stuart Piggott on the occasion of his sixty-fifth birthday*, 135–43. London, Thames and Hudson.

Yalçın, Ü., Pulak, C. and Slotta, R. (eds) (2005) *Das Schiff von Uluburun. Welthandel vor 3000 Jahren. Katalog der Ausstellung des Deutschen Bergbau-Museums Bochum vom 15. Juli 2005 bis 16. Juli 2006*. Bochum, Deutsches Bergbau-Museum Bochum.

Chapter 6

Innovation through recoil from networks

Julie Hruby

Members of both recent and ancient cultures have recognised drawbacks to increasing network integration. These range from psychological discomfort, economic competition and social upheaval through the spread of infectious disease, slavery and death. These challenges can trigger conservative impulses toward local identity formation. Such impulses can be seen in cases where older, useless objects are retained as a matter of nostalgia or in cases where a culture intensifies its local traditions. Criteria for identifying recoil against networks using archaeological and epigraphic data are established and demonstrated. The Mycenaean Palace of Nestor at Pylos provides evidence for both nostalgic maintenance of 'useless' objects, including Linear B records of tripods that are no longer functional, and for a tendency to intensify traditional material characteristics such as the apparently increasing miniaturisation of small vessels. The learning process behind this kind of localisation is explored.

Key words: networks, localisation, nostalgia, Mycenaean, Pylos, miniaturisation

1. Introduction

Members of recent cultures have often reacted to high levels of cultural, political and economic engagement with broader networks by embracing their own local and regional traditions. In so doing, they can transform those local customs. For example, some shift local or regional dialects to emphasise differences from neighbours or distant political powers; others shift from glorifying exotic foods to celebrating local ones but transform and elaborate their traditionally simple foods. The goal may range from the positive construction of local identity to active resistance to sociopolitical forces. This paper asks one methodological question and one theoretical one: how might we identify similar phenomena in antiquity, and what was the learning process behind those changes that emerge from the rejection of novelty?

We will begin with a brief discussion of the goals and approaches this paper will use, then examine a range of drawbacks to large-scale or increasing-scale network integration, any of which can provoke resistance. Then we will discuss modern examples of how peoples' and cultures' reactions to increasing levels of network interaction have led to backlash in the form of embracing the local and traditional, and how what is considered to be 'traditional' has changed as a result. We will establish criteria for identifying comparable reactions to perceptions of increasing levels of interaction in antiquity (especially on the basis of material culture) and list a few of the domains in which such shifts in the 'traditional' might theoretically be found. Then we will examine a case study to demonstrate how this approach might work and list a few impediments to recognising this kind of shift.

The goal is to recognise the impact that interactions with macro-scale networks have on mid- and micro-scale ones, such as the impact of eastern Mediterranean political and economic networks on the people within the prehistoric state of Messenia, in the southwest of what is now Greece. Obviously, this topic reaches well beyond what a single paper can, but Late Mycenaean Messenia will provide us with evidence that it can be possible to see when people in the past perceived themselves to be engaging with increasing levels of macro-scale integration by looking for evidence of localist backlash.

In approaching this project, it is necessary to utilise methodologies from a broad range of fields, including sociology, political science, economics and psychology, that discuss the contemporary world, its increasing levels of globalisation and resistance to that globalisation. This is not due to a belief that the contemporary world order *proves* anything about the past, though many scholars of globalisation do look to earlier periods for the origins of the phenomenon (Held *et al.* 1999, 152–4). As so many modern scholars, most notably Manuel Castells (1997; 2006, 159–6), have pointed out, both the global reach of contemporary interactions and the bulk and speed of communications via new technologies make the problems of the contemporary world unlike what has come before. Indeed, it is clear that modern resistance to globalisation has itself taken a wide range of forms. Instead, scholarship on the modern world's increasing levels of network integration provides a basis for generating questions about how people may have reacted to similar but smaller-scale and slower increases in the past. This paper, then, is intended to serve as much as a mechanism for asking new questions as it is a medium for generating answers.

'Tradition' is a critical concept to this endeavour, and in this context it is useful to reject Eric Hobsbawm's (1997, 2) distinction between what he calls 'tradition' – defined as an invented, relatively recent phenomenon of what he describes as 'responses to novel situations which can take the form of reference to old situations' – and that which he calls 'custom' – described as dominating so-called 'traditional' (*i.e.* more genuine) societies. Hobsbawm's approach can be rejected for several reasons, ranging from the fact that his approach to 'so-called traditional societies' seems unnecessarily romantic to those who do in fact work with those societies to the fact that this distinction clearly breaks down when all societies under discussion are, to one extent or another, 'traditional'. Instead, a more traditional (as it were) definition proves more useful; the Oxford English Dictionary (2018) defines 'tradition' as, among other things, 'a belief, statement, custom, etc., handed down by non-written means (esp. word of mouth, or practice) from generation to generation'.

2. Networks as challenges

It is unsurprising that many modern scholars of socio-economic, technological and political network systems in the past tend to view increasing levels of engagement with these systems as a generally positive thing and decreasing levels of engagement as a negative one. There are clear benefits to such engagement, including the transmission of ideas, technologies and goods (LaBianca and Scham 2006). Yet as Appadurai (2001, 1–5) points out, academia and globalisation have a complex relationship, and the fact that many of us come from relatively successful positions within states that have recently stood and may still stand as major imperial powers allows us the luxury of underestimating the drawbacks of increasing integration into macro-scale networks, and as a result to ignore the fact that one of the major ways in which networks can affect culture is through conservative backlash. While the benefits of heavy integration in large-scale networks are potentially substantial, the drawbacks are as well. They include factors like the spread of infectious disease, economic competition, social upheaval, the threats associated with being invaded or subjected to foreign hegemony and a range of cognitive threats.

For example, it is common for history books to treat the plague that struck Athens at the beginning of the Peloponnesian War as a direct result of crowded and unsanitary conditions caused by the state of emergency and by a pre-existing high population density (*e.g.* Garnsey 1988, 90). While this view is reasonable and no doubt true, it fails to incorporate another critical factor: that the plague was likely to have been the result as much of high levels of Athenian network integration as of warfare *per se* (see Garnsey 1988, 96–105 for the necessity of importing large quantities of food even in normal years; 139–40 for factors favouring trade). Both the speed with which the plague spread and the high death-toll, as reported by Thucydides and confirmed by the recent excavation of the remains of apparent plague victims in a mass grave outside the Kerameikos cemetery (Baziotopoulou-Valavani 2002), suggest that the plague was the result of the introduction of a novel pathogen (see National Intelligence Council 2000, 5, 13 for the impact of novel pathogens) to a population without immunity; after all, diseases tend to travel the same networks that ideas do. The fact that Thucydides reports that the plague entered Athens via its port city, Piraeus, reinforces the idea that the plague must initially have come from outside the city. He suggests that its source was Africa, and that it reached Greece through Egypt and Persia (Thucydides 2.48). While the actual point of origin of the pathogen cannot be confirmed until its genetic identity is widely agreed upon. (Unfortunately, Papagrigorakis *et al.*'s 2006 DNA-based identification of it as typhoid fever has not met with universal acceptance within the medical community; their methodology was questioned by Shapiro *et al.* 2006.) It is clear that the idea that novel disease could come from abroad and threaten even a major polis was understood already in Classical antiquity (Garnsey 1988, 171–3, 192–3, 195, 220 on infectious disease causing food crises in the Roman Republic (lack of farm workers); cf. imports as a mechanism for ameliorating those crises, 231–5).

Other drawbacks, while less concrete than infectious disease, are no less real. Economic competition, for example, can increase inequality and threaten the economic wellbeing or livelihood of those whose technological competencies or equipment become outmoded as a result of contact with people whose technological skills are superior. One example might be the introduction of the potter's wheel. A wheel represents both new physical infrastructure and a potentially steep learning curve (Berg 2007, 244–6). Berg (2007) has documented that at Phylakopi on Melos, the potter's wheel was introduced late in the Middle Cycladic period and that the range of wheel-made pots increased gradually, generation by generation, reflecting the slow acquisition of new skills, by potters who had limited access to instruction or who were working only seasonally and part-time. It is fairly easy to imagine an older, more experienced potter supporting herself in some part through the manufacture of coil-built vessels when the wheel was first adopted, but even if the first wheel-made pots in Greece were in fact coil-built and only finished on the wheel, as now seems to have been the case in at least some contexts (Choleva 2012), our potter would have faced increasing competition. She must either have competed at a disadvantage, being restricted to the more conceptually limited range of traditional Melian forms, or invested in new equipment and learned new, potentially uncomfortable, skills.

The potters at Ayia Irini on Kea were apparently obligated to adopt more efficient production methods as they came into increasing contact with Minoan culture in the Late Cycladic II period; Davis and Lewis see this as a result of direct economic competition from Cretan potters (1985), though Berg (2004, 82) points out that there were virtually no Minoan conical cups on Kea or Kean ones on Crete, and she hypothesises that the increase in economic competition may have been caused by internal Kean developments triggered by 'exposure to a more technologically efficient society'. Either way, new economic pressures arose, potentially forcing some producers out of the field.

Additionally, consumers seeking the kinds of goods that are exported or that serve as the medium of taxation to a distant government may face higher 'prices' (regardless of whether the price is monetary or in barter) than they would have, had there been no mechanism for export. Had we sufficient evidence, we might find this to have been the case with textiles or other goods taxed and exported by Mycenaean palatial elites, or with grain in Egypt under the Roman Empire (see Erdkamp 2005, 10 for the coercive, non-market movement of grain). This is likely to have been a particular problem for those dependent on the market alone for foodstuffs, insofar as it may have made either availability more sporadic or prices more volatile.

Other economic drawbacks to integration into large-scale networks, especially for those who are not among the wealthy and powerful, that are well-documented in modern contexts include brain-drain and brawn-drain; migrants are likely to be among the better educated, more skilled, younger and stronger members of their own societies, and if enough emigrate, they leave their home-communities without access to their skills. Even remittance, the practice of sending wealth home, is unlikely to have made up for the loss of skilled craftsmen; in light of the state of the ancient banking industry, it is difficult to imagine Athenian metics, for example, sending money back to their places of origin on a frequent basis. Even if they did, remittance would have been a mixed blessing, stabilising poorer economies but increasing income inequality (much as it does today, for which see Orrenius *et al.* 2010).

There were political threats from network incorporation as well; many examples of such drawbacks are known from the classical world, including loss of life, enslavement, exile and being subject to looting and plundering. We might think here of the Ionian cities drawn into the Persian Empire (Herodotus 1), or of the Melians who rejected the opportunity to be drawn into the Athenian empire, at great cost (Thucydides 5. 84–116).

Cognitive threats, while less concrete, would also have been significant. The familiar is typically judged to be less threatening than the unknown, and it is increasingly clear that, contrary to what we intuitively believe, human decisions precede cognition, with decisions rationalised rather than reasoned (Zajonc 1980; see also Lerner *et al.* 2015). Since the familiar is less threatening, many individuals out of any group are likely to prefer the familiar to the novel. Indeed, the term 'status quo bias' refers to a widely documented cognitive bias toward the familiar (Nicolle *et al.* 2011). There are other drawbacks to becoming increasingly integrated, but the overall point should already be clear: the opportunities for death, doom and destruction, or at least discomfort, are extensive and therefore can provide an impetus for backlash.

3. Identifying recoil from networks

Backlash from network integration can manifest itself in a variety of forms. Scholars of sociology and political science primarily discuss large-scale, violent, resistance movements, such as the Mexican Zapatistas, American militias and Islamic fundamentalism. They point out that at times of substantial social and technological change, some people gain and others lose, and they are interested in understanding the reactions of those who have lost. Castells (1997, 68), for example, discusses what he calls 'Social Movements against the New Global Order'. He investigates the identities, political strategies and discourse of the Mexican Zapatistas, the American militia movement and Japan's Aum Shinrikyo, finding that for each of these groups, 'resistance confronts domination, empowerment reacts against powerlessness, and alternative projects challenge the logic embedded in the new global order' (Castells 1997, 69).

The detection of violent resistance to imperialism and to network integration should theoretically be possible in antiquity; the destruction sequence at Masada, located in an area newly incorporated into the Roman Empire but comfortably within its borders, for example, might even in the absence of Josephus's text be interpreted as evidence that violent revolt might have occurred, and in this case a variety of other factors make the revolt archaeologically visible, including the coinage of the rebellion (Deutsch 2011). The identification of violent and large-scale revolt is at least a familiar problem, though it can be methodologically challenging to differentiate among causes of instability. Factors that suggest armed revolt against integration might include large caches of weaponry in private homes, and the frequent burial of caches or hoards of wealth well within established state borders but shortly after integration. Burned destructions solidly within the borders of states may also reflect resistance, especially when they are focused on elite structures, though they must be differentiated from external incursions. But non-violent or limited-violence resistance is much more difficult to identify archaeologically. Political protests against the WTO, IMF and World Bank are a staple of the contemporary anti-globalisation movement (Carroll and Coburn 2003, 96–100), but they leave little physical evidence that will be identifiable 3000 years from now.

Most scholarship on resistance focuses on those who have *lost* rather than on those who have *lost something*, but even those who have on balance gained may turn toward the traditional out of nostalgia. Even elites, perhaps especially elites, have a great deal to lose at times of upheaval and new technologies, but violent resistance is both costly and risky. In many situations, backlash can instead take the form of shifts, often by elites, that transform the traditional. One hint that nostalgia may have been a part of a culture is a tendency for members to maintain heirloom objects that have become useless for their original functions. For example, the Palace of Nestor at Pylos possessed and inventoried vessels that had apparently ceased to be functional, like an antique tripod of Cretan workmanship with legs that had been burned away (Tablet PY Ta 641; see Bennett and Olivier 1973, 230).

A stronger indication may come from reflections in material culture and language of sudden or strong or highly symbolic turns toward (or maintenance of) older ways. One modern example of such a transformation is the adaptation of traditional languages in ways that either increase the frequency with which they are spoken or intensify their distinctive characteristics. For example, the Xinca language, an obsolescing indigenous language in Guatamala, had already been substantially more glottalised than Spanish, and its last speakers have shifted toward glottalising more than did earlier speakers (Campbell and Muntzel 1989, 189, 198). Campbell and Muntzel view this shift as a function of imperfect learning of the tongue rather than as intentional resistance to the non-glottalised Spanish ways of speaking, but it is worth noting that these are not mutually exclusive factors; people who have gone to some trouble to learn to speak a traditional language are inherently engaged in a form of resistance.

A similar case can be made for the use of French in Quebec (Heller 1999, 144), or for the use of Irish in Ireland (Coulmas 2005, 176), or for the maintenance of African American Vernacular English (Rickford and Rickford 2000, 224), or for the historical restriction of indigenous American languages (Little and McCarty 2006). More recently, this accounts for the growth in schools in indigenous languages like Cherokee, where instruction has been catalysed by the work of Tom Belt (among others), a native speaker known for his work building Cherokee-language textbooks and schools (*e.g.* Belt 2013; WCU 2018). We are also able to identify the use of regionally specific, archaic languages in the past as a method of identity formation. One example is the continuation of the use of the cuneiform script and Akkadian language long after the far-simpler, alphabetic Aramaic became standard (McCall 1990, 33); another is the Vatican's maintenance of Latin long past its decline as a vernacular language.

Another modern example of recoil from networks is the localisation movement. This broad-based movement, supported by those across the political spectrum, serves as a positively framed alternative to the anti-globalisation movement; the withdrawal of the UK from the EU is an interesting national example of this phenomenon. Thousands of different bumper stickers, car magnets, and Facebook memes proclaim support for local music, local craft and especially local food. Popular authors proclaim that the average item of food has travelled 1500 miles, arguing that this is environmentally disastrous (*e.g.* Pollan 2006, 239). This movement is in no way restricted to the members of lower socio-economic classes and is in fact far more prevalent among elites, who have actually benefitted tremendously from globalisation (Govindasamy *et al.* 1998; Eastwood *et al.* 1999).

While many claim localism, and especially the local food movement, to be a branch of the environmental movement, local production of food can sometimes be far worse for the environment than production of food in places where it can be done efficiently. For example, tomatoes for consumption in Sweden have lower carbon footprints when they are grown in Spain than when they are grown locally in heated greenhouses, because transportation is a minor part of the energy cost of food production (Carlsson-Kanyama 1998). Similarly, it has been argued that lamb shipped to the UK from New Zealand may be more energy-efficient than lamb produced in the UK, because production in New Zealand is done in environmentally sounder ways (Saunders *et al.* 2006, 83–92; though see Schnell 2013, 618 for a methodological critique). The fact that those who shop at local markets will pay more for local products than for those that are guaranteed to be fresher suggests that the movement is a nostalgic one (Darby *et al.* 2008), as the quaint scenes of barns and chickens that are often paired with local foods on menus and bumper stickers would indicate.

This kind of gentle nostalgia for days past can in theory be found in any number of realms: foodstuffs, cooking styles, music, storytelling, dance, manners and mannerisms, religious practice, athletic competition, clothing, adornment and archaism in the style or technology of art or craft in any medium. Despite methodological challenges to finding some of these in antiquity, especially in prehistory, it can be done. The process of recoil against network integration can be identified on the basis of the following characteristics:

- A pre-existing local tradition exists, though it need not be particularly old.
- That tradition should be distinguishable from the traditions of other proximate nodes.
- The tradition must intensify over time, in frequency or in distinctiveness, or be maintained while other practices shift.
- The transformation should either move local practice away from the practices of other, relationally close nodes of the network, or maintain pre-existing distance.

- There must have been an audience, even if only the practitioner.
- Recoil in one aspect of practice does not preclude the adoption of novel practice or imported goods in others (just as today one might purchase local honey in jars manufactured in China).
- The recoil should coincide chronologically and spatially with increases in levels of long-distance network integration, or at least with an increase in the perception of integration.

Many of these characteristics are archaeologically visible, though they can only be identified through close attention to detail and to both spatial and chronological patterns.

4. Case study

One example of this kind of identification is of prehistoric miniature vessels from the southwest Peloponnese. One of the many distinctive features of the ceramic assemblage from the Palace of Nestor at Pylos is its uncommonly large number of unusually tiny miniature vessels, especially kylikes. The destruction level, often assigned to the Late Helladic III B/C transition (c. 1180 BC) (Mountjoy 1997), includes at least 7 miniature bowls, at least 24 miniature dippers and at least 163 miniature kylikes (Blegen and Rawson 1966, 356, 363–4, 366) (Fig. 6.1).

The production of many tiny miniatures once seemed to have been character-istic only of the era of the palace's destruction around 1180 BC, but evidence has recently begun to accumulate that this was in fact a pre-existing local tradition of the palace and region. We discovered among sherds from below the floor of room 18 the remains of an earlier miniature dipper and a kylix, and from the sherds below room 20 another kylix (Fig. 6.2). The dipper from room 18 is datable to LH IIIB1 on the basis of its painted decoration, and the kylix from under room 18 can be tenta-tively dated to LH IIIA on the basis of its everted rim. The kylix from under room 20 can be dated tentatively to LH IIIA2 to earliest LH IIIB1 on the basis of its foot shape.

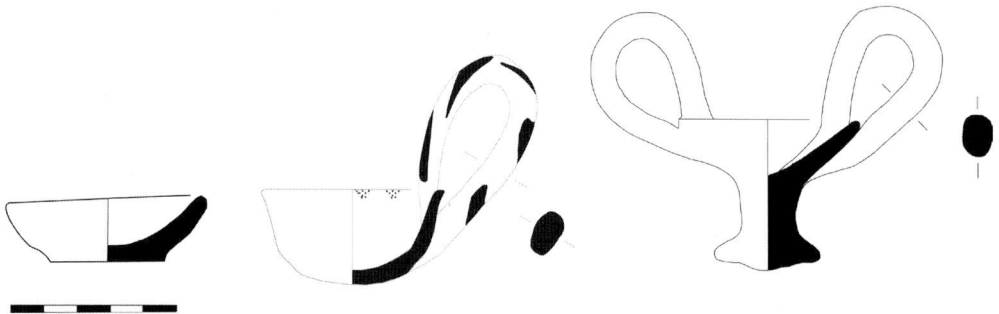

Figure 6.1 Destruction-level miniature vessels from the Palace of Nestor, including a bowl, dipper and kylix (the equivalent of a wine glass).

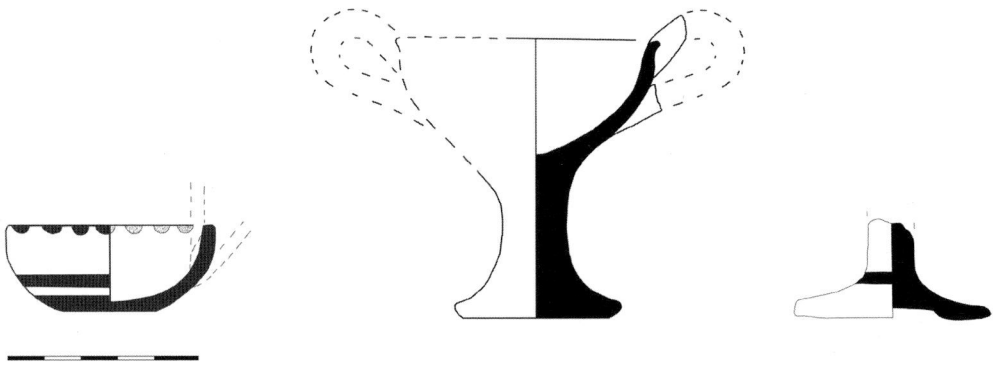

Figure 6.2 *Pre-destruction miniature vessels from the Palace of Nestor, including the bowl of a dipper and two kylix sherds.*

These earlier vessels suggest that Pylos's tiny miniatures are characteristic of the site and not a destruction-era anomaly. A longer regional tradition can increasingly be established as well; excavations at the nearby site of Iklaina have found a wide range of miniatures, some of which Gulizio has tentatively dated to the Late Helladic I period (personal communication). This tradition is visible also at the nearby sites of Nichoria (Shelmerdine 1992, 515, fig. 9–67) and Malthi (Lólos 1987, 20, 22).

It is helpful to create a local, chronologically specific definition of miniaturisation. Fortunately, discovering a Pylian palatial, emic differentiation between miniatures and full-sized vessels is straightforward. The pottery recovered from the site comes in a wide range of sizes, from a diminutive kylix with a capacity of 10 ml through pithoi with capacities of at least 180 l (Palmer 1994, 146). One mechanism for recovering emic (indigenous) size classes is to look at a ceramic type and create a histogram representing each of many single variables (height, rim diameter, capacity, etc.). When any resulting histogram is multimodal, each mode and the surrounding data should represent the members of one emic size class, particularly when there is a distinct break between modes (Hruby 2010; the rationale for this argument is established meticulously by Read and Russell 1996).

As a result, we can define miniatures in either of two ways. The first is applicable in cases where we have multiple size classes for a shape. For example, kylikes come in a range of different size classes, and the smallest class ranges in capacity from 10 to 35 ml, then there is a substantial gap in capacity before the next-smallest kylix at 135 ml. It would be reasonable to refer to the smallest class of kylikes (or bowls or dippers) as miniature on the basis of this definition. According to this definition, Pylos has miniature bowls (capacities 17–29 ml; the next smallest bowl has a capacity of 143 ml) and dippers (capacities 11–40 ml; the next smallest dipper has a capacity of 80 ml) as well as kylikes. The second mechanism for identifying miniatures, a more restrictive one but applicable when the very small vessel type does not exist in larger format, would be to identify a break in the capacity levels of all vessels. If we wish to scale the data, so that comparatively small differences in very large vessels are minimised while similar sizes in very tiny vessels become more visible, one mechanism would be to use the natural log. By this measure too, the diminutive bowls, dippers, and kylikes at Pylos can be defined as miniatures; at Pylos, all are vessels with capacities the natural log of which is less than 3.69. (A single uncommonly small, pedestaled amphora also has a capacity of 40 ml (with a natural log of 3.69), but because the Pylos pantries were largely shelved by type and it was found stored with larger examples of its type, it may have been an outlier rather than a true miniature.) The next smallest natural log is 4.09. By contrast, while capacities are rarely included, the published dimensions of 'miniature' or 'diminutive' vessels, especially kylikes, identified outside of Messenia at sites like Tiryns, Mycenae and Orchomenos can be substantially larger regardless of their date, suggesting that some of those vessels (even though they are smaller than the full-size examples of vessels of their own types) can fall into, or even above, the size range that is absent from the Pylos pantries (*e.g.* Mountjoy 1986, 49 fig. 56, 50, 101, 102 fig. 123, 126; Damm 1997. It is possible that the Pylos examples follow Minoan size prototypes).

This is not to suggest that all diminutive vessels shared a single function; they almost certainly did not. The contexts in which they were found suggest that miniature bowls and dippers were functional equipment for the serving of foods intended to impart flavour in small quantities, perhaps salt or spices or honey. All of the miniature bowls and dippers come from the palace's pantries, where the paraphernalia for large-scale feasts was stored (Hruby 2010).

By contrast, miniature kylikes seem to have been particularly significant, with clear symbolic value. They have been discovered in a range of contexts, including in storage, but also in several other contexts, many of which imply ritual significance: in tombs at Volimidia near the palace, on a plaster 'table of offerings' in the throne room and burned, in an administrative context shared with the burned animal bones that bore witness to a large-scale sacrificial event (Blegen and Rawson 1966; Blegen *et al.* 1973; Stocker and Davis 2004). They occur in much greater numbers than do other miniatures; the 163 kylikes are more than five times the number of bowls and dippers combined. Tellingly, they cannot have simply been tiny drinking vessels, for children or for the consumption by adults of substances that were dear; the high-swung handles, of which each vessel had two, would have hit anyone, even a small child, in the face in such a way as to make drinking completely impossible.

These miniature kylikes suggest a nostalgic tradition embraced by palatial elites and transformed by their esteem. There is a little suggestive evidence, though it is by no means conclusive, that they may have been made in increasingly distinctive diminutive dimensions over time within the LH III period. The destruction-level kylikes are uniformly tiny, and when graphed with the examples from earlier in the LH III period found beneath the floor, the earlier vessels are clear dimensional outliers, as demonstrated by histograms representing capacity (Fig. 6.3), height (Fig. 6.4), rim diameter (Fig. 6.5), and base diameter (Fig. 6.6). While this may not be coincidental, relying on

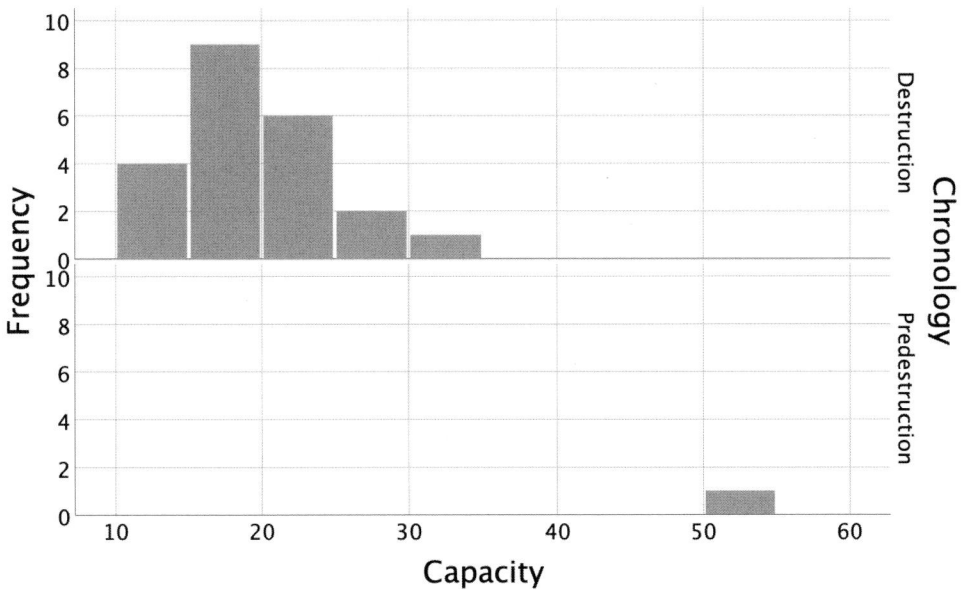

Figure 6.3 Histogram of the capacities of all prehistoric kylikes from the Palace of Nestor. N=23.

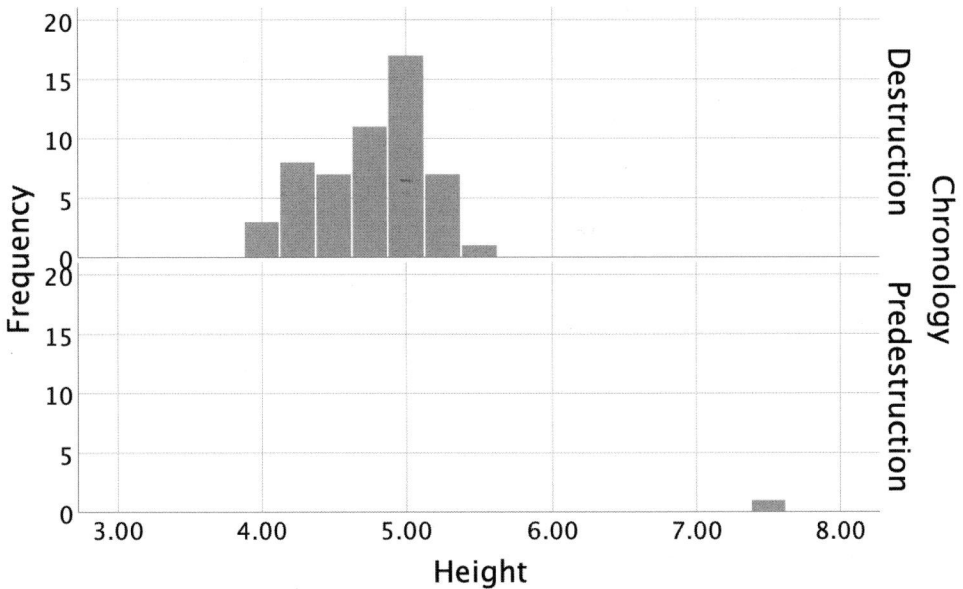

Figure 6.4 Histograms of the heights of all prehistoric kylikes from the Palace of Nestor. N=55.

only two earlier examples, one of which is fragmentary, to demonstrate a pattern is risky. This hypothesis requires more evidence, which may be forthcoming shortly; a team has been excavating earlier levels of the palace, including just outside room 20.

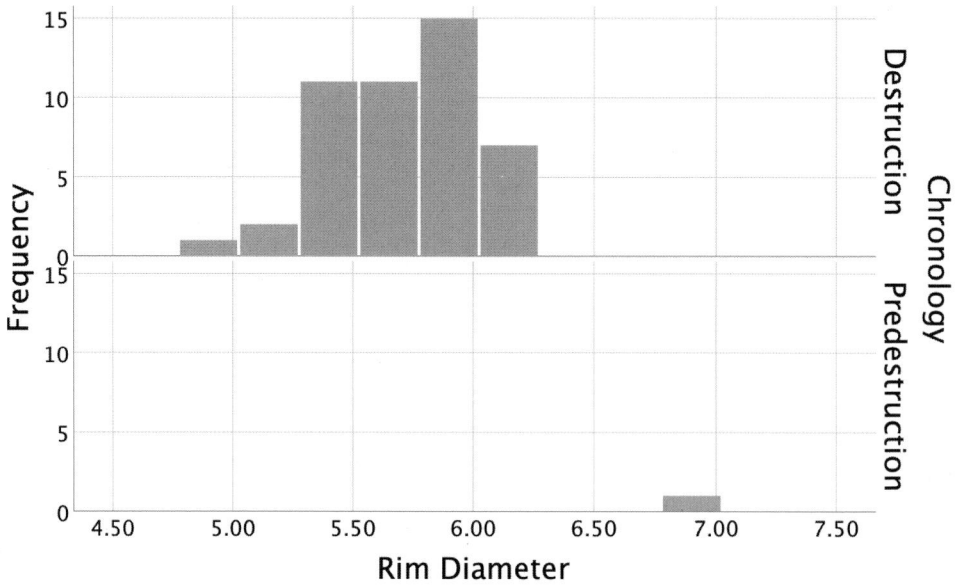

Figure 6.5 Histograms of the rim diameters of all prehistoric kylikes from the Palace of Nestor. N=48.

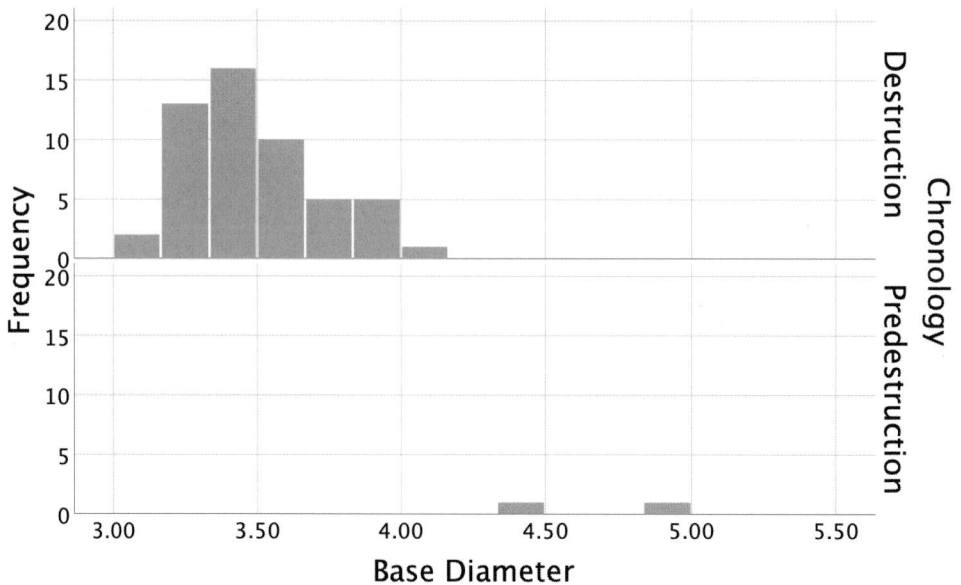

Figure 6.6 Histograms of the base diameters of all prehistoric kylikes from the Palace of Nestor. N=54.

If indeed kylikes were shrinking within the LH III period, there are two possible explanations. One is that the Pylians were being stingy, either the potter with his clay or the elites with their wine; the other is that this was an act of nostalgia for an older way, leading to increasingly distinctive local objects. Of the two, nostalgia is the more likely hypothesis. The amount of clay conserved by forming a smaller vessel was offset by the substantial increase in the size of the vessels' handles in the later examples. The amount of wine conserved (less than 30 ml per vessel) could have been conserved just as effectively by careful pouring and would, in any case, have been minuscule. If all 163 miniature kylikes at the palace had been the size of the earlier LH IIIA example, then assuming the vessels were not reused (and they seem unlikely to have been), only 4 or 5 litres of wine would have been saved by all of the vessels combined. When compared with the 11,808 litres of wine listed on one single tablet, a saving of 4 or 5 litres seems hardly worth mentioning.

Regardless of any shift in the size of these vessels, or of its cause, it also seems that the *number* of diminutive kylikes may have peaked in the LH IIIB period. This is inherently an intuitive judgement, perhaps skewed by the excavation history of the region; it is difficult to establish in any meaningful statistical sense. The trend of miniatures peaking in frequency in the LH IIIB period, however, is not limited to Messenia, and Mountjoy (1986, 101) has remarked on the phenomenon in Greece at large.

5. Implications

We might also note that, despite their (perhaps) increasingly diminutive sizes, the Pylos kylikes maintained their visual distinctiveness through the mechanism of enhancing the size of their handles. Indeed, it is possible that the increasingly tall high-swung handles made the bodies of the newer kylikes look even smaller by comparison, while maintaining the space occupied by, and so the visual impact of, the vessel as a whole. Furthermore, as we have already discussed, some of the diminutive vessels appear in symbolically charged contexts. If the *distinctiveness* of the vessels was the attribute that had intensified, for instance by their becoming increasingly small over time, that might suggest that the Pylian elites were self-identifying as people-with-tiny-minia-ture-vessels. If their *numbers* increased, that might instead reflect the fact that the Pylians were engaging in an activity using those vessels, and that the activity was the focus of identity-building, rather than the vessels themselves. If their contexts became more distinctive or significant, then we have an indication that either the vessels or the activities that relied upon them, perhaps both, were important to their practitioners. The diminutive kylikes, at least, seem to have been used in heavily ritualised contexts, and the practices for which they were used may actually be a better candidate for regional identity formation than are the kylikes *per se*, though the kylikes themselves may also have been seen as a critical attribute of local identity.

The learning process behind the transformation of or stasis in local tradition is relatively straightforward. A practitioner (potter, dancer, etc.) must be familiar with local ways, must come into contact with new practices (through contact with practitioners, or with new tools, or with new products), and must make a decision, perhaps not a conscious one, to reproduce familiar practices rather than new ones. That reproduction of familiar practice may, however, exaggerate local or region-specific attributes, through a conscious or subconscious attempt at identity-construction, shifting local practice in an increasingly reactionary way.

As the above example shows, finding this kind of shift in antiquity, especially prehistoric antiquity, can be difficult for a variety of reasons. First, while ideologies of the traditional may be strong, they may not necessarily affect the majority of behaviours; the pull of external ideologies or economic factors may simply be stronger. Second, it requires a high level of chronological resolution in a wide range of artefacts; we have this kind of resolution for some kinds of ceramics but not yet for faience plaques or for cooking wares. Third, it requires a sense of relative frequency of object-types over time, which in turn requires knowledge of both the length that time periods last and a reasonably high level of chronological continuity in excavated sites within a single region. Fourth, it requires that we correlate artefacts with behaviours in addition to typologies, though even the thought structures behind ancient typologies may themselves have shifted over time, another topic that is potentially worthy of investigation.

In short, while network analysis is itself a useful tool, it is important not to conflate its value as a modern analytical approach with the value or lack thereof of increasing network integration for those who experienced it. Surely some must have benefitted, but not all, and even those who did benefit must have missed aspects of their earlier lives. Change can be uncomfortable, unhealthy, frightening, even deadly; if we fail to consider its negative impacts, and how those affect culture, we do our predecessors a grave disservice.

Acknowledgements

I would like to thank Shari Stocker and Jack Davis for access to the material on which the end of this paper is based, Joann Gulizio for sharing her knowledge of the relevant material from Iklaina, and Michael Cosmopoulos for making it possible for her to do so. Susanne Friedberg kindly offered bibliographic recommendations, and all illustrations are by Eric J. Chatterjee. Not least, I would like to thank the organisers of the conference for the invitation to join this conversation and for their hospitality.

References

Appadurai, A. (2001) Grassroots globalization and the research imagination. In A. Appadurai (ed.) *Globalization*, 1–21. Durham, NC, Duke University Press.

Baziotopoulou-Valavani, E.A. (2002) Mass burial from the cemetery of Kerameikos. In M. Stamatopoulou and M. Yeroulanou (eds) *Excavating Classical Culture. Recent archaeological discoveries in Greece*, 187–201. BAR International Series 1031. Oxford, Archaeopress.

Belt, T. (2013) Vocal and verbal arts archives. (http://languagematrix.com/bio/thomas.shtml, accessed 26 August 2018).

Bennett, E.L. and Olivier, J.-P. (1973) *The Pylos Tablets Transcribed.* Incunabula graeca. Rome, Edizioni dell'Ateneo.

Berg, I. (2004) The meanings of standardisation: conical cups in the Late Bronze Age Aegean. *Antiquity* 78, 74–85.

Berg, I. (2007) Meaning in the making: the potter's wheel at Phylakopi, Melos (Greece). *Journal of Anthropological Archaeology* 26, 234–52. doi: 10.1016/j.jaa.2006.10.001.

Blegen, C.W. and Rawson, M. (1966) *The Palace of Nestor at Pylos in Western Messenia.* Vol. I. Princeton, Princeton University Press.

Blegen, C.W., Rawson, M., Taylour, W. and Donovan, W.P. (1973) *The Palace of Nestor at Pylos in Western Messenia.* Vol. III. Princeton, Princeton University Press.

Campbell, L. and Muntzel, M. (1989) The structural consequences of language death. In N.C. Dorian (ed.) *Investigating Obsolescence: studies in language contraction and obsolescence,* 181–96. Cambridge, Cambridge University Press.

Carlsson-Kanyama, A. (1998) Food consumption patterns and their influence on climate change: greenhouse gas emissions in the life-cycle of tomatoes and carrots consumed in Sweden. *Ambio* 27, 528–34.

Carroll, W. and Coburn, E. (2003) Social movements and transformation. In W. Clement and L F. Vosko (eds), *Changing Canada: political economy as transformation,* 79–105. Montreal, McGill-Queen's University Press.

Castells, M. (1997) *The Power of Identity.* Malden, MA, Blackwell.

Castells, M. (2006) Nothing new under the sun? In Ø.S. LaBianca and S.A. Scham (eds) *Connectivity in Antiquity: globalization as long-term historical process,* 158–67. Approaches to Anthropological Archaeology. London, Equinox Publishing Ltd.

Choleva, M. (2012) The first wheelmade pottery at Lerna: wheel-thrown or wheel-fashioned? *Hesperia* 81, 343–81.

Coulmas, F. (2005) *Sociolinguistics: the study of speakers' choices.* Cambridge, Cambridge University Press.

Damm, U. (1997) *Die Spätbronzezeitlichen Miniaturgefässe und Hohlgeformten Stiere von Tiryns : eine Analyse der Form und Funktion.* PhD Thesis. Universität Bonn.

Darby, K., Batte, M.T., Ernst, S. and Roe, B. (2008) Decomposing local: a conjoint analysis of locally produced foods. *American Journal of Agricultural Economics* 90, 476–86. doi: 10.1111/j.1467-8276.2007.01111.x.

Davis, J.L. and Lewis, H.B. (1985) Mechanization of pottery production: a case study from the Cycladic Islands. In A.B. Knapp and T. Stech (eds) *Prehistoric Production and Exchange: the Aegean and eastern Mediterranean,* 79–92. Los Angeles, UCLA Institute of Archaeology.

Deutsch, R. (2011) Coinage of the first Jewish revolt against Rome: iconography, minting authority, metallurgy. In M. Popović (ed.) *The Jewish Revolt against Rome: interdisciplinary perspectives,* 361–71. Supplements to the Journal for the Study of Judaism. Leiden, Brill.

Eastwood, D.B., Brooker, J.R. and Gray, M.D. (1999) Location and other market attributes affecting farmers' market patronage: the case of Tennessee. *Journal of Food Distribution Research* 30, 63–72.

Erdkamp, P. (2005) *The Grain Market in the Roman Empire: a social, political and economic study.* Cambridge, Cambridge University Press.

Garnsey, P. (1988) *Famine and Food Supply in the Graeco-Roman World: responses to risk and crisis.* Cambridge, Cambridge University Press.

Govindasamy, R., Zurbriggen, M., Italia, J., Adelaja, A.O., Nitzsche, P. and van Vranken, R. Farmers markets: consumer trends, preferences, and characteristics. The State University of New Jersey Rutgers (1998). (http://ageconsearch.umn.edu/bitstream/36722/2/pa980798.pdf, accessed 28 August 2018).

Held, D., McGrew, A., Goldblatt, D. and Perraton. J. (1999) *Global Transformations: politics, economics and culture*. Stanford, Stanford University Press.

Heller, M. (1999) Heated language in a cold climate. In J. Blommaert (ed.) *Language Ideological Debates*, 143–70. Berlin, Mouton de Gruyter.

Herodotus (2003) *The Histories*. Tr. A. de Sélincourt. London, Penguin Group.

Hobsbawm, E. (1983) Introduction: inventing traditions. In E. Hobsbawm and T.O. Ranger (eds) *The Invention of Tradition*, 1–14. Cambridge, Cambridge University Press.

Hruby, J. (2010) Mycenaean pottery from Pylos: an indigenous typology. *American Journal of Archaeology* 114, 195–216.

LaBianca, Ø.S. and Scham, S.A. (2006) Introduction – ancient network flows. In Ø.S. LaBianca and S.A. Scham (eds) *Connectivity in Antiquity: globalization as long-term historical process*, 1–5. Approaches to Anthropological Archaeology. London, Equinox Publishing Ltd.

Lerner, J.S., Li, Y., Valdesolo, P. and Kassam, K.S. (2015) Emotion and decision making. *Annual Review of Psychology* 66, 799–823. doi: 10.1146/annurev-psych-010213-115043

Little, M.E.R. and McCarty, T.L. (2006) Language planning challenges and prospects in Native American communities and schools. Arizona State University. (http://nepc.colorado.edu/files/Report-EPSL-0602-105-LPRU.pdf, accessed 28 August 2018).

Lólos, Y.B. (1987) *The Late Helladic I Pottery of the Southwestern Peloponnesos and its Local Characteristics*. Studies in Mediterranean Archaeology Pocket Books. Göteborg, Paul Åströms Förlag.

McCall, H. (1993) *Mesopotamian Myths*. London, British Museum Publications.

Mountjoy, P.A. (1986) *Mycenaean Decorated Pottery: a guide to identification*. Studies in Mediterranean Archaeology. Göteborg, Paul Åströms Förlag.

Mountjoy, P.A. (1997) The destruction of the palace at Pylos reconsidered. *Annual of the British School at Athens* 92, 109–37.

National Intelligence Council (2000) The global infectious disease threat and its implications for the United States. National Intelligence Estimate No. NIE 99-17D), (2000), 1–60. National Intelligence Council. (http://www.dni.gov/files/documents/infectiousdiseases_2000.pdf, accessed 28 August 2018).

Nicolle, A., Fleming, S.M., Bach, D.R., Driver, J. and Dolan, R.J. (2011) A regret-induced status quo bias. *Journal of Neuroscience* 31, 3320–7. doi: 10.1523/JNEUROSCI.5615-10.2011.

Orrenius, P.M., Zavodny, M., Canas, J. and Coronado, R. (2010) Do remittances boost economic development? Evidence from Mexican states. Federal Reserve Bank of Dallas. (http://www.dallasfed.org/assets/documents/research/papers/2010/wp1007.pdf, accessed 28 August 2018).

Oxford English Dictionary Online (2018) *s.v.* tradition (June 2018). Oxford, Oxford University Press. (http://www.oed.com/view/Entry/204302?rskey=bH3V9G&result=1, accessed 28 August 2018).

Palmer, R. (1994) *Wine in the Mycenaean Palace Economy*. Aegaeum. Université de Liège, Histoire de l'art et archéologie de la Grèce antique, and University of Texas at Austin Program in Aegean Scripts and Prehistory. Liège and Austin, TX.

Papagrigorakis, M.J., Yapijakis, C., Synodinos, P.N. and Baziotopoulou-Valavani, E.A. (2006) DNA examination of ancient dental pulp incriminates typhoid fever as a probable cause of the plague of Athens. *International Journal of Infectious Diseases* 10, 206–14. doi: 10.1016/j.ijid.2005.09.001.

Pollan, M. (2006) *The Omnivore's Dilemma: a natural history of four meals*. New York, Penguin.

Read, D.W. and Russell, G. (1996) A method for taxonomic typology construction and an example: utilized flakes. *American Antiquity* 61, 663–84.

Rickford, J.R. and Rickford, R.J. (2000) *Spoken Soul: the story of Black English*. New York, John Wiley.

Saunders, C., Barber, A. and Taylor, G. (2006) Food miles – comparative energy/emissions performance of New Zealand's agriculture industry, 1–105. Christchurch, NZ, Lincoln University. (https://researcharchive.lincoln.ac.nz/handle/10182/125, accessed 12 January 2021).

Schnell, S.M. (2013) Food miles, local eating, and community supported agriculture: putting local food in its place. *Agriculture and Human Values* 30, 615–28. doi: 10.1007/s10460-013-9436-8.

Shapiro, B., Rambaut, A. and Gilbert, M.T.P. (2006) No proof that typhoid caused the plague of Athens (a reply to Papagrigorakis *et al.*). *International Journal of Infectious Diseases* 10, 334–5. doi: 10.1016/j.ijid.2006.02.005.

Shelmerdine, C.W. (1992) Mycenaean pottery from the settlement. In W.A. McDonald and N.C. Wilkie (eds) *Excavations at Nichoria in Southwest Greece.* Vol. II, 495–517. Minneapolis, MN, University of Minnesota Press.

Stocker, S.R. and Davis, J.L. (2004) Animal sacrifice, archives, and feasting at the Palace of Nestor. *Hesperia* 73, 179–98.

Thucydides (1972) *History of the Peloponnesian War.* Tr. R. Warner. London, Penguin Group.

WCU (Western Carolina University) (2018) Cherokee studies experts. (https://www.wcu.edu/learn/departments-schools-colleges/cas/humanities/world-languages/world-languages-faculty-staff/tom-belt.aspx, accessed 28 August 2018).

Zajonc, R. (1980) Feeling and thinking: preferences need no inferences. *American Psychologist* 35, 151–75.

Chapter 7

Networks and assemblages: a view from Archaic Sicily

Carla M. Antonaccio

This chapter uses assemblage theory to explore the complex network of identities at the site of Morgantina, Sicily both during the period of Greek occupation but also predating it. For this site, which displays a complex constantly shifting range of identities through the material cultural record that do not divide neatly into the traditional 'ethnic' categories assigned by archaeologists working to traditional culture histories, hybridity seems to offer a good interpretative fit for understanding the material record. This is manifest both of terms of agency seen in the manufacture and constituent elements of individual objects and in the way objects are deployed together in specific contexts. Assemblage theory allows for a broader, more complete picture of the constituent elements – human, material, natural, built, cultivated and wild – that come into place and time but are essentially unstable and liable to recombination.

Key words: networks, indigeneity, Sicily, assemblage, identity

1. Introduction

Archaeologists are primarily concerned with things and the people with which they are in relationship, as well as the systems, including environmental, in which they function. Archaeologists have long been using some form of network model to represent and explain the past for a variety of societies, places and times, addressing topics such as trade and exchange, gift giving, hospitality, ritual practice, social complexity and many other features of human societies (Wolfe 1978–1979; Renfrew and Cooke 1979). These network models are derived from those used in the social and life sciences in particular. The networks with which archaeologists work are 'sociomaterial networks', as Knappett clarifies, including both human beings and things (Knappett 2016, 24). In a related development, the importance of things, including the relationships among or between things, and not just humans and things, has been captured by the notion of 'entanglement' as enunciated by Nicholas Thomas and further worked out by Ian Hodder (Thomas 1991; Hodder 2012). Entanglement also captures the oft-times short term intersection of threads of culture. Assemblage theory, the work especially of the philosophers Deleuze and Guattari, is also coming into play, a development that will be explored below.

An effusion of work on network thinking in Classical and Mediterranean archae-ology, especially applied to the Aegean Bronze Age, has marked the past decade (Knappett 2011; 2013, Brughmans *et al.* 2016). One of the most stimulating recent books in classical history postulates that the spread of Greek culture throughout the Mediterranean in the post-Bronze Age can be understood as a small world network (Malkin 2011). As Malkin's book heralded for the study of Archaic Greece, the dom-inance of network thinking now confronts the recent preoccupation in archaeology (and other disciplines) of discerning identity through material culture. The very notions of cultures and of ethnicity, ingrained in archaeology, are derived from per-ceived or asserted differences among human groups, and an assumed idea of how these are expressed materially. Since the development of post-processual archaeology, archaeologists have also pointed to the reflexive relationship of material culture, individuals and societies, and insisted on the agency of individuals in the past. Still, much recent work has focused on understanding ethnicity and other forms of identity. Some scholars have also sought to refine our categories, disentangling ethnicity from cultural or other forms of identity, trying to integrate written narratives that bear on emic and etic views of identity, and suggesting how to read them against discourses of material culture and human action.

Any consideration of identity and the material record contends with an old par-adigm: that of culture-history, which posits that styles and forms of material culture are a direct index of cultural and/or ethnic identity. These identities are crystallised by mythological and historical narratives that define them, using criteria of descent and homeland, and in this view, material cultural traits may constitute the tangible indicia of this identity – but not reliably. New work on archaeogenetics is now engaging how to mesh the physical anthropological evidence from ancient DNA for population movements and intermingling with cultural groupings established from distinctive artefacts or assemblages, with many caveats (Eisenmann *et al.* 2018).

In the ancient Mediterranean, bounded communities distinguished by distinc-tive material culture traits were linked together with colonial discourses, *e.g.* about Greeks and indigenes, with more sophisticated and technically advanced Greeks assimilating less complex, 'barbarian' cultures. This oppositional paradigm, rooted in Greek thought itself, has shifted because of the internal dissonance that tends to accompany such a shift. Archaeologists working in the Mediterranean at places like Morgantina simply could not make such a bimodal system of opposites work as more sites were excavated and published, presenting complex assemblages that could not all be explained by Greeks bearing pots (and more). Yet we are fundamentally still in thrall to the culture-history model of studying, defining and discerning cultural and ethnic identity through material culture. One of its features is diffusionism, the flow of persons and their attendant cultural attributes from an original homeland (cf. Hackenbeck *et al.*, this volume). An important contribution of network theory is to model connectivity challenging the culture-history view of material culture as a signal of the movement of a people carrying its culture outward from an original homeland, in a diffusionist mechanism that also fits colonialist narratives. Networks are formed of flows structured by connections between nodes and for our purposes they may, or may not, signal ethnicity, nationality, cultural affiliation and territoriality (see more on the latter below). But a salient feature of networks is their decentralised nature and collapse of distance since links are not predicated on territorial proximity.

Archaeologists studying Roman trade have also utilised network thinking (Scheidel and Meeks 2014; Leidwanger 2017), as have historians and economists. The variety of these projects and their network approaches demonstrate that network theory, or network thinking, is firmly established as an important, even dominant, paradigm in archaeology. As such, it runs the risk of becoming a totalising strategy, applied to everything and explaining little. There is not even agreement on whether networks are a quantitative computational model, or more of a metaphor.

As noted above, network theory has clearly pointed out the persistence of the old culture history model, in which distinct boundaries for cultural groups could be read off distinctive forms of material culture. In the Greek case, archaeologists and historians now think more about the diversity of Hellenicity, and the nature and effects of the Greek diaspora of the early Archaic period, but also the genesis of Hellenicity itself. The advent of network theory as currently conceived has also meant engaging with notions of centre and periphery, authentic and derivative, original, indigenous and colonial.

2. Post-coloniality without colonialism

Archaeology has taken a turn to post-coloniality and concepts such as hybridity to suggest a way forward from the structuralist polarities of Greek and barbarian, or Greek and Other, and to account for the distributions of things, as well as the ways in which they become enmeshed in pre-existing systems of meaning, and also changed those systems. Hybridity also seems like a good fit for the 'inbetweenness' that results when things from elsewhere are emulated, adapted and incorporated into societies both indigenous and colonial (Gunaratnam 2014). Hybridity has come in for much criticism as well on a variety of grounds; a major question has been whether hybridity, formulated as a response to modern imperialism and colonialism, is applicable to the independent city-states and societies of the Archaic Mediterranean. In particular, are Greek or Phoenician settlements in the central and west Mediterranean even colonies at all, without an empire behind them?

In Sicily, the example that is the focus of this paper, later Greco-Roman historical sources relate that there were three indigenous populations with their own languages and material traditions before Greeks and Phoenicians arrived in the ninth and eighth centuries BC and created permanent settlements (colonies), as they did elsewhere in the Mediterranean. This information itself is a demonstration of culture-history *avant la lettre*. Yet, indigenous settlements existed in Sicily long before the colonising activities of these other groups, and those living in these settlements spoke languages with links to, and shared material cultural traits with, contemporary communities in mainland Italy and elsewhere in the Mediterranean. It is also the case that the material culture in Sicily shows local variations and long and short distance interaction well before the Archaic period.

As examples of culture history, broadly speaking, the Greeks, their culture and material culture, were a default for archaeologists dealing with the period of population movements and new settlements. Greek pottery and other artefacts are ubiquitous in the Mediterranean during this period, to a greater or lesser degree, but ultimately it had to be recognised that this ubiquity could not definitively indicate the presence of Greek individuals *per se* on a given site. We hereby beg the question of who or what is a Greek, and how we can discern the presence of such people. Greek pottery is well known for being in great demand and being appreciated by other Mediterranean populations, for example, the Etruscans, who consumed it in quantity, the Celts and the Iberians. Roughly the idea was that Greek material culture was desirable, elite, a marker of status – a standard colonialist discourse. But the corollary assumption was that local, or indigenous, artefacts would not be sought or appreciated by others, and so one could be confident that the presence of indigenous objects indicated the presence of ethnically and/or culturally distinctive users of these objects. In short, indigenous material culture was marked.

3. Case study: Morgantina

Morgantina in east central Sicily was inhabited continuously from the late Bronze Age and sporadically since at least the Early Bronze Age. In the eighth and seventh centuries BC, its material culture exhibits the impact of the development of networks carrying objects, practices and technologies by sea and by land (for example, ceramics and scented oil, comestibles, burial customs, drinking and dining practices and architectural forms and technologies). Morgantina presents an interesting case study in two respects. First, recent work on the site in all periods has focused, at least in part, on issues of communal or civic and ethnic identity, as well as acculturation and consumption and production; and relationships with other communities inside and outside Sicily (Antonaccio 2015 for a summary). Second, for the present paper, Morgantina's archaeology features heterogeneous assemblages of artefacts, present in all periods. The conventions of archaeological study and publication divided material first into media, then focused on centres of production and decorative traditions, as well as function and date. Greek imports were privileged over local artefacts.

Diverse archaeological assemblages were often downplayed in early work and analysis on the site. One notable exception was the Archaic cemeteries, predominantly chamber tombs used for multiple burials. Tomb groups accompanying burials were published as assemblages, as well as analysed according to the long-standing categories noted above; from this work the particularities of Archaic Morgantina's compound material culture, and its interpretation, first took shape (Lyons 1996). Most of the questions that were asked were focused on trying to identify the ethnicity – Greek or Sikel – of the burials from the objects buried with the dead. This debate extended during the 1990s to the Archaic settlement, and ultimately to the status of the settlement as it was re-founded in the mid-fifth century BC as an orthogonally planned city complete with agora, theatre and several types of public buildings typical of Greek cities. These seemed complete proof of a Greek political and cultural identity, but at the same time, the persistence of non-Greek names and objects pointed to the persistence of indigeneity. Recent work has drawn on postcolonial theory to suggest that Morgantina's material culture is neither Greek nor Sikel, but hybrid. Hybridity is not merely a mixture of cultures, but a space of negotiation in between that challenges the hard boundaries of fixed and essential identities. It may also be the result of the agency of indigenes, rather than a form of mimicry of Greek culture or the passive acceptance of self-evidently superior or more elite forms, upending old ideals of the dominance and desirability of Hellenic culture. And, ethnogenesis may result from such processes, rather than pre-exist them.

4. Assemblages and networks

The heterogeneity in Morgantina assemblages has thus far been approached through the conventional archaeological definition of assemblage: a group of artefacts (and sometimes ecofacts) that occur in a specific context. Some assemblages occur regularly and the pattern and context are usually thought to include intentionality (Joyce and Pollard 2010). But there is another meaning of the term *assemblage* that has made its way into archaeological discourse that comes from the work of philosophers Gilles Deleuze and Felix Guattari, refined by Manuel DeLanda; this is also part of a broader discourse about social ontology (DeLanda 2016; Epstein 2018). As summarised by Julian Thomas, their use of *assemblage* shares a basic definition with the archaeological one – 'a composition made up of disparate elements that cohere for a greater or lesser period, and to a greater or lesser extent, under specific historical conditions'. Further, however, *assemblages*

> have no essence or organising principle, and it is the assemblage as a whole that acts ... [it] deliberately blurs the conventional boundary between culture and nature, so that both ecologies and societies can, together and independently, be assemblages ... assemblages are alive even though they are not bounded organisms. (Thomas 2015, 1295)

Thomas heads his discussion of this approach by speaking of 'assemblages and archaeologies of life'. DeLanda emphasises the 'emergent properties' of assemblages, that they are more than individual entities and also more than merely the sum of their parts; their emergent properties arise from the interaction of an assemblage's parts (2016, 19–22).

There are, therefore, three aspects of network thinking that figure in this particular examination of the complex material record of Archaic Morgantina: 1) the interoperation of networks, in this case, indigenous networks and Greek (see van der Leeuw 2013); 2) how these multi-nets account for the heterogeneous assemblages we find at Morgantina, and Morgantina as, itself, an assemblage; and 3) what such an approach tells us about other categories that we infer from the archaeological record, especially types of social identity and structure. The implications of examining the operation of multi-nets – despite the challenges noted above – and a broader conceptualisation of assemblage may illuminate in a new way several issues that have dominated the archaeological discourse in recent years.

5. Populating assemblages

Because of the ways that archaeological artefacts are recovered, sorted, stored and studied, Morgantina's assemblages must, themselves, be assembled, or reassembled, and choices made about what to include, in the present. In other words, the agency of archaeologists, in addition to their assumptions about the markedness or power of any particular artefact or class of artefacts, is part of the *agencement*, the French word that is translated by English *agency* (Müller 2015, 28). It also becomes clear that context, as understood by archaeologists as the physical matrix in which assemblages occur, is included in the wider definition of assemblage under discussion here.

It would be ideal to include the full context of Archaic Morgantina in a comprehensive assemblage. This Assemblage would include buildings, tombs and the occupants of the tombs, animals and plants, landscape and water, urban infrastructure, every artefact and ecofact of whatever origin, and all of the persons. This is not possible – much of Morgantina's data is legacy data, the product of a research agenda of half a century ago that was not concerned with collecting environmental data, could not identify some of the artefacts, and was less concerned with archaeological assemblages than presently is the case.

Constrained by the limits of what is possible, then, we turn to a reasonably well-documented archaeological assemblage that can be placed in the larger Morgantina Assemblage of the sixth and early fifth centuries BC. It is a complete mortuary assemblage from Tomb 4, one of the unlooted chamber tombs in Necropolis II, on the east scarp of the ridgetop that forms the known core of the Archaic city (Fig. 7.1). Excavated in 1957, this large tomb was used for five inhumations and was used between 525 and 475 BC. The first publication of this tomb (Sjöqvist 1958) neatly illustrates how assemblages with archaeological context were reconfigured, in fact to become new assemblages based on two principles: the origin or tradition of the tomb's contents (principally ceramics), also grouped by shape. Chronology was not considered as important. The categories were Attic, Corinthian, Lakonian and 'Sikeliote' or Colonial (presumed to have been made in a coastal colony). A grouping designated 'local' or plainware included many which are indigenous in shape: askos, three-handled basin, cup with high-swung handle, cooking mugs, and one badly slipped krater

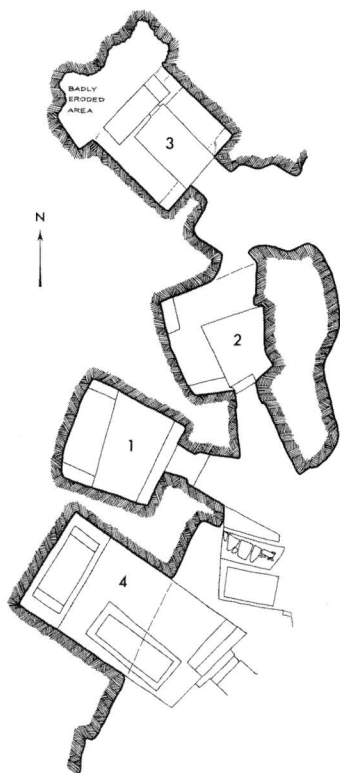

Figure 7.1 Necropolis II, Tombs 1–4 (Lyons 1996, 137 fig. 3, courtesy Department of Art and Archaeology, Princeton University).

clearly of Lakonian type, presumably deemed 'local' because of its lesser quality. In the final publication, a separate plate was devoted to metal, glass and stone objects: beads, hair ornaments, rings, a die, fibulae, in silver, bronze and iron (Lyons 1996, 138–52).

Some of these choices were made because individual burials and their offerings were in disarray at the time of the excavation, but nevertheless the notebook of the excavator allowed a plan of the finds' positions as found to be published (Lyons 1996, 139, fig. 4). The overall effect of the presentation is of abundance and diversity in the assemblage. The context is the entirety of the tomb, situated in a group of tombs of similar type, five in all in this part of the burial grounds. This too constitutes an assemblage. It is possible that those making the burials thought of the tomb as an assemblage constituted over the time it was in use. It is only by reading the catalogue of finds, arranged by presumed origin of the ceramic material (often imprecise or uncertain) that we can find contexts within contexts, for example, that within a single three-handled bowl was another bowl, both of Sikeliote manufacture, and within the second was a third vessel – a black gloss oenochoe, also presumably a local product imitating imported wares in shape and surface (black slipped).

Before proceeding further, a caveat: the categories and conventions of an archaeological catalogue form assemblages with the assemblage of the tomb groups that reflect the choices and values assigned by archaeologists in the present. We privilege shape, for example, and decoration as indicative of ethnic or regional identity. It is easier to identify imports, but we then privilege the place of manufacture without considering that a Lakonian (or Tarentine) krater's origin may not mean the same thing to those including it in the tomb as it does to us in the present. The meaning of an object, including the significance of its origin, is not fixed and may shift with its use and recontextualisation. Objects of indigenous tradition (certain shapes, fabrics and decorative schemes) as well as those we gloss with terms such as *colonial* or *Sikeliote* are particularly tempting to see as emblems of resistance, persistence, ethnicity, indigeneity, and more.

One also finds that nearly all the metal was found with the earliest burial, c. 550 BC, in a rock-cut sarcophagus at the back of the tomb chamber. A cist tomb in the floor was also early, c. 525 BC, and similarly contained mostly metal offerings. As noted, the metal and other small, non-ceramic items were gathered into an assemblage in a single illustration. Finally, a note at the end of the entry records, fragmentary material, never inventoried, and not illustrated, but including many more examples of the shapes and traditions of pottery published in the catalogue, as well as a not otherwise attested transport amphora fragment. So, even the comprehensive publication of the assemblage does not present a complete assemblage. It is interesting to realise how much conventions of ordering and including or excluding, in the present, affect the literal picture of an assemblage, even before our assumptions about what belongs or does not belong, or how to define the assemblage.

The heterogeneity of the assemblage of this one tomb is also relative. The groups of pottery have heterogeneous origins and represent several local, Greek traditions; they evince the operation of networks that brought these objects to Morgantina. Whatever motivated those who received them and the connections between the node formed by Morgantina and Athens or Corinth or any place on the coast, the results are visible. We may note the preponderance of drinking shapes, also local cooking mugs which may speak of commensality and others suitable for dining (stemmed dishes and plates). Others are 'votive', *e.g.* the terracotta female protomes, miniature drinking and pouring vessels. Some, however, stand out because of their other associations, if not actual place of manufacture: a carinated cup, local very large closed and spouted pouring vessels (askoi) used for serving something in large quantities, possibly a local beverage. These two are indigenous in origin: not made abroad, nor from Greek traditions, but in form and function local to Italy and to Sicily.

6. Assemblages, typologies, indigeneity

The presence, in a tomb of the sixth century BC, of distinctive local forms besides others made locally but incorporating Greek forms, as well as Greek imports, references another assemblage constructed by archaeologists that, as noted earlier, has been marked as indigenous. Within this indigenous tradition there is also diversity: what we in the present assign a particular valence is based on assumptions about what it is signalling. The local traditional ceramic repertoire could produce truly transcultural objects – Greek in form, local in fabric and eclectic in decoration (Fig. 7.2). Tomb 4 contained other forms in plain or slipped wares that are less influenced by imports (Fig. 7.3).

But, in addition, there are other fabrics and decorative traditions, identified with west Sicily and the Elymian ethnic group, that make their appearance at Morgantina (Antonaccio 2015). Examples may be found in Morgantina's tombs, especially from the late seventh and early sixth centuries BC as well as the settlement. The fabrics are generally a distinctive light or dark grey, gritty and hard, and the surface decoration is incised, combed or stamped. Materials science has helped us, to a degree, to go beyond suppositions about the origins of indigenous ceramic forms based on visual analysis. At Morgantina a programme of pXRF analysis started in 2007, attempting to understand if fabrics that were visually distinctive were chemically distinctive. A variety of assumed Greek imports and imitations, and indigenous ceramics

Figure 7.2 Inv. no. 59-2175, local kernos composed of three trefoil oinochoai, from the Cittadella settlement (Photo: C. Williams).

from a variety of periods, were analysed to understand something about pre-existing networks of production and technologies before the Greek period of intensive settlement in Sicily. pXRF was chosen because it is non-destructive, inexpensive, does not require the transportation of samples to a lab; the equipment used is portable and can take a reading very quickly. pXRF can also be misleading and requires known clay sources to match the origins of a ceramic clay fabric with its place of manufacture.

Some interesting results emerged: for example, very high-quality black gloss pottery, assumed to be either Athenian or 'colonial', has a local origin. pXRF has also shed some light on the grey wares found in the tombs and settlement. As noted above, this grey or dark and gritty fabric takes varied forms: pitchers, cups and large bowls are the most common. Both the forms and the decoration seem to be rooted in much older Italic and Mediterranean traditions going

Figure 7.3 Local pottery from Tomb 4 (Lyons 1996, pl. 13, courtesy Department of Art and Archaeology, Princeton University).

back to the Neolithic, and also Bronze Age traditions. Grey wares, including incised and carinated forms, are also found in the Balkans and northern Italy, and made well into the Iron Age. The repertoire of decorative motifs is widely shared among sites in west Sicily, and, in addition to the similarities in form, fabric and surface treatments, these similarities have been seen as an index of regional interaction; meanwhile the distinctive combinations of shared motifs, have been explained as an index of local expression. Even within the grey wares, there is a wide range of variation in fabric, finish and decoration.

While much more prevalent in the west, this ware is also found in central Sicily, where its type-site is Sant'Angelo Muxaro near Agrigento, on the edge of the territory of a second indigenous ethnic group, the Sikans. Thus, while this type of ceramic is 'at home' in western Sicily, there are some examples of incised grey wares in Late Bronze Age and Iron Age Morgantina, and Leighton (1993) notes several examples of this type of pottery in contexts transitional to the Archaic period, where it persists.

pXRF undermines the notion that grey wares are definitively 'Elymian', and/or a marker for a chronological period. Grey wares do constitute one, recurring element in the assemblages in Sicily over some centuries, as does the continued presence of ceramic containers in local fabrics with carinated profiles, which may influence a marked local preference for imported black gloss drinking cups with sharply profiled lips (Walsh and Antonaccio 2014). But it is also clear that other aspects of assemblage theory, such as territoriality, could be applicable here. While archaeologists have concerned themselves with hierarchies of all kinds, in assemblage theory, 'strata' are not inherent expressions of value but the result of how the heterogeneous components are organised – something not predetermined, but emergent. To utilise the very helpful points made by Müller, assemblages are *relational* (the independent parts are autonomous and their individual properties do not account for how they function as a whole); they are *productive*, generating new social formations and not merely reflective of society or reality; they are heterogeneous: anything can be related, and therefore 'socio-material' (see above); they participate in a dynamic *deterritorialisation* and *reterritorialisation*: 'Assemblages establish territories as they emerge and hold together but also constantly mutate, transform and break up' (Müller 2015, 29). Finally, there is an aspect of *desire*: it is this human physical attraction that joins things that are fundamentally fragmented in this way of thinking.

7. Time and assemblage

An assemblage as defined by Deleuze and Guattari is a temporary coming together of things, people, animals etc. situated in space. Time of course is a prime archaeological concern, and here perhaps archaeology may make a contribution to assemblage theory as it has developed outside our discipline. Deleuze and Guattari reject 'filiations', instead stressing symbiosis in the sense of co-functioning in an assemblage, which allows for the breaking apart and recombination of elements. For the assemblage as a whole, they explicitly reject any kind of descent or succession. But archaeologists can actually trace descent and evolution of things in the past, and this is one aspect of examining the constituents of an archaeological assemblage – even one defined very broadly as assemblage theory does – attending to the power of time and how the past functions in the present, within the whole (Müller 2015, 27).

Grey wares and other elements from the indigenous strand had a particular role to play in the heterogeneity, or hybridity, of ceramic assemblages at Morgantina. These assemblages, of course, were deployed within specific contexts that were, themselves, heterogeneous: large buildings with stone foundations and mudbrick walls featuring clay rooftiles and painted architectural terracottas of Greek style, in use by a populace still burying in chamber tombs of indigenous derivation (Antonaccio 1997). Some elements of Greek urban design exist – *e.g.* stone and mudbrick houses with clay rooftiles, and the aforementioned sacred or public buildings – but few other features in the excavated settlement that usually signify a Greek *polis*. With better data, we could extend our consideration of the Morgantina Assemblage to include its natural environment, architecture, cultural habits and practices, and much more. Indeed, to deploy assemblage theory fully requires this. But this exercise at least points to the assemblages within assemblages – including those created in our present modes of inquiry – and their impact on our interpretations. Finally, post-processual archaeology has insisted on the agency of individuals and of things in reflexive relationships. These relationships may be modelled by network thinking that, even with our limited data, is quite complex. It must include networks that pre-exist those of Archaic Greece, which do not arise *ex nihilo*; networks incorporate elements from different strata, and are conditioned by time, identity and other networks. Assemblage theory says that assemblages behave like contagion and the wind. We can accept this if we think of the mutability of assemblages as networks evolve, and the effects of networks, and assemblages, on each other cannot be predicted or controlled. But this principle does not mean that agency or intention is of no account.

To conclude, at a place like Morgantina layered networks, or multi-nets, that pre-existed the formation of Greek and other networks and then interact with them, can be brought into dialogue with assemblage theory. This concept of assemblage is interesting to juxtapose with the suggestion that hybrids are networks: we might say that hybrids are assemblages and brought about through networks.

Assemblage theory allows for a broader, more complete picture of the constituent elements – human, material, natural, built, cultivated and wild – that come into place and time but are essentially unstable and liable to recombination. To take full advantage of the possible insights of assemblage theory would naturally require more data in order to widen the assemblage: it would include understanding the economic, ecological and many other elements that constitute an assemblage. It would, archaeologically speaking, fold context into assemblage, so that the built environment is included, and not just a conditioning factor or matrix. But recognising that at a certain scale, the effects of the coming together of an assemblage are as impersonal (or supra-personal) as the wind or contagion (to cite Deleuze and Guattari), we must also retain our focus on the intentions and actions of humans. While humans do not determine, or control, assemblages in all their possible complexity, the recurrence of certain artefacts, symbols, behaviours and rituals marks many human societies and piques our curiosity. No universals are possible or advisable, no essential or original, or immutable meanings can be deduced. But still we ask, what happened, how and why, and thereby understand something about ourselves in the past, as well as the present.

References

Antonaccio, C. (1997) Urbanism at Archaic Morgantina. *Acta Hyperborea* 7, 167–93.

Antonaccio, C. (2015) Re-excavating Morgantina. In D. Haggis and C. Antonaccio (eds) *Classical Archaeology in Context: theory and practice in excavation in the Greek world*, 51–69. Berlin and Boston, de Gruyter.

Brughmans, T., Collar, A. and Howard, F. (eds) (2016) *The Connected Past. Challenges to network studies in archaeology and history.* Oxford, Oxford University Press.

DeLanda, M. (2016) *Assemblage Theory.* Edinburgh, Edinburgh University Press.

Eisenmann, S., Bánffy, E., van Dommelen, P., Maran, J., Lazaridis, I., Mittnik, A., McCormick, M., Krause, J., Reich, D. and Stockhammer, P. (2018) Reconciling material cultures in archaeology with genetic data: the nomenclature of clusters emerging from archaeogenomic analysis. *Scientific Reports* 8. 13003. doi:10.1038/s41598-018-31123-z.

Epstein, B. (2018) Social ontology. In E.N. Zalta (ed.) *The Stanford Encyclopedia of Philosophy.* Summer 2018 edn. https://plato.stanford.edu/archives/sum2018/entries/social-ontology/.

Gunaratnam, Y. (2014) Rethinking hybridity: interrogating mixedness. *Subjectivity* 7.1, 1–17. https://doi.org/10.1057/sub.2013.16.

Hodder, I. (2012) *Entangled: an archaeology of the relationships between humans and things.* Malden and Oxford, Wiley-Blackwell.

Knappett, C. (2011) *An Archaeology of Interaction. Network perspectives on material culture and society.* Oxford, Oxford University Press.

Knappett, C. (2013) Introduction: why networks? In C. Knappett (ed.) *Network Analysis in Archaeology. New approaches to regional interaction*, 3–15. Oxford, Oxford University Press.

Knappett, C. (2016) Networks in archaeology: between scientific method and humanistic metaphor. In T. Brughmans, A. Collar and F. Howard (eds) (2016) *The Connected Past. Challenges to network studies in archaeology and history*, 21–33. Oxford, Oxford University Press.

Leidwanger, J. (2017) From time capsules to networks: new light on Roman shipwrecks in the maritime economy. *American Journal of Archaeology* 121, 595–619.

Leighton, R. (1993) *The Protohistoric Settlement on the Cittadella.* Morgantina Studies 4. Princeton, Princeton University Press.

Lyons, C. (1996) *The Archaic Cemeteries.* Morgantina Studies V. Princeton, Princeton University Press.

Malkin, I. (2011) *A Small Greek World. Networks in the ancient Mediterranean.* Oxford, Oxford University Press.

Müller, M. (2015) Assemblages and actor-networks: rethinking socio-material power, politics and space. *Geography Compass* 9.1, 27–41.

Renfrew, C. and Cooke, K. (eds) (1979) *Transformations: mathematical approaches to culture change.* New York, San Francisco and London, Academic Press.

Scheidel, W. and Meeks, E. (2014) ORBIS Stanford Geospatial Network Model of the Roman World. (https://orbis.stanford.edu/, accessed 15 January 2021).

Sjöqvist, E. (1958) Excavations at Serra Orlando (Morgantina). Preliminary report II. *American Journal of Archaeology* 62, 155–64.

Thomas, N. (1991) *Entangled Objects. Exchange, material culture, and colonialism in the Pacific.* Cambridge, MA, Harvard University Press.

Thomas, J. (2015) The future of archaeological theory. *Antiquity* 89, 1287–96.

Van der Leeuw, S. (2013) Archaeology, networks, information processing, and beyond. In C. Knappett (ed.) *Network Analysis in Archaeology. New approaches to regional interaction,* 335–48. Oxford, Oxford University Press.

Walsh, J. and Antonaccio, C. (2014) Athenian black gloss and consumer preference in the Mediterranean. *Oxford Journal of Archaeology* 33, 47–67.

Wolfe, A. (1978–1979) The rise of network thinking in anthropology. *Social Networks* 1, 53–64. https://doi.org/10.1016/0378-8733(78)90012-6.

Index

manufacture, production 79, 92
  terra sigillata 3, 4, 7, 8–10
  table ware 7, 9, 70, 72, 73, 74, 75, 76, 77
  See also ceramic
power 60, 74, 77, 78, 80, 91, 99, 101, 103
  of things 13, 18, 122, 127
practice(s) xii, 23, 25, 31, 34–6, 38–9, 57–8, 60,
  72–3, 77, 78, 93, 100, 102, 105–6, 111–12, 117,
  120, 127
practitioner(s) 74, 106, 111
Primal Point Analysis 18, 91
production 9, 52, 55, 56, 70, 73, 74, 77, 78, 79,
  80, 92, 102, 105, 106, 120, 125,
Pylos, 99–112 *passim*

rank 60
residence 52. *See also* house
ritual 6, 31, 56, 57, 60, 74, 108, 111, 117, 128
rivers 48, 70, 72, 86, 92
Roman 3, 6, 7, 8–10, 18, 34–8, 101, 102, 103, 119
Romania 86, 87
routes 36, 48, 60, 61

scale xii, 2, 22, 24–5, 28, 34–5, 38, 39, 48, 59, 60,
  61, 70, 80, 85, 99–100, 101, 102, 103, 108, 127
Scandinavia(n) 32, 37, 89, 91
settlement(s) xii, xiii, 11, 27, 28, 36, 49, 53, 55,
  56–7, 59, 70–1, 80, 119, 120, 121, 124,
  125, 127
  defended, enclosed, fortified 27, 29–30
  hilltop 52
  location 13
  mounds, tells 28–9, 70, 72
  organisation 29, 30, 78
  pattern 29, 30, 51, 59, 60, 61
ships 32, 86
shipwreck 85, 86,
Sicily 117–28, *passim*
Sikel 121, 122, 123
silver 36, 38, 52, 55–6, 58, 123
slave 16, 52, 99. *See also* enslavement
smiths 36–7, 39
social change 24, 26, 80, 103
  contacts 39 55, 58
  conventions 57
  differentiation 59
  fragmentation 40
  interaction xii, 1, 58, 79

instability 39
  organisation 32, 60, 61, 72, 75
  ontology 121
  relationships xii, 3, 17, 34, 36, 49, 60, 79
  stratification 32, 52
  upheaval 21, 101
Social Network Analysis (SNA) xi, 1, 2, 4, 6, 7,
  18, 39
soil 31
Spain 47–61 *passim*, 105
spatial 2, 8 17, 31, 48, 52, 106
stability, stable 25, 37, 75, 79
status 16, 32, 33, 36, 37, 74, 77, 120, 121
storage 5, 15, 52, 70, 72, 108
sun 32, 34
system(s) 23, 24, 30, 51, 53, 55, 72, 74, 75, 77, 78,
  79, 80, 85, 91, 92, 101, 117, 118, 119

table ware. *See* pottery
technological 5, 7, 32, 36, 74, 75, 101–2, 103
technology, technologies 4, 17, 24, 27, 34, 36,
  38, 39, 100, 101, 104, 105, 120, 125
tell (site). *See* settlement
terra sigillata. *See* pottery
territorial, territoriality 52, 53, 55, 58, 119, 126
territory, territories 35, 52, 53, 55, 57, 126
time 12, 18, 22–7, 38, 40, 105, 126–7
tin 86
Tiryns 86, 88, 93, 108
trade 9, 34, 36, 48, 52, 60, 86, 90, 101,
  117, 119
trader(s) 8, 9, 11
tradition 70, 76, 77, 100, 105, 106–8, 111, 122,
  123, 124

urban 9, 16, 122, 127
Urnfield 32, 70, 92

violence, violent 28, 52, 103–4
votive 16, 124

warrior(s) 32, 33, 36
water 29, 33, 122
weapons 35, 36, 50, 52, 89, 103
wine 106, 110, 111
World Systems Theory 91

Zeitgeist 21–40, *passim*